Globalization and Belonging

Theory, Culture & Society

Theory, Culture & Society caters for the resurgence of interest in culture within contemporary social science and the humanities. Building on the heritage of classical social theory, the book series examines ways in which this tradition has been reshaped by a new generation of theorists. It also publishes theoretically informed analyses of everyday life, popular culture, and new intellectual movements.

EDITOR: Mike Featherstone, *Nottingham Trent University*

SERIES EDITORIAL BOARD
Roy Boyne, *University of Durham*
Mike Hepworth, *University of Aberdeen*
Scott Lash, *Goldsmiths College, University of London*
Roland Robertson, *University of Aberdeen*
Bryan S. Turner, *University of Cambridge*

THE TCS CENTRE
The *Theory, Culture & Society* book series, the journals *Theory, Culture & Society* and Body & Society, and related conference, seminar and postgraduate programmes operate from the TCS Centre at Nottingham Trent University. For further details of the TCS Centre's activities please contact:

Centre Administrator
The TCS Centre, Room 175
Faculty of Humanities
Nottingham Trent University
Clifton Lane, Nottingham, NG11 8NS, UK
e-mail: tcs@ntu.ac.uk
web: http://tcs.ntu.ac.uk

Recent volumes include:

Sex and Manners
Cas Wouters

The Body and Social Theory
Chris Shilling

Religion, Realism and Social Theory
Phillip A. Mellor

The Body in Culture, Technology and Society
Chris Shilling

Globalization and Belonging

Mike Savage
Gaynor Bagnall
Brian Longhurst

SAGE Publications
London • Thousand Oaks • New Delhi

© Mike Savage, Gaynor Bagnall, Brian Longhurst 2005

First published 2005

Published in association with Theory, Culture & Society,
Nottingham Trent University

 SAGE Publications Ltd
1 Oliver's Yard
55 City Road
London EC1Y 1SP

SAGE Publications Inc.
2455 Teller Road
Thousand Oaks, California 91320

SAGE Publications India Pvt Ltd
B-42 Panchshell Enclave
Post Box 4109
New Delhi 110 017

British Library Cataloguing in Publication data

A catalogue record for this book is
available from the British Library

ISBN 0-7619-4985-2
    0-7619-4986-0 (pbk)

Library of Congress control number available

Typeset by C&M Digital (P) Ltd., Chennai, India
Printed and bound in Great Britain by Athanaeum Press, Gateshead

Contents

List of Tables and Maps

Preface and Acknowledgements

The origins of this book date from 1996 when the Economic and Social Research Council (to whom we are duly grateful) funded our project called 'Lifestyles and Social Integration: a study of middle-class culture in Manchester'. The aims of the research project were influenced by what Rosemary Crompton (1998) has identified as the 'employment aggregate' approach to class analysis. This perspective, associated with sociologists such as John Goldthorpe and Gordon Marshall, considers how people's class position within employment relationships affects their life chances and actions, such as their educational achievement (famously, Halsey et al. 1980), or political orientations (Heath et al. 1985, 1991; Evans 1999). We were aware that this perspective had not been much applied to the study of consumption, leisure practices and lifestyles (though see Savage et al. 1992, and subsequent discussions in Butler and Savage 1995; Chaney 1996; Lury 1997; Warde 1997 for partial exceptions), and were especially interested to map differences in middle-class lifestyles. Our plan, therefore, was to use qualitative methods to expand our understanding of consumption patterns and lifestyles within the middle-class, focusing on four local areas chosen to exemplify potentially different forms of middle-class culture. We were concerned to pay particular attention to the local contexts in which consumption took place, drawing upon Gaynor Bagnall's and Brian Longhurst's earlier research on audiences (Longhurst and Savage 1996; Bagnall 1996, 1998; Abercrombie and Longhurst 1998).

The research was conducted between 1997 and 1999, and duly led to a clutch of papers (Longhurst et al. 2001; Savage 2000; Savage et al. 2001; Savage et al. 2004a; Bangnall et al. 2003). However, we did not have time to fully write up our research immediately after completing the fieldwork. Gaynor took up her first lecturing post at Liverpool John Moores University, with all the demands that a new job entailed. Brian became Director of the Institute for Social Research (and later Head of the School of English, Sociology, Politics and Contemporary History) at the University of Salford, and Mike became Head of the Sociology Department at the University of Manchester. In addition, we all had the demands of young children! While we had time to 'mine' the data for issues of particular interest, such as class identity (Savage et al. 2001), or radio listening (Longhurst et al. 2001), we did not have the chance to analyse the interview data as a whole, much of which was left untouched until 2002. The bulk of the data was analysed and the book written from summer 2002 to summer 2003 when Mike had a year's sabbatical. Mike therefore took the lead, with input from Gaynor and Brain, in writing up what had been very much a team project.

When we came to write this book, our framing concerns had shifted. Mike's *Class Analysis and Social Transformation* (2000), written after we collected the data but before we fully analysed it, saw him becoming more sceptical of the scope of the 'employment aggregate' approach to class analysis for the understanding of consumption and lifestyle. He argued that while close relationships between class position and life-chances could be detected, there was little evidence that identity, values and lifestyles were so directly linked. This was of course a familiar (though largely untested) claim in much sociological writing of this period (see for instance Chaney 1996). We became increasingly interested in understanding the local contexts in which we carried out our interviews, and understanding the relationship between locale, lifestyles and identities. Rather then seeing class cultures and lifestyles as fundamentally the product of occupation and employment, could we instead see them as arising out of residential processes?

This new interest chimed in with research demonstrating the significance of place for outcomes in the areas of health, political alignments, and so on. But it raised its own can of worms. We needed to consider how our research related to older debates in community studies and urban sociology regarding the significance of place, neighbourhood and community. More seriously still, it was not clear what theoretical warrant there was for emphasising local processes when, in a globalised world, people and objects were held to be mobile. Furthermore, given the general acceptance that neighbourhoods are not now (even if they ever were) face-to-face communities, how could we understand the salience of place? We became preoccupied by resolving these issues, which led us to put the analysis of middle-class cultures, consumption and lifestyles into a different theoretical frame.

In the end we have written a book about the nature of local belonging in a global world. We hope that we have cast our local case studies in a way that will be interesting to a wide audience, including people who have no interest in, or knowledge of, the North West of England. The strength of our book, we would like to think, is in the quality of the interviews we carried out. There is no shortage of sophisticated theoretical frameworks, but there is very little empirical research which allows us to explore what globalisation 'on the ground' entails. This is the gap that we hope our book addresses in an interesting – and perhaps provocative – way!

The first chapter rehearses our theoretical concerns and lays out our methodology. Chapter 1 argues that while globalisation theory is deeply concerned with understanding the relationship between the global and the local, we need to distinguish those approaches which see the local simply as an instance of epochal global change, and those which see the local as irritant. Taking up the latter approach through the insights of Arjun Appadurai, Walter Benjamin and Doreen Massey, we show how Pierre Bourdieu's social theory might be extended to understand how people might feel they belong in certain contexts. Chapter 1 also briefly outlines and defends our methodology, and introduces our choice of Manchester as a suitable place to examine these issues.

Chapter 2 is possibly the most important chapter in the book in introducing our core concept of elective belonging. We show that people's feeling of belonging is not linked to any historical roots they may have in the area. Indeed, those relatively few people who are 'born and bred' in the place where they still live often feel ill at ease there. However, we also show that people are critical of those who they see as transients, with no ties to the place they now live in. Our concept of elective belonging argues that places are not characterised by tensions between insiders and outsiders but that instead they are defined as locales for people electing to belong (and not just reside) in specific places.

This argument is elaborated in later chapters. Chapter 3 shows that bringing up children plays a key role in this process of electing to belong. In-migrants who bring up children, talk about the way that this makes them feel at home. However, following the work of Ball (2002) and Butler and Robson (2003a) we show how such groups are concerned with the local politics of schooling, and how belonging is therefore related to the wider spatial organization of the educational field. Choosing to belong to a place hence involves comparing places and invoking a relational frame of awareness.

Chapter 4 takes this argument further by showing how people's sense of feeling at home depends not on their attachment to some kind of face-to-face community but to the way that they connect their location to other places that they prize. In a world with global connections, residents routinely associate the place that they live with other places, sometimes places at a significant distance such as London. However, we also show that these kinds of networks of the cultural imaginary are not fully global in scope: the spatial references rarely stretch beyond the British Isles.

Chapter 5 considers how our respondents talked about the city of Manchester. For all our four areas, Manchester was the nearest major city, and most respondents had very clear and emotive views about the city. We show, however, that the significance of Manchester is not that where people feel loyalty to a community with which they are bound. Rather, people's perceptions of the city are related to their visualisation of its special sites and its role as centre of high culture. We use these findings to criticise arguments associated with the 'LA School' regarding the fragmentation and decentralisation of urban space, and lend critical support to Le Gales's recent emphasis on the distinctive character of European cities.

Chapter 6 considers how work cultures affects the nature of social ties, and allows us to examine the extent of class formation in our four areas. We show that people's friendship patterns and interaction with work colleagues is remarkably differentiated, with little overlap between these spheres. There is relatively little spill over between work and social life, leading us to doubt that there are any marked processes of class formation currently visible.

Chapter 7 explores the role of the media in the cultural imaginary of our respondents. The media is often seen as central to the organisation of global cultural flows, yet we show how people's media use is more complex than such a view might suppose. People distance themselves from media use, and emphasise their agency choosing what they watch. We show how people are concerned to mark place in their narratives of the media use, and we demonstrate, against the claims of globalisation theory, that the spatial range of most cultural references is highly delimited.

Chapter 8 focuses specifically on people's global reflexivity to consider how they talked about global issues and connections. We argue for the value of seeing our respondents as part of a British imperial diaspora, with connections spread to other parts of the English speaking world, but with little other contact. We show how limited people's sense of global reflexivity actually is, and argue that the concept of cosmopolitanism has little value in accounting for global awareness. Finally, we lay out our main arguments with respect to globalisation theory in the Conclusion.

Turning to our acknowledgements, we would like to thank Sage (and Chris Rojek and the Theory, Culture and Society team in particular) for agreeing to publish our book. In a period when it is ever more difficult to publish research-based books, we sincerely thank them for their support, and hope they are happy with the result. Sage's reader, Frank Webster, helped us to sharpen our final manuscript. It should be noted that we have not had space to report all the findings germane to our concerns. Readers who are interested in how our arguments relate to debates on social capital might therefore wish to consult Bagnall et al. (2003), Savage et al. (2004, 2005), on social class (Savage et al. 2004b).

Needless to say, we have learnt much from many people during this project. First and foremost we are obviously grateful to the ESRC for their support (and more particularly, the support of its referees) without which this book could not have been written. During the early stages of the research project we were guided by a steering group which included Steve Edgell (Salford), Ronnie Frankenberg (Brunel/Keele), Karen Evans (Liverpool), Rosemary Mellor (Manchester), Roger Silverstone (LSE), Derek Wynne (Manchester Metropolitan University) and Roger Burrows (University of York). Rosemary and Derek have both sadly died since the project began and we would like to think that there are traces of their influence in this study. Paul Joyce helped with data analysis. As the book took shape we have benefited enormously from the conversations and interest of Nick Abercrombie, Lisa Adkins, Stephen Ball, Tony Bennett, Talja Blokland, Tim Butler, Eamonn Carrabine, Garry Crawford, Nick Crossley, Fiona Devine, Rob Flynn, Peter Halfpenny, Sylvia Hayes, Helen Hills, Johs Hjellbrekke, Tony Kearon, Dan Laughey, Patrick Legales, Annemarie Money, Bev Skeggs, Alan Warde, and Paul Watt. We certainly have not been able to satisfy them on all the points they have raised, but we are flattered that from their diverse positions they have wanted to engage with our work. Mike would particularly like to thank Fiona Devine, Bev Skeggs and Alan Warde for helping him to explore many of the issues about class, stratification and culture – often over a congenial glass of wine!

Versions of chapters have been given to the following audiences who we thank for their comments: British Sociological Association Annual Conferences (1997, 1999, 2002); *The Legacy of the Frankfurt School in Cultural Studies* conference (Salford 1998) *Cultural Studies and Interdisciplinarity: Difference, Otherness, Dialogue, Translation* conference (Leeds 2000) *Cultural Change and Urban Contexts* conference (Manchester, Manchester Metropolitan and Salford 2000) *Crossroads in Cultural Studies* conference (Tampere 2002) the Turkish Oral History Foundation (Istanbul 2003); the Institute of Social and Economic Research, University of Essex; Liverpool John Moores University; University of Manchester University of Salford University of Sheffield University of Leicester Open University University of Lancaster and Unilever.

Finally, Mike would like to thank Helen and Isambard for sharing the experience of 'elective belonging' in Withington, South Manchester. Gaynor would like to thank Graham, Claire, and Jack for all their support and especially for 'dancing on a Saturday night' and her Mum, Doreen for always being there. Brian would like to thank Bernadette, James and Tim for continuing to share it all.

1

Global Change and Local Belonging

Over the past two centuries sociologists have frequently pronounced the
end of local identities, and yet attachment to place remains remarkably
obdurate. This obstinacy endures even though the terms of the sociological
debate have changed radically in the past decade. The early social theorists
Marx, Weber, Durkheim and Simmel argued that capitalist modernity shattered the personal bonds of face-to-face community (see generally, Kumar
1978) and their concern animated sociological reflection for much of the
20th Century. Yet, despite these prophetic accounts, many urban sociologists emphasised that community ties could be reconstructed even in a
modern, complex world (see Gans 1962; Wellman 1979; Fischer 1982;
Savage et al. 2002). Since the early 1990s, however, globalisation theorists
have re-energised these old debates. These writers emphasise that in a
world characterised by virtual communication, institutional deregulation,
and the movement of capital, information, objects and people at great
speed across large distances, social life cannot be seen as firmly located in
particular places with clear boundaries. Identities are therefore diasporic,
mobile and transient. The leading British sociologist John Urry (2000) has
issued a manifesto for the 21st Century centred on a new sociology of flows
to replace a sociology of 'territory', arguing that belonging 'almost always
involve(s) diverse forms of mobility', so that people dwell 'in and through
being at home and away, through the dialectic of roots and routes' (Urry
2000: 132–133).

Although these issues are widely discussed, they have rarely been subject
to systematic empirical examination. Our book explores how far-reaching
global changes are articulated locally through examining the cultural practices, lifestyles and identities of 182 residents in four locations around
Manchester, England, in the late 1990s. Our study is timely. It is widely
recognised that local case studies, if not conceived as studies of fixed and
bounded communities, but as studies of sites from which forms of mobility
as well as fixity can be empirically observed, are vitally necessary for elaborating the nature of contemporary social change. This is a point of agreement between those writing from within the community studies tradition,
such as Graham Crow (2002) who claims that local studies have always
been crucial for generating insights regarding social change, and Ulrich Beck
(2002: 23), who insists that 'you cannot even think about globalisation
without referring to specific locations and places'. The issue, however, is
how to elaborate these programmatic statements into viable empirical

research. This first chapter lays out the theoretical and methodological basis for our study. Firstly, we show how globalisation theory conceives of the 'local'. Many globalisation theorists want to abolish the distinction between the global and the local, yet it is also clear that without some reference to the 'local', the meaning of the 'global' also becomes obscure. This unstable tension between the local and global goes to the core of globalisation theory. In the second section we explain how Pierre Bourdieu's social theory can be developed to provide a distinctive way through these uncertainties by offering a spatially sensitive, but non-reductive account of social practice. The third part of this chapter explains our research methodology, showing why Manchester is a telling site in which to study global change and local belonging, and justifying our use of qualitative methods. Finally, we explain why we chose our four locations within the Manchester area, and offer brief pen portraits of them which will serve as a foundation for the more detailed analyses in later chapters.

1.1 Globalisation and the problem of the local

Globalisation theory emerged from the later 1980s in response to new forms of capitalist hegemony (Robertson 1992). The collapse of most state socialist regimes, as well as the weakening power of labour movements and socialist politics within many capitalist nations removed the main political alternative to free-market capitalism (Bauman 1989). Economic restructuring, state deregulation, the power of large transnational corporations, and the proliferation of new technologies facilitating the mobility of goods, capital, people and symbols, led to a new sense of global connectivity. New kinds of consumerist post-modern aesthetic, and intensified forms of individualised identities, were heralded as indications of new social relations generated by global flows (see Harvey 1987; Lash and Urry 1987; Bauman 1989; Jameson 1991). By the early 1990s it was possible to conceive of one world organised around common capitalist parameters, for the first time since the First World War (see Fukuyama 1992).

Early globalisation theorists used these dramatic developments to repackage longer standing concerns regarding the fate of community (Nisbet 1953; Therborn 1970). For Giddens (1990, 1991) 'the concept of globalisation is best understood as expressing the fundamental aspects of time-space distanciation' (1991: 2). Communication was no longer confined to the boundaries of particular places as practices became increasingly detached from their local settings. Giddens relied on Heidegger's existential ontology which saw insecurity resulting from the loss of face-to-face certainty (Thrift 1993). New information and media technologies played a crucial role here. Giddens drew on Meyrowtiz's (1985) arguments that new media generated 'no sense of place', with people defining their salient relationships not in terms of face-to-face contacts but in terms of media characters and celebrities. The geographer David Harvey, whose best-selling

The Condition of Postmodernity (1987) emphasised how global flows were related to cultural change, was himself influenced by Raymond Williams's concern about the instability and fragmentation of the face-to-face community in contemporary life (Harvey 1993). Harvey's own work engaged with the humanist argument that social life is most secure in face-to-face, communal situations, and his criticisms of post-modern culture was in large part related to his fears about its evisceration of communities, especially industrial, working-class communities (Harvey and Layter 1993). Harvey's arguments were paralleled by Jameson's (1991) lament on the emergence of a new depthless post-modern culture, anchored neither in the co-ordinates of time and place, and dependent on a superficial pastiche of signs. Other work in this vein pointed to the transient spaces of shopping malls, fast food joints, and airport terminals to emphasise the rise of new kinds of 'non-places' (Auge 1995). The culmination of this early work came with Robertson (1992), who developed the first major account of globalisation as the rise of a 'global awareness',[1] and Albrow's (1996) account of the Global Age as marking the end of modernity.

This early period of globalisation theory was, however, short lived. By the early 1990s any simple sense that a new world order might be generated was dissipated behind growing national and cultural conflicts. It became clear that major global tensions, between religious blocs and between national and ethnic groups, only served to highlight entrenched divisions around the globe. A subtly different approach to globalisation and spatial change emerged by the mid-1990s, represented in the later work of Robertson (1995), in the writings of Lash and Urry (1994), Massey (1993; 1994), and Castells (1996a and b, 1997). These writers did not emphasise the erosion of place but rather focused on new forms of connection and mobility, and their potential to rework social relationships and to re-construct localism. A key point made by these writers was that the local is not transcended by globalisation, but rather that the local is to be understood through the lens of global relationships. Globalisation, therefore, produces new forms of localisation in a dialectical relationship that Robertson (1995) popularised as 'glocalisation', where 'globalisation has involved the reconstruction of "home", "community" and "locality"' (Robertson 1995: 30). This argument is indebted to Lefevbre's claim that 'the worldwide does not abolish the local' (cited in Brenner 2000: 369). Versions of this account are now standard fare in globalisation and urban theory. For Ulrich Beck (2002: 17) 'Globalisation is a non-linear, dialectic process in which the global and the local do not exist as cultural polarities but as combined and mutually implicating principles'. For Michael Smith (2001: 182) 'the global and local are not separate containers but mutually constitutive social processes'. For John Urry, 'the global and local are inextricably and irreversibly bound together through a dynamic relationship' (2002: 84).

This attempt to recover the 'local' as an intrinsic aspect of globalisation raises a host of problems. If we do not rely on the outmoded view that the local is defined in terms of face-to-face community, it is unclear what the local is supposed to be. Its scale is also uncertain. The urban is often identified as the local site for global processes (for instance Sassen 1991; Smith 2001), but as Brenner (2000) indicates, there is no theoretical warrant for this. Is the local not also the nation, the neighbourhood, the house, the bedroom? Lurking behind this, it is often unclear what global and local 'principles' (Beck) or 'processes' (Smith) are. What exactly is at stake in understanding the local from within the terms of globalisation theory? There are in fact five distinct ways of construing the 'local' which need to be unpacked: firstly the local as context, secondly the local as the 'particular' in opposition to the global 'universal'; thirdly the local as historical residue, fourthly the local as hub in a network and fifthly the locality as bounded construction.

Firstly, the familiar idea of context offers what might seem a straightforward way of conceptualising the local. John Urry (2002: 137) for instance, argues that cosmopolitanism involves 'comprehending the specificity of one's local context'. However, it is not clear what this means when globalisation theory argues that social relationships are stretched over space and are organised through flows and forms of movement. Insofar as this is true, it is not clear how contexts are local, as some anthropologists have noted. Appadurai (1996) thus argues that localities are not contexts, but that contexts define the boundaries of localities. Franklin et al. (2000) argue further that globalisation alters the historically significant way that 'nature' serves as a horizon against which human life (or culture) can be defined. Rather than nature being a 'given', it is itself produced by culture, allowing a proliferation of meanings and values. This is possible in large part because the global becomes its own context (there are no boundaries other than its own). Instead of seeing agency as linked to the contexts of everyday life routines, 'emergent global networks offer the chosen – or rather, choice itself – as the origin of the imagined community of global citizenship' (Franklin et al. 2000: 75). It therefore seems difficult to appeal to the idea of local context within the terms of globalisation theory.

A second possibility defines the local as a 'particular' in opposition to the global 'universal'. This idea is related to conceptions of globalisation as an overarching, social process related to epochal social change. Construing the local as concrete in opposition to an abstract universal makes it difficult to avoid an infinite regress in which the local becomes the empirical, so that any concrete instance of anything is 'local'. It provides no warrant for seeing the local as 'small scale'. It entails a view that different particulars can at best be seen as contingently inter-related, with the universal standing above and outside such interactions. The idea of the 'local' does no analytical work in this account, and could therefore easily be dropped from the analysis (if not the description) of globalisation. This is an account which appears to give the local some significance, but in reality the power of the overarching, universal processes is reaffirmed through the architecture of the conceptual framework. It is not clear that the local matters other than as an instantiation of such global powers.

This is a problem with all epochal, generalising conceptions of globalisation, such as is evident in the work of Beck (2000), Bauman (1998) and Albrow (1996). The work of Manuel Castells is perhaps the most interesting, and bears some attention here. Castells is careful to situate globalisation geo-politically, and he distances himself from 'simplistic versions' of the globalisation thesis (Castells 1996: 97) by defining globalisation in terms of information flows made possible by technological developments, especially as linked to global financial markets. He sees global information flows existing in tension with other kinds of more localised processes, paying particular importance to the distinction between economic globalisation and political regionalisation. 'Historically rooted political institutions' seek to restrict global economic forces, with the result that:

> while dominant segments of all national economics are linked into the global web, segments of countries, regions, economic sectors and local societies are disconnected from the processes of accumulation and consumption that characterize the informational/global economy. (Castells 1996a: 102–103)

For all Castells's sophistication he thereby upholds a unilinear view of globalisation in which local societies can somehow be disconnected from global processes, and are defined as a historical residue, not themselves motors of change, the sources of which are held to come from elsewhere. These he sees as 'globalisation and informationalisation, enacted by networks of wealth, technology and power, (which) are transforming our world' (Castells 1997a: 68), which appear to operate outside any particular 'locality'.

This formulation leads him to view local identities ultimately as a response to globalisation, and this account of the local as defensive historical reaction is a third way of rendering the significance of the local. The tension between the local and global means that 'reflexive life planning becomes impossible. ... Under such conditions, civil societies shrink and disarticulate ... (and) the search for meaning takes place then in the reconstruction of defensive identities around communal principles' (Castells 1997a: 11). There is thus a new concern to establish community, in which globalising social relations accentuate localised communal identities. This is a kind of change and response model, whereby the motor of change is global informational capitalism, while invoking the local is a reaction to this (see further, Smith 2001).[2]

The problem here is that the global is thereby removed from any particular local instance, working through an abstract space of flows (see also Allen 2003). For all his careful empirical detail, Castells is thereby still subject to the same kinds of problems found in the work of Albrow, Beck and Giddens, which have been most powerfully exposed by Walter Benjamin's critique of historicism:

> It is very easy to establish oppositions ... within the various 'fields' of any epoch, such that on one side lies the 'productive', 'forward-looking', 'lively', 'positive' part of the epoch, and on the other side the abortive, retrograde and obsolescent. The very contours of the positive element will appear only insofar as this element is set off against the negative. (1999: 459)

Benjamin's point is that in such accounts the present is defined with respect to a past constructed in its shadow. This 'present' becomes a product which the powerful use as a means of denying truths they would rather not face. It thus becomes part of a moral project in which globalisation constructs its own truths, rendering the local as a repository of the defensive past. Using Benjamin's insights, we can recognise that globalisation is a means for particular people, with specific interests and identities, to proclaim universal rights and powers. Faced with the implications of Benjamin's insights, we see it as morally essential to champion the local. Rather than seeing the local as an instance of global social change, in which case it has no analytical importance and functions mainly as a cipher within globalisation theory, it is important to champion the idea of the local as an 'irritant' to the epochal and speculative character of much contemporary social theory. We can do this by building on two further renderings of the local in recent social theory.

A fourth way of construing the local adopts network approaches.[3] Network approaches vary immensely, but both in the form of social network analysis, as well as in actor network theory they insist that global processes do not work at a general level, but operate through specific proximate ties and connections. The global thus does not stand above the local, but are a particular set of network ties, with the result that there is no 'one' global, but an infinite multiplicity of global relationships, all constituted in various forms through particular local configurations.[4] The power of network thinking is that it construes the local as hubs in networks connecting other locals, and thereby the local is not seen as a concrete particular in opposition to a general, but as articulated with other local particulars through its networks with them. It is not the purpose of our book to use formal network analysis, as elaborated by Wellman (1979) or Wasserman and Faust (1994), though we are interested in how places can more generally be understood in network terms. Similarly, although our book is not an application of actor network theory, we are certainly sympathetic to its stance which insists on the provisional and contingent nature of ties, its emphasis on fluidity, and its scepticism towards macro-epochal claims (see for instance Latour 1993 on modernity).

Rather, in developing this general approach, we are indebted to the powerful arguments of Doreen Massey regarding a 'progressive sense of place' (Massey 1993, 1994). Massey (1994) shows that people move into and out of places, both on a regular and an irregular basis, and this coming and going is crucial to understanding how people come to perceive their relationship to place. Similarly Amin and Thrift's (2002: 7) application of actor network theory to the understanding of cities as 'a place of mobility, flow and everyday practice' is useful. This leads them to develop an account of the city that is based on the 'instituted, transhuman and distanciated nature of urban life', which allows them to recognise the importance of mobility and flows without invoking a theory of globalisation.

Arjun Appadurai (1996) offers probably the most developed and subtle alternative to that of the epochalists, and his account of the construction of contemporary neighbourhoods marks a fifth perspective. He argues that localities are not 'given' primordially but are socially produced through processes of boundary definition. 'Neighbourhoods are inherently what they are because they are opposed to something else and derive from other, already produced neighbourhoods' (Appadurai 1996: 183). Thus, global flows allow neighbourhoods to be reproduced as people's imagination is used to differentiate their neighbourhood from the outside. Appadurai thereby insists that neighbourhoods are not to be seen as passive, static products, with the implication that the dynamic of change comes from outside. As residents go about their daily life they encounter images, people and technologies from outside their neighbourhood which provide the potential for neighbourhood itself to be redefined. Appadurai's approach squares with important anthropological work on the construction of symbolic boundaries (e.g. Cohen 1985) and emphasises how global flows thereby allows the proliferation of rich imaginary and symbolic resources to allow people to construct their 'local' in a range of ways. He is thus able to see globalisation not as an epochal change but in a more nuanced way. 'The production of locality – always, I have argued, a fragile and difficult achievement – is more than ever shot through with contradictions, destabilised by human motion, and displaced by the formation of new kinds of virtual neighbourhoods' (Appadurai 1996: 198).

We have seen how globalisation theory reaches an impasse in its understanding of the local. Early globalisation theorists continued to expound long standing sociological concerns regarding the eclipse of community, seeing globalisation as the culmination of such processes. In its more recent formulations, however, globalisation is seen to involve the construction of the local, but we have pointed to the problematic conceptions of this within epochal globalisation theory. It is necessary to invoke the local to sustain the claims of globalisation, but there is no obvious theoretical foundation for it. Insofar as space is a matter of indifference, it is not clear how 'local' spatial units can be a 'principle', or a 'process', with the result that the local can only be defined as a result of globalisation (where it becomes a particular), or as a kind of weakly theorised 'residue'. By contrast we have drawn upon network and relational conceptions to suggest the need for an account of the local which is not contrasted with the global, but which situates the local against other locals in an environment where comparisons and references are multiple and complex. In the next section, we develop this approach through reference to the work of Pierre Bourdieu.

1.2 Capital, habitus and field

It remains important, we argue, to recognise the ongoing significance of territoriality for social relationships. If we abandon the view that the local is the privileged site of face-to-face community, then we need an alternative way of understanding the stakes that fixed sites bring. Two necessary elements are a theory of embodiment and a theory of property. A theory of embodiment, which focuses on the relative immobility of humans vis-á-vis flows of goods and symbols, allows us to recognise the relative significance of territory for people.[5] A theory of property, as found in Marxist perspectives, importantly sees that territory defines landed property and capital (Lefebvre 1991; Harvey 1983). In the work of Harvey this perspective has been elaborated through the idea of a spatial fix (Harvey 1985).[6] These two points can then be connected with a third, which is that global flows do not eclipse embodiment and property, but overlay them, so that the social world becomes more complex but does involve a simple transition from one dominant form of organisation to another.

We do not need to develop an account along these lines from scratch, since Pierre Bourdieu has already elaborated a sophisticated social theory which recognises both the salience of embodiment and the power of property, or in his terms, capital. However, Bourdieu himself has rarely talked much about globalisation, and where he has, his comments are naïve and unreflexive.[7] In addition his sociology of space is strikingly underdeveloped, although his perspective is strongly indebted to spatial metaphors, such as the 'field' (Lopez and Scott 2000).[8] In this section we show how Bourdieu's conceptual armoury can be used to elaborate an analytically powerful account of the local and the global.

Early interpretations of Bourdieu's work defined it as either neo-Marxist or as hybrid Marxist/Weberian which relied on a predominantly instrumental theory of cultural capital. Those who were socialised by family and upbringing into the appropriate cultural resources were better able to advance their interests, especially through being able to perform well in the educational system (see Jenkins 1992). Such interpretations fit works such as Bourdieu and Passeron (1973), but in the past decade, and perhaps especially since the appearance of *Pascalian Meditations* (Bourdieu 1999a) it has become clear that Bourdieu's theoretical framework marks a fundamental break from such instrumental thinking, through his re-working of phenomenological philosophy (see generally Swartz 1997, Dreyfus and Rabinow 1999; Crossley 2001) in which everyday life is at the bedrock of social existence. In this context, Bourdieu's concept of capital can be placed in broader context where its interplay with 'habitus' and 'field' is crucial.

The starting point for this interpretation of Bourdieu is his notion of habitus which insists that people's dispositions are embodied, and thereby necessarily territorially located. Rather than see self-interest as the main mechanism for action, Bourdieu's embodied sociology leads him to focus more on feelings of 'comfort' in place. In some cases there seems no break between the actor and the world around. This is due to the 'practical sense of a habitus', in which

'the agent engaged in practice knows the world but with knowledge which ... is not set up in the relation of externality of a knowing consciousness. He [sic] knows it, in a sense, too well ... takes it for granted, *precisely because he is caught up in it, bound up with it; he inhabits it like a garment or a familiar habitat.* (Bourdieu 1999a: 142/3: italics ours)

There are echoes here of the existentialist concern with physical proximity as the bedrock of human existence. However, there is nothing intrinsic about what places one feels comfortable in, and in this respect Bourdieu departs from existential assumptions that view the 'home', or 'nature' as being inherently more conducive to feeling at one with one's surrounds. Instead, it is important to understand how different kinds of places are incorporated into fields, so that, as Lefebvre (1991) observes, space is not just an arena for conflict but forms part of the stakes over which conflict takes place. Fields define hierarchical spaces of social and spatial positions, specifying the stakes involved in such positions. In this respect, Bourdieu's account is consistent with network approaches, and echoes the well-known arguments of Massey (1984).

> 'the capital city is ... the site of capital, that is, the site in physical space where the positive poles of all the fields are concentrated along with most of the agents occupying these dominant positions; which means that the capital cannot be adequately analysed except in relation to the provinces (and 'provincialness'), which is nothing other than being deprived (in entirely relative terms) of the capital and capital. (Bourdieu 1999b: 125)

The mechanism which links habitus and field, or 'the feel for the game, and the game itself' (Bourdieu 1999a: 151), is the sense of bodily comfort and ease which people experience in different social situations – *which are also physical situations.*

> Just as physical space ... is defined by the reciprocal externality of positions ... the social space is defined by the mutual exclusion, or distinction, of the positions which constitute it. ... Social agents, and also things insofar as they are appropriated by them and therefore constituted as properties, are situated in a place in social space, a distinct and distinctive place which can be characterized by the position it occupies relative to other places (...) and the distance (...) that separates it from them. (Bourdieu 1999a: 134)

Thus, fields require spatial separation so that different kinds of stakes involve various kinds of location.

> The dispositions occupied involve an adjustment to the position – what Erving Goffman calls the 'the sense of one's place'. It is this sense of one's place which in a situation of interaction, prompts those whom we call in French les gens humbles, literally, 'humble people' – perhaps 'common folks' in English – to remain humbly in their place, and which prompts others to 'keep their distance' or to 'keep their station in life'. (Bourdieu 1987: 5)

People are comfortable when there is a correspondence between habitus and field, but otherwise people feel ill at ease and seek to move – socially and spatially – so that their discomfort is relieved. For Bourdieu this is crucial to the 'dialectic of positions and dispositions'. Mobility is driven as people, with their relatively fixed habitus, both move between fields (places of work, leisure, residence, etc.), and move to places within fields where they feel more comfortable. Mobility and stability are hence reciprocally inter-related through the linkage between fields and habitus.

Various fields differ in the ways they articulate with physical space. Capitalist modernity involves fields becoming more differentiated, separated from each other (Fowler 1997). This involves the diversification of the audiences for various kinds of cultural practices. Thus Abercrombie and Longhurst (1998) argue, contemporary capitalist societies are increasingly characterised by the interaction between simple (e.g. theatre), mass (e.g. television) and diffused audiences (of everyday life). Extant paradigms for the study of audiences are unable to cope with the varied empirical and conceptual demands of the understanding of these relations. This diversification means that we use an increasing variety of spaces in our lives as we move between fields, such as those of work, different leisure pursuits, and so on. There is thus no one space where we feel at home all the time. A secretary may feel at ease working alongside a senior executive in neighbouring offices, but ill at ease if she is invited to her home for a meal. There are disjunctures between fields, and the spaces associated with them. This has numerous implications.

As each field becomes clearly demarcated from others, so it becomes the object for specific strategising and discursive awareness (see generally McNay 1999). Discursive consciousness, and reflexivity in general, is amplified through the multiplication of fields. Residential fields become subject to more strategic reflection, and are less interpreted as 'where one happens to live', or 'where one was brought up'. In addition, fields vary in the extent to which they depend on spatially situated practices. At one extreme, some fields, notably those which are strongly characterised by struggles over distinction, depend on stakes located uniquely in space. Thus cultural capital involves the separation of the territory of high culture (theatres, museums, cultivated homes, etc.) from that of low or popular culture (pubs, music halls, etc.). However, this is not to say that all fields are organised in this way. When cultural production and reception become more detached from specific sites, when in the arguments of Walter Benjamin (1973), they are more subject to mechanical reproducibility, they are less likely to generate distinction. Thus, recent American research demonstrating that increasing numbers of Americans are 'cultural omnivores' who participate in both 'high' and 'low' culture (e.g. Peterson and Kern 1996) draws frequently on examples from music. As listening to music becomes less dependent on live performance, and is possible in a wider range of spaces (from one's bedroom to the car stereo and the personal hi-fi), so it becomes less a marker for distinction. Precisely because it is a relatively easy matter to put different CDs on inside your home, musical taste becomes more mobile and less organised around fixed hierarchical tastes.

Furthermore, within any field, those practices that continue to rely on spatial fixity are most likely to be tied up with claims to distinction than those that do not. The audience at the 'premier' of a film, which is fixed at one point in space and time, is necessarily more exclusive than the audiences in later performances which are shown multiply in a variety of locations. Claims to social and cultural distinction continue to rely on an auratic concern to preserve particular, unique locations as 'natural' for specific practices. Global processes involve the 'overlaying' of territorially based fields with fields which are less territorially organised (see Brenner 2000). There is increasing differentiation between those fields – often organised through mass communication – that are relatively spatially indifferent, and those that remain very largely rooted in place. The friction, or disjuncture, between these fields is of crucial importance. Those cultural fields that are still dependent on fixed spaces are likely to remain as significant as ever in generating cultural distinction.

Appadurai's (1993, 1996) arguments regarding the organisation of the imagination are pertinent here. He argues that we live in a world with a global imaginary, where our imaginations roam far over space and time. 'Electronic mediation and mass migration mark the world of the present not as technically new forces but as ones that seem to impel (and sometimes compel) the work of the imagination' (Appadurai 1996: 4). The social organisation of imagination is linked to five separate kinds of global cultural flows based around the movement of people (ethnoscapes), media technologies and images (mediascapes), technologies (technoscapes), finance and investment flows (financescapes), and political ideologies and narratives (ideoscapes). Appadurai insists that these five flows are in disjuncture from one another, and that the tensions between these flows account for the complexities of globalising processes. Appadurai's focus on flows has been highly influential, and has been developed by later writers who have sought to develop further kinds of flows held to be characteristic of globalisation (e.g. Urry 2000). However, his emphasis on imagination has been less extensively developed (see Abercrombie and Longhurst 1998); a limitation which we seek to redress in the main body of this book.

Disjunctures between fields, as well as the emergence of new more mobile fields, generates a somewhat different dynamic from the struggles for distinction analysed by Bourdieu. 'Ordinariness' becomes a key arena around which people seek to establish the commonality of their shared position with various others (Devine 1992; Erickson 1996; Black 2001; Longhurst et al. 2001; Savage et al. 2001). People claim ordinariness in order to 'opt into' a range of shared practices and activities in a situation where the multiplicity of fields may pull them into separate practices. This ordinariness codes new kinds of distinctions and hierarchies, though these may be implicit rather than stated overtly. We are interested in this book in exploring how residential location is related to different cultural fields, and the spatial organisation of these fields.

Our book is therefore a study of the contemporary significance of local belonging. This encapsulates Bourdieu's interest in how people may feel comfortable or not in any one place, relating this to the habitus and capital of its residents. This allow us to explore local belonging as fluid and contingent, in a manner consistent with Probyn's (1996) and Fortier's (2000) insistence that belonging is not a given but is itself unstable, positing both states (of unbelonging) from which one comes, and possible future states of belonging to which one may aspire. Probyn's formulation of 'outside belonging' usefully indicates some of the tensions around this term:

> the desire that individuals have to belong, a tenacious and fragile desire that is …
> increasingly performed in the knowledge of the impossibility of ever really and
> truly belonging, along with the fear that the stability of belonging and the sanc-
> tity of belonging are forever past. (Probyn 1996: 8)

Belonging should be seen neither in existential terms (as primordial attachment to some kind of face-to-face community), nor as discursively constructed, but as a socially constructed, embedded process in which people reflexively judge the suitability of a given site as appropriate given their social trajectory and their position in other fields. There is thus a kind of paradox which is that residential space remains relatively fixed yet also the subject of increasing temporal instability as people reflect on its ability to act as marker of their home. Residential place continues to matter since people feel some sense of 'being at home' in an increasingly turbulent world. Thus, even though continuing to be relatively fixed, housing is also thoroughly the subject of reflexivity. It follows that in a mobile, global environment, location in fixed physical space may be of increasing relative significance in the generation of social distinction.

1.3 Researching Manchester neighbourhoods

Much attention has focused on the role of 'global cities', such as New York, Los Angeles, and London (e.g. Sassen 1991; Buck et al. 2002). There are differences of view here as to whether such cities can be seen as increasingly distinct global cities differentiated from 'second tier' cities. Hannerz (1996) insists on the cultural significance of only a few global cities, and this argument is supported by the claims of Friedmann and Wolff (1982), Castells (1996) and Sassen (1991) that global cities are becoming increasingly important sites for global mobility. These claims have been disputed theoretically by Smith (2001), and empirically through Buck et al.'s (2002) argument that the development of London in the past 20 years owes more to its regional and national role than to its global position.

In all this work, there is a danger that debates about globalisation become conflated with studies of a few 'global cities', and that we lose sight of the numerically more significant middle ranking urban spaces. During the 1980s numerous studies of industrial cities portrayed a bleak picture of de-industrialisation and redundancy (Smith and Feagin 1996), with such cities being seen in relative decline. However, just as the prime role of global cities has been questioned in recent years, so there has been greater interest in the global role of 'second tier' cities. Castells (2002: 372) argues that 'all large metropolitan areas in the developed world, and all of the largest in the developing world, are thus global to some extent'. In this context, Manchester is a very revealing case study. It remains a leading European city: its population of nearly four million people (Le Gales 2002:

Table 2.3) marks it as the seventh largest conurbation in Europe in 2000. There are only two other non-capital cities in Europe greater in size (Essen in Germany and Barcelona in Spain).

Manchester is also a highly pertinent case study because of its history as the first industrial city. For Peter Hall (1998: 347) 'Manchester in 1770 was the first true innovative milieu', with its unique combination of technical skill, transport networks, and capital availability allowing the rapid growth of the cotton textile industry which was the most dynamic sector in Britain's industrial revolution. For much of the 19th Century, Manchester was seen by observers as diverse as Alexis de Tocqueville, Frederic Engels, and Mary Gaskell as the epitome of the new capitalist industrial order. Manchester retained this dynamic momentum even after the textile industry began to contract from the early 20th Century. It built one of the widest canals in England to allow ocean-going ships to use neighbouring Salford docks in the 1890s and became a major port until the 1960s. The Trafford Park Industrial Estate pioneered a new form of industrial development, with large factories being leased out to multi-national companies from the first decade of the 20th Century. This was the site of Ford motor company's first British plant and many other American firms, such as Colgate and Kellogs invested in the area. Its scientific expertise was considerable. It was the original home of Rolls Royce engine makers, and was a pace maker in the development of computer technology until the early 1950s, through the expertise of electronic engineering firms such as Ferranti and the close links they established with scientists at Manchester University.

This innovative industrial tradition, however, began to fail in the 1950s, and collapsed with remarkable speed from the 1970s (see generally Peck and Ward 2002). The textile industry virtually disappeared, with marked employment decline in engineering and other manufacturing sectors. In the Greater Manchester region as a whole, male full-time employment declined by 32% between 1971 and 1997, and all forms of employment by 11% (compared to a 5% rise in England as a whole, see Giordiano and Twomey 2002). Unemployment levels reached over 20% in the 1980s, and although they declined thereafter, this was largely due to the unemployed ceasing to look for work as they left the labour market through disability, sickness or early retirement. Giordano and Twomey (2002: 68) calculate a real unemployment rate of 29% in 1997. Parts of the inner city saw deteriorating housing and high levels of poverty and deprivation.

However, amidst this industrial decline, a new mode of urban regeneration programme was championed from the mid-1980s (see Taylor et al. 1996; Peck and Ward 2002). This involved re-branding the city as an attractive site for capital, well-qualified professionals and visitors, redeveloping its urban core through service led provision, and modernising its transport and retail infrastructure (see Devine et al. 2000; Robson 2002, Mellor 2002; and Peck and Tickell 1995). Manchester sought to define itself as a major European city, second only to London in England. It made a respectable bid for the Olympic Games in 2000, it hosted the Commonwealth Games in 2002,

13

and its airport became a major international hub. This was all backed by the success of Manchester United Football Club, which dominated English soccer from the early 1990s, when it became the world's most profitable football club. Its popular culture enjoyed a glorious period from the late 1970s to the mid-1990s when its home grown musical talent, in the form of bands such as New Order, the Smiths, the Stone Roses and Oasis defined it as the 'happening' city, and a leading centre of the rave and dance culture. Young people flocked to the city. For much of the 1980s and 1990s Manchester University was one of the most popular universities in the UK, and the city saw the largest concentration of students in Western Europe in its four Universities. A particularly dramatic development in Manchester from the early 1990s was the attraction of affluent residents back into central urban locations through the conversion of warehouses and offices into apartments (see Wynne and O'Connor 1996), and the generation of a café bar, club and restaurant scene. Manchester's gay village became one of the world centres of gay consumer culture (Binnie and Skeggs 2004)

The recent history of Manchester, therefore, clearly exemplifies the tensions and ambivalences of globalisation itself. It witnessed the loss of its old role as centre to a regionally based industrial economy, but it pioneered new kinds of urban development drawing on global flows and post-industrial symbols (see Hills 2000 and Tyrer 2000; 2002). Most studies of the city have hitherto focused on central sites within it, taken to represent its extreme facets. At one extreme these include studies of its deprived neighbourhoods such as Hulme (Harding 1997 and more generally Griffiths 1998). There have been rather more studies of the dynamic city centre, including O'Connor and Wynne's (1996) ode to the cultural dynamism of the new city dwellers, and Skeggs's research on aspects of the gay village (e.g. Binnie and Skeggs 2004). While such research is invaluable, the challenge for understanding contemporary urban processes is to recognise the spatial extension of activities in what Castells defines as the metropolitan region:

> These settlements blur the distinctions between cities and countryside, and between cities and suburbs. They include, in spatial discontinuity, built up areas of various density, open space, agricultural activities, natural areas, residential expanses and concentrations of services and manufacturing activities. (2002: 374)

Although leading global cities such as Los Angeles, with its diverse neighbourhoods, are the epitome for these metropolitan regions, our challenge is to investigate whether 'second tier' cities such as Manchester can also be seen to have such defined zones, and if so, how such zones relate to the habitus of different kinds of urban residents. Rather than attempting to understand the city 'as a whole', we can take a selection of different neigbourhoods to consider the degrees of commonality and difference within them. This allows us the potential to examine the interplay between global processes and the formation of distinct local milieux.

We therefore selected four contrasting residential areas in and around Manchester, whose residents had different combinations of economic and/or cultural capital and we deliberately did not seek to examine those in poor or working-class areas. This strategy allowed us to recognise the possible diversity within the city, yet without sacrificing detailed knowledge of the particularity of each area. In each area we took the electoral register as our sampling frame, took a one in three sample of particular streets, and arranged interviews by letter, telephone and through knocking on doors, finally achieving between 43 and 47 interviews in each place. In households with male and female members we alternated who we approached to obtain roughly similar numbers of men and women, though we actually ended up interviewing more women then men because men were more likely to refuse to be interviewed. Our overall response rate of 34% is in line with other research of this type. The interviews lasted between 45 minutes and 2 hours and covered the following topics: interaction and perception of neighbourhood and locality; leisure practices and household relationships; work and work histories; and social and cultural attitudes and values. Half the interviews were conducted by Gaynor, the project's Research Associate, with the remainder being carried out by Brian and Mike. We each interviewed in every area so that we could compare our thoughts on the four areas between ourselves. The Appendix lists all our interviewees (anonymised), including their occupation and income, and also indicates the pages of this book where we have quoted from or referred to them, so that readers can see how we have not 'cherry picked' but have drawn on the wide array of material from across most of the sample.

It is central to our concerns that, like Burawoy et al. (1991; 2000) and Layder (1993), we wanted to use qualitative research to address 'macro' issues of global change, and we did not conceive our research as committing us to a view that social relations are organised on a micro basis, as within the grounded theory and interactionist tradition (Glaser and Strauss 1967; Seale 1999; May 2001). This allowed us to do justice to Bourdieu's emphasis on a reflexive sociology that captures the intersection of structure and agency (Bourdieu and Wacquant 1992), society and the individual. In the absence of any obvious British exemplars for this kind of research (though see the parallel study of Butler and Robson 2003a, and to some extent Buck et al. 2002), we loosely drew on the evocative American models of Bellah et al. (1996) and Wolfe (1998), both of which used around 200 in-depth interviews to explore the values and culture of middle-class Americans in a period of major social change.

Central to our concerns was to explore people's own narratives of connectivity and global ties, rising out of their daily routines of work, residence and leisure. We are not persuaded that it is a useful exercise to ask people directly about global issues, their sense of global belonging, and so forth. Respondents who are asked questions about global issues will be able to answer with varying degrees of sophistication and clarity, but their replies may not be salient to their everyday lives. Here we support Silverman's (2001) invocation to use naturally occurring data wherever possible, which in the context of our research involved looking at how the local and the global was articulated in the various questions on aspects of everyday life and identity. Our interview schedules were concerned to ask people about their daily routines around work, household, kin, friends and leisure, so that we could ascertain both the kinds of spatial ranges of such practices, and the extent to which people's narratives spontaneously invoked any kinds of global issues as they talked.

It is clear that conducting 182 interviews involved some quantitative, as well as qualitative elements. We had nearly 1.5 million words of transcription, coded up in ways detailed in the chapters of this book. All our interviews in Wilmslow were coded to QSR-Nudist as a means of facilitating analysis. However, we found Nudist only as helpful as the codes that we used permitted it to be, and for writing this book we coded interviews using Excel spread sheets and by the extensive coding of transcripts around particular themes or issues. Our analysis involved both looking at the range of answers across the cases, as well as the way that answers were related to other parts of the narrative within cases. In addition to our interpretative analysis, we were concerned to establish whether there were general patterns in each of our four areas. We therefore report simple frequencies for the practices and values of interest to us. We realise that this strategy may displease both quantitative and qualitative researchers. Qualitative researchers frequently emphasise that their research does not depend on generating a large sample or trying to generalise (see Mason 1996; Sayer 1992) and they may fear that it becomes difficult to do justice to the complexity of particular cases when 182 interviews were conducted and analysed. With so many interviews there may be a danger that data analysis takes the form of 'cherry-picking' from a large number of possible interviews those few quotes that conform to ideas or hunches, so that a rigorous qualitative testing of data actually becomes more difficult. Quantitative researchers, on the other hand, may worry that 182 cases are not enough to allow any kind of statistical analysis, especially given our sampling strategy which is not on a random basis.

Despite these understandable concerns, we think it is useful to generalise about broad differences, and similarities, between our four areas, by reporting frequencies and patterns, even though such generalisations need to come with a 'health warning' that they might not be sustained by more statistically representative survey analysis. Given that we do not seek to establish correlations between variables, and that we are more sympathetic to a descriptive research strategy rather than one premised on the assumptions of general linear reality (Abbott 2000), we do not see this as a major problem. The simple frequencies we use are mainly checks so that readers can assess how we are using qualitative material from across the range of cases. In each of the four areas, our analysis centred on showing how particular individuals exemplify certain core processes, and developing typologies around which individuals could be meaningfully linked, following the lead of Layder (1993). Our elaboration of such typologies depended on assessing whether the distinctions we delineated on the basis of our reading of the transcripts were also salient to respondents themselves. We were especially interested in exploring the view of those who were ambivalent. In our analysis, as well as reporting general findings, we use extended individidual case studies, which we place in boxes for emphasis. These cases are reported in greater detail so that readers can see how our account of key processes are instantiated in the narratives and life histories of respondents. We do not seek to extrapolate issues which are not germane to respondents themselves: rather, our account organises narratives which are salient and meaningful to respondents. Our extensive use of quotation is therefore deliberate, and although readers can chose to skip the boxed accounts if they wish, they are warned that these accounts have been chosen not to illustrate but to demonstrate the force of our arguments. The respondents we have used for these extended case studies are identified by name, and a full list is provided in the Appendix.

1.4 Our case study areas

The four areas were chosen to exemplify different kinds of social mix, differentiating the areas in terms of the extent of their economic and cultural capital within a range of loosely 'middle-class' neighbourhoods. Following scrutiny of MIMAS small area statistics and local investigations we chose the following locations near Manchester (see Map 1.1).

Wilmslow was an old market town 12 miles south of Manchester, located in the desirable north Cheshire suburban belt between Macclesfield and Altrincham. This area became a Victorian gentleman's suburb of Manchester from the later Victorian period, with regular train services allowing professional commuters to get to the city centre in under half an hour. From the 1980s the area benefited from the decentralisation of employment from the city centre, with many large corporations setting up operations in the vicinity. Its proximity to Manchester airport, ten minutes drive away, further increased its popularity. Despite this development, planning controls ensured that large tracts of rural land were preserved in the vicinity, and with the hills of the Peak District being only a few miles away, this ensured that the town maintained something of its rural feel. Nonetheless, the town centre had itself been subject to redevelopment, with many new shops and café bars opening in the period just before we conducted our interviews. This was one of the most affluent areas in the UK and we interviewed respondents in detached housing where properties were valued in 1997 at between £250,000 and £750,000 (see Savage et al. 2004a).

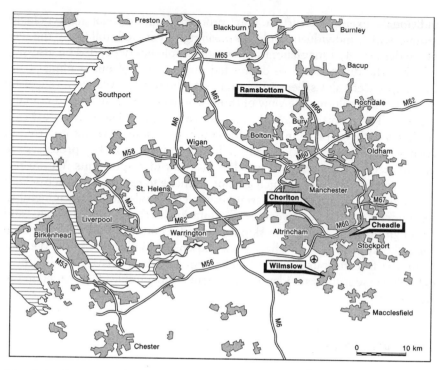

Map 1.1 *Location of case study areas*

Cheadle was an 'ordinary' inter-war suburban estate of three bedroom semi-detached housing, situated six miles south of Manchester. The village itself retained its medieval church and its old high street, though in contrast to Wilmslow its shopping centre looked distinctly faded and down at heel. Situated only a mile away from the major city of Stockport, a process of suburban infilling had meant that there were few green spaces which separated the town from its neighbours. We interviewed in one of these infill developments half a mile from the village centre. In 1997/98 houses were valued at between £50,000 and £65,000 (see Savage et al. 2004b). Here we expected to find lower levels of economic and cultural capital.

Chorlton was a district of urban gentrification in an area of Victorian terraced streets three miles from the centre of Manchester, clustered around new cafés, wine bars, restaurants and specialist shops. Although Chorlton merged into other parts of inner city Manchester to the north and east, on the west and south it faced the River Mersey which gave it a sense of identity and separated it from Manchester's outer suburbs. In the 1960s, the area had been relatively poor, with a predominantly working-class population, and a considerable Irish presence, but from this period there had been a steady influx of professionals, attracted to the close proximity to the city centre, the green spaces adjoining the River Mersey and dotted throughout the area, and the bohemian feel linked to the existence of its distinctive shopping centre. Properties ranged in price from £50,000 for small terraces to £200,000 for the largest terraced houses.

Ramsbottom was selected as an area of rural gentrification with relatively affluent households but relatively few highly educated respondents. It is an old Lancashire mill town 12 miles north of Manchester. Until the 1980s the town was relatively cut off from Manchester and its closest ties were to its neighbouring towns in the Lancashire textile belt, Bolton, Bury and Rochdale. However, a new motorway had dramatically improved access to the area and it had emerged as a popular commuter belt location. The old town centre retained a lively, bustling, small town feeling, with a number of new shops aimed at the affluent middle classes opening in recent years, in part drawing on the success of the East Lancashire steam railway which led to a significant influx of day visitors. The town was situated in an attractive valley at the foot of moors rising a thousand feet above the town, giving it an air of being in the countryside. We interviewed in an area of large older terraces situated close to the town centre, and a range of newer semi-detached housing built for commuters, which sold for between £50,000 and £150,000.

Each of the four areas had its own distinct history and characteristics, yet we also selected them expecting them to have residents with different stocks of economic and cultural capital. Table 1.1 indicates that our respondents do indeed fall into very different kinds of profile according to the ACORN postcode classification. The ACORN classification is loosely hierarchical, with 1 indicating the wealthiest, and 54 the least wealthy postcode areas. Table 1.2 indicates the key features of our achieved sample, including the occupational class distribution of respondents, levels of household income, and the educational qualifications of respondents. We briefly refer to the main characteristics of our sample, and to give a little more flavour of these four places, which will be unknown to most of the readers of this book, we will use four personal vignettes which exemplify some of the aspects of local residents that we unpack in greater detail in later chapters.

Nearly all the *Wilmslow* addresses come from the most affluent postcode grouping, with the majority of this population being in the top 3% of the income distribution. The average household income of our sample was over £70,000,[9] but in nearly all cases men earned the vast bulk of this: the average male income was £68,000 and the average female income was £10,000.[10] Many men worked in manageral positions in the large corporations based in North Chesire. As Stuart indicates, respondents exemplified affluent suburban conventionality, organised around a marked gendered division of

Table 1.1 *Percent of households in each area falling into various ACORN postcode categories*

Acorn classification	Cheadle	Chorlton	Ramsbottom	Wilmslow	% of UK pop.
1 – wealthy suburbs, detached housing				93	2.6
3 – mature affluent home owning areas				7	2.7
9 – Private flats, elderly people	9				0.9
10 – Affluent working families with mortgages			43		2.1
13 – Home-owning family areas			13		2.6
14 – Home-owning family areas, older children	42				3
18 – Furnished flats and bedsits, younger single people		4			0.4
19 – Apartments, young professionals, singles and couples		23			1.1
20 – Gentrified multi-ethnic areas		62			1
28 – Established home-owning areas	35				4
29 – Home-owning areas, council tenants, retired	9				2.7
30 – Established home-owners, skilled workers	5				4.5
31 – Home-owners in older properties, younger workers			40		3
33 – Council areas, some new home-owners			2		3.8
37 – Multi-occupied town centres, mixed occupations		11			1.8
N =	43	47	47	45	

labour with a male corporate breadwinner, and a female domestic carer (see Savage et al. 2004a for further detail). All households except one in Wilmslow had either currently or in the past contained a heterosexual couple and children.[11] There were only three women who earned above £20,000, and only one of these, a dentist, earned a salary (around £50,000) approaching the male norm. There were only two households with male and female partners where the women earned more than the men. One of these was that of the dentist, whose partner was now retired, but had had a very senior executive job in the past. In the other case, a female trainer earned very slightly more than her male partner. In both cases these households were distinctive in seeing younger women living with older men who had children from previous marriages.

Table 1.2 *Statistics of achieved sample*

Dimensions	Cheadle	Chorlton	Ramsbottom	Wilmslow
Mean Household income	£23k	£30k	£36k	£70k
% Graduates	14	60	19	45
% Upper service class	3	18	26	42
% Service class	24	60	62	63
% Female	35	53	45	62
Mean age	46	40	45	54
% Ethnic minority	2	2	4	4
No. of interviews	43	47	47	45
Response rates	29%	39%	30%	41%

Stuart: Wilmslow corporate cultures and suburban conventionality

Stuart (W74) is exemplary of the corporate executive culture evident in Wilmslow. He was a physician who had chosen to work for a private company as a means of maximising his salary. His interview reveals the centrality of his work and its impact on his household relations.

I talk to my contemporaries and I came back from a London trip last Thursday and I was on the train ... (with) a senior doctor on the train who is a friend of mine and we spent two and a half hours chatting as we came back together, again in a very similar role to myself and he said all the things that I'm talking about now he would repeat and it's fairly common that we all find ourselves under pressure, there's nowhere to run away too, I mean my wife and daughter sat on that settee where you are several months ago and my wife was having a bit of a complain about the hours I was working and I said yes OK I can back off, I can go in at 9 and I've been going in at 7 and I can come home at 5 instead of 6 or 6.30 and at my next salary review my company will say you've not achieved as much this year, so your salary is a little less and your bonus not so good and forget about the share options, and the following year the same will happen and over a number of years I'll get really shaded down, it might not be so bad that I lose my job, but I get really shaded down and I said when you want to have that new bedroom fitted that we've just had done and you want that extra holiday, or you want to change your car, I'm awfully sorry we won't be able to do it, you can't have it both ways, tell me which one you'd like, and my daughter for once sat there and said to my wife, you know mum, dad's right you can't have it both ways, make your mind up, don't complain unless your prepared to sacrifice something and I thought for a 19 year old it was quite good. I could make a change, I could sell this house and go for a much smaller house, but I've always had this little thing inside me, I'm an achiever, I like to achieve.

Stuart relates his household relations and work as fair to himself and his wife. Men work longer hours but women can spend more. However, as his last sentence reveals, Stuart actually wanted to work long hours because he wanted to achieve, and so really sacrificed nothing. For his wife, the possibility of spending money was a compensation for Stuart's absence from home.

Chorlton was very different. Most of the ACORN postcodes are for gentrifying areas. Twenty-six households, more than half of the total, did not have, and never had had children. Among this group there was considerable diversity of household form, including sharing with housemates, heterosexual partners, gay partners and single households. A further four households were comprised of single parents. There was no sense therefore of a dominant household type, and childrearing was a less central activity than in Wilmslow. Only 8 of the 41 households had incomes above £40,000 and there were no households where incomes rose above £70,000. Male breadwinner dominance was not marked. Eleven households with different sex partners had men earning the majority of the household income, compared to 9 with women earning the most, and 8 where incomes were similar. In addition there were 8 male- and 8 female-only households. Twenty of our respondents, nearly half, worked in what might be termed the cultural sector, in education, the media and a range of cultural businesses, and a further 8 worked in the health and social services. Susan is an interesting example. A small minority were manual or routine white-collar workers. Only 3 worked for large private corporations, whereas 15 worked in the public sector. There was a remarkable degree of fluidity, between genders, between work and leisure, and a strong sense of engagement with cultural activities.

Susan: Chorlton domestic egalitarianism and the home–work overlap

Susan (D109) worked in her husband's pottery* business and also taught part time at a local College.[12] When asked how she became interested in stained glass, she replied:

> Well that goes back quite a long time. Many years ago when the children were just starting at school I opened a toyshop,* strangely enough on Leighton Road,* and a colleague of mine brought along some terrarcotta and a few bits and bobs of stained glass to sell in the shop, and they were actually selling better than the toys*, so I thought I'd like to get involved in that. So we chatted and talked and I learned how to do it and then later on someone who was actually a potter* taught me and my husband how to really do it, it was a bit like an apprenticeship. Since then it's been a main part of our living really. Today I was working at Peter's studios* which is attached to Stockport infirmary*, working with people recovering from mental health problems, and they come along to the artist's studio and work alongside, I just carry on working and they have their own projects that they're working on.

Susan's interest in pottery* grew out of her contacts, and then how the pottery* work feeds through into her teaching and other activities. She was clear that she preferred this informal mode of working and related how she had dropped out of several teaching courses and 'I don't think

> I'll ever become a qualified teacher because something always aggravates me to the point where I can't continue, either in the classroom or the political situation'. She added, 'I have never felt like an orthodox worker, really'. This sense of alienation from organised bureaucratic work was widely shared.

Ramsbottom respondents were intermediate between Wilmslow and Chorlton. The ACORN codes were drawn in part from group 10, 'affluent working families', which are seen to be 'a particular feature of the 1980s boom areas' and 31 'blue-collar neighbourhoods', in 'older terraced housing'. These respondents had slightly higher household incomes than households in Chorlton, but considerably less than those in Wilmslow. Eight households did not have children, but the nuclear, male breadwinner household dominated, with 26 households comprising male and female partners with men earning the majority of the income, 3 households having equal incomes between men and women, and 5 having a female breadwinner. Only 5 women earned more than £20,000 compared with 26 men. Like Joanne (see below), women were largely employed in routine white-collar work, or occasionally in auxilliary professions such as nursing. A key feature of the sample is their relative lack of exposure to higher education, with only 9 having an undergraduate university degree (in 2 cases, from the Open University). On the whole, male residents were in managerial, technical IT and sales occupations rather than professional ones. Only 6 worked (or had worked) in professional occupations (2 teachers, 1 lecturer, 1 accountant and 2 chartered engineers). There was also a small minority of manual workers, especially in the older parts of Ramsbottom.

Joanne: Ramsbottom administrative work cultures

Joanne (R21) was atypical of most Ramsbottom respondents since she was bought up in the South of England, in Essex. She moved north when, 'I met my husband in Colchester* and he was not a happy man down South – he spoke a different language … it's quite a serious different language!'. She came from a farm labourer's background and left school with no qualifications. Her husband was a qualified accountant and she followed him back north. Despite her own lack of formal qualifications she had been promoted over time into a responsible job in the insurance industry.

> Well, when I came up to Manchester I went to an Employment Agency and said ... they said 'what can you do?' and I said 'not a lot' and they said 'well, try this insurance broker'. So I started off with the Broker and then became interested in the loss adjustment* side of things and then started looking for (other) work. I mean in those days you were allowed to ... you didn't need a degree or anything. I haven't got an 'O' level to my name.

You've learned your stuff as you've gone along?

Yes. I've lied a bit on occasions when it came to interviews – yes I've got ten 'O' levels and I didn't colour my lips' til I was fourteen-and-a-half, you know.

She had a strongly practical orientation to her work, where she tracked professional expertise.

Well, there's a lot of in-house training, you know, I have ... to a certain degree I'm expected to have the same sort of knowledge of Case Law as a solicitor – in fact I know I've got to have because I've got to cross words ... you know, cross words with them all the time and if I don't know what I'm talking about then I'd be taken to the cleaners. So there's continuous in-house training. Apart from that it's been a seat-of-your-pants job and sort of from experience.

Her own pride in her achievements was tempered by her strong concern not to let her work life dominate her social life. She had no children and an active social life based on her enthusiasm for walking, exercise, and eating and drinking out. Although she was now in a responsible position, she was ultimately instrumental about her work.

No. No, I just want to be paid a reasonable sum for what I do and then bugger off and enjoy my social life; I think that's been my ... my problem in life.

Why is it a problem? That sounds quite good really.

Well, I'd probably ... I'd probably be in a more responsible position being paid more if I'd have put a bit more effort into it when I was younger but work always hampered your social life, you know. Work was something you had to do ... I don't look forward to it (work) but I don't hate it; I quite enjoy ... I enjoy the work and I enjoy the people I work with, you know, I'm quite fortunate.

Joanne has a very different narrative to that found in Wilmslow, where men mostly have considerable autonomy because they direct organisations, or Chorlton, where cultural work is more central. To use the terms developed by Savage et al. (1992), Ramsbottom respondents are largely dependent on organisation assets.

In *Cheadle* most respondents came from two middle-income postcode areas. Area 14 are 'established family areas with relatively low levels of population migration', while group 35 notes that 'you are more likely to find the classic "mum, dad and two children" in these neighbourhoods than anywhere else in Britain'. There was a strong sense gained from the interviews in Cheadle that life was pretty tough. Admittedly, there were only 2 unemployed respondents in our sample, and only 4 households with incomes of under £10,000. In this sense, there was little absolute deprivation in the area. However, the moderate incomes of most residents were clearly hard earned. Only 3 households had incomes above £40,000, and three quarters were earning less than £30,000. Only 2 men earned more than £30,000, while 26 earned less than £20,000. Only 4 women earned above £20,000, and in general their paid employment was seen as subsidiary income to that of the male breadwinner: there were only 4 cases where women were the main earners in the household. Working respondents tended to work long hours, with many households having complicated shift arrangements to allow both partners to work while covering childcare responsibilities. In most cases there were strongly demarcated gender roles, with women being primarily responsible for domestic work, shopping and caring. Although the area is occupationally diverse, as Edward's story indicates below, there is a strong culture of manual labour which predominates in nearly all households, and which gave the area, as one respondent put it 'a practical flavour'. No less than 8 of the self-employed were involved in manual labour in building or other outdoor work, and the other self-employed were also involved in manufacturing activity. Some of these were involved in franchising arrangements that to all intents and purposes made the workers dependent on the franchising firm. Even 6 of the 9 service class respondents also were strongly steeped in the experience of manual labour.

Edward: Cheadle grafting skills

Edward (C34), was a further education lecturer in plumbing*, whose work history exemplified many of the difficulties faced by manual labourers since the 1980s. His story is worth relating at length...

Yes, I had my own business for a number of years and for one reason or another it failed, probably my own fault more than anything else, I had a period of unemployment, I then out of the blue just went to the Job Centre in Manchester, for no reason, I just felt that I wanted to go that day, and there was a job advertised for a youth training supervisor in plumbing.* I went for the interview, they called me up the next day saying you've got the job, and I found myself having half a dozen lads round me without any real experience or knowledge of how to train. So I was then encouraged by my wife to go and get some training, which I did at Salford University*, I did a one year course in further education for teachers, which was a City & Guilds, which I achieved, while I was working. At the end of that I was recommended to do the Certificate in Education. I then went to the boss at that time and said I need to go on this course one day a week, what about letting me go for day release on it and after a lot of hesitation he said yes you can go on it. So I got on the first year of the course in

Manchester, I had the second year of the course at Widnes Institute of Higher Education* and I became a CertEd at the end of it. Towards the end of that course the job was advertised that I'm in now, I applied for it, got it and I've been there ever since.

And how long is that?

Twelve years.

And before you had your own business, what did you do?

Well if you want to start from when I left school, from leaving school at 15 and a half, without any qualifications I went into an apprenticeship as a plumber*, living in Chester*. A year after I started there they closed down, I then spent the rest of my apprenticeship with a building company. I served my time there. I went to college for four years and got advanced crafts in plumbing*, building science, and about six months after coming out of my time we moved from where we were living in Chester* to Warrington*. I got a job with a building company, just as a plumber*, worked my way up to chargehand, from chargehand to foreman, I was then asked to become general foreman on site. So at the age of 32 I worked my way up to general foreman. From there at that point we were just about to get married and I had an argument one day with the contracts manager and I walked off the job. My mother and father at the time were on the shops* and said, instead of going back into the trade, come into the shop* with us. I didn't do that but we opened up a workshop*. From there I ran that for about three and a half years and then sold the business and moved into something else which failed completely had a period of unemployment. We then started moving around the country a little bit because of the problems that we had. I actually had a job as a shop* manager for a while, which moved us round the country, we were living in the north east for a while, and we moved to Ashton*, from Ashton* we left the shop* business and moved into a flat in Longsight* and had a job as a newspaper man*. From there, because I was home half nine, ten o'clock finished for the day, I thought I'd do a few jobs … put adverts in newsagents windows, and it led to getting quite a bit of work. I finished up doing two jobs and I thought I'd give my newspaper* job up and go plumbing* full time as my own business. And that's how I started off in business doing plumbing* and from there, just all of a sudden going out with some friends one night, he said just in conversation, I said I had to go out and buy my pipes* and he said, what about if you had a place to make your own pipes*, would you be able to make money out of it. I said probably, so he said I've got an empty warehouse, look at it. So I decided after looking at it to set up in business, we got money out of the government to set it up and I was then making pipes*, working six in the morning 'til nine at night and getting very stressed. I became very ill with it, it's the only time I've ever been on tranquilisers because I was so ill and I gave that up. It was making pipes*… for the DIY market and it was also an idea that was just about to be sold abroad because of the easy way of transporting pipes* to other parts of the world and we were getting all sorts of specifications in to have me make pipes* for places where they could be transported in containers. It was at that time I became ill because of the pressures we were under and I gave the business up. At that point I became unemployed, I then got a job with a building firm … and it was six months before Christmas. I was alright 'til then,

> after Christmas the work dried up, they made me unemployed again. And that's my life story!
>
> In one sense, Edward's work history was very turbulent, as he moved between different sectors of employment, into and out of self-employment, into further forms of training and finally into professional employment. In another sense, however, his work had been rather stable, as he sought different kinds of outlet for his skills in plumbing*.

We can see that our four case study areas are analytically different. Their residents have different stocks of economic and cultural capital. There are different kinds of gender relationship in these areas, and residents vary in their age. In the next chapter we begin our study by examining whether there were any commonalities in how these diverse groups of respondents identified with their own neighbourhoods and defined their sense of local belonging.

Notes

1 Featherstone and Lash (1995) argue that even the first generation of globalisation theory differentiates homogenisers from particularisers, and cite Said, Bhabha, and Hall as examples of the latter. However, these theorists were not particularly prominent in developing concepts of globalisation, though their work was always pertinent to such concerns, as Featherstone and Lash make clear.

2 For other examples of this rendering of the local as resistance to the global, see Urry (2002: 87) who reports that 'the power of the attractor of glocalisation can also be found in the more general development of local brands and of the often localised resistances that develop against them'.

3 We should note that we do not use the idea of networks in the same way that Castells does, where he draws on the metaphor of networks within IT to emphasise the significance of instantaneous flows between inter-connected nodes, focusing especially on the significance of capital mobility. Only on one page does he draw on a theoretical discussion of the nature of networks (Castells 1996: 470). See also the pertinent criticisms of Urry (2002: 8–12).

4 Our approach uses the idea of network in a broad way: for our purposes it includes mobility such as flows, (Urry 2000: Chapter 2), fire (Law and Hetherington 1999), etc.

5 To be fair, elements of this argument can be detected in the work of Castells (1996) but it is then occluded through arguments regarding the remaking of the self which pick up on the disembodiment of the human agent in globalising conditions.

6 The concept of the spatial fix refers to the fact that flows depend on the existence of a fixed infrastructure (of roads, communication technologies, etc.) and thereby provides a useful way of seeing a dialectical relationship between flows and fixity.

7 For instance his account of the 'international circulation of ideas' (Bourdieu 1999b) seems to assume that the context of intellectual ideas is fundamentally shaped by their national origins, while his attack of globalisation as a form of Americanisation (Bourdieu and Wacquant 1999) rarely rises above the level of a polemical intervention. This latter intervention sparked a major critical review in *Theory, Culture and Society* but the crucial point is that Bourdieu's intervention is political, linked to his role as 'public intellectual', rather than theoretical, and that it is therefore misplaced to see the limitations of his intervention as discrediting his theoretical stance.

8 See for instance his argument that: 'The task of science, then is to construct the space which allows us to explain and predict the largest possible number of differences observed between individuals ...' (Bourdieu 1987: 3)

9 This is an approximation. Respondents were asked to state which income group they fell into, and since each income band was at £10,000 intervals this does not allow precise measurement. In addition, six of the households stated that they fell into the top income bracket of 'over £100,000', but there is no way of knowing how much they exceeded this.

10 Average male and female incomes sum to more than the average household income because there are some sole earner female households. Female incomes are total incomes and do not take account of whether the worker was full or part time.

11 The exception being a heterosexual couple without children.

12 Here, and in subsequent quotations we have changed or omitted any specific details that might permit a respondent to be identified. We indicate any alterations with an asterix.

2

The Limits of Local Attachment

The genre of community studies is currently in crisis. These studies of local social relations have a long and venerable history stretching back to the Victorian social inquiries of eminent observers such as Mayhew, Booth and Rowntree (see Abrams 1968; Yeo 1996). During much of the 20th Century this tradition matured as it became more sophisticated in its methodology, and the period between 1950 and 1970 in particular witnessed a series of path-breaking studies (see the overview in Crow 2002). However, as we identified in Chapter 1, since the 1970s it has become increasingly uncertain how local communities are to be theoretically understood in a period of dramatic global change, while its case study methodology has looked outdated with advances in sampling theory and the elaboration of more sophisticated qualitative methods not premised on face-to-face interaction.

We show in this chapter that we do indeed need to fundamentally break from any lingering conceptions of local social relations as defined by the activities, values and cultures of those 'born and bred' in an area. Here we agree with proponents of globalisation theory. Although in our four locations there continue to be people who live in the vicinity of where they were brought up, these are not necessarily the people who feel they belong there. It is the perceptions and values of incoming migrant groups, which more powerfully establish dominant place identities and attachments. We therefore criticise the idea that places are characterised by tension between 'born and bred' locals and migrant incomers, a standard view of post war community studies. Rather, people's sense of being at home is related to reflexive processes in which they can satisfactorily account to themselves how they come to live where they do.

In developing this argument we begin to elaborate our core idea of 'elective belonging', which articulates senses of spatial attachment, social position, and forms of connectivity to other places. Belonging is not to a fixed community, with the implication of closed boundaries, but is more fluid, seeing places as sites for performing identities. Individuals attach their own biography to their 'chosen' residential location, so that they tell stories that indicate how their arrival and subsequent settlement is appropriate to their sense of themselves. People who come to live in an area with no prior ties to it, but who can link their residence to their biographical life history, are able to see themselves as belonging to the area. This kind of elective belonging is critically dependent on people's relational sense of place, their ability to relate their area of residence against other possible areas, so that the meaning of place is critically judged in terms of its relational meanings.

This chapter is divided into two parts. In the first part we examine residents' perception of the social tone of place, in order to assess the kinds of people they think live near them. This allows us to show that their perception of divisions between locals and migrants is premised on an ethics of 'elective belonging', in which both born and bred locals, and also transient migrants, are treated with suspicion in favour of those who have migrated into the area, usually from within Northern England, and who have made a decision to stay. Although we develop this argument at a general level, we also show how this ethic varies in subtle ways between our four locations. We pay particular attention to Ramsbottom, where the sense of a division between locals and immigrants is unusually strong, and to Cheadle, which is the only area to see a sizeable population of 'local' residents. In the second part of the chapter we develop our argument that it is actually those who are 'born and bred' in their area of residence who now feel 'out of place'.

2.1 Discourses of localism and transience

Since the 1950s it has become increasingly recognised that communities were not self-contained and that large-scale migration meant that significant proportions of the population were not native to the area. The significance of work-related migration linked to the emergence of large-scale organisations and credentialism, and the rise of suburbs and long distance commuting was deemed to erode the fundamental significance of place. Watson (1964) saw non-locals as 'spiralists', employees of bureaucratic organisations moving around the country as directed by their employers (see also Pahl and Pahl 1971). Others defined this relationship as a new form of class relationship, with migrants being seen, in uncomplimentary terms, as members of the middle class, distant from more 'genuine' working class locals (Stacey 1960; Frankenberg 1966). Many accounts lamented what they saw as the decline of communal social relationships this entailed (Mills 1951; Whyte 1957; Bellah et al. 1996). Nonetheless, especially in British work, it was still argued that the locally embedded population continued to be the kernel of community. It became commonplace to see a divide between locals and non-locals (defined variously as 'cosmopolitans', 'spiralists', 'incomers' and the like) as fundamental to the organisation of local social relationships, with the 'locals' retaining moral possession over place (for a well-known account see Elias and Scotson 1965 and generally, Crow and Allan 1994: Chapter 4). For Ray Pahl (1970: 97), for instance, 'middle class people come to the countryside in search of a meaningful community and by their presence they help to destroy whatever community was there'.[1] Only a few studies denied the salience of some kind of a distinction between locals and incomers.[2]

A particularly interesting and influential rendering of this view was deployed in the work of anthropologists such as Strathern (1981, 1990), Cohen (1982, 1985) and Edwards (2000). Strathern's (1981) account of Elmdon is probably the most detailed and thorough account of the idea that long-term local residents have moral ownership over place. 'Within the village, then, a cluster of families is designated "real Elmdon", and of people who have lived most of their lives there it is birth members of these families, men and women alike, who are unambiguously "real Elmdon"' (Strathern 1981, 12). Although Elmdon was a small rural village of only 321 people when it was studied in the 1960s, Strathern nonetheless generalises from this study in her accounts of how kinship practices and values continue to define Englishness (Strathern 1990), and how this invokes proliferating the boundary between nature and culture. Through Strathern's influence, this idea can be found at the heart of Franklin et al.'s (2000) study of global nature. Jeanette Edwards invokes the centrality of kinship in her study of Bacup, an old industrial town in Rossendale (similar in several respects to Ramsbottom from which it is only ten miles distant). Edwards shows how Bacup residents refer to the past, and how they enact kinship as a means of establishing their connection to place. 'The perception of the unique locality is itself a function of the way in which idioms of relatedness, by no means exclusive to Bacup, are put to work. ... Idioms of kinship fashion places and pasts as well as persons and, of course, relationships' (Edwards 2000: 248).

Edwards evokes a second important anthropological contribution. Unlike sociologists, they have been less concerned to map social differences between locals and incomers in favour of a concern to emphasise the fluidity and constructed nature of symbolic boundaries themselves (see Cohen 1985; Munro 1998). Insiders and outsiders do not exist as fixed categories, but rather Strathern and Edwards show how kinship can be used to enact such boundaries.[3]

Given the centrality of this divide in existing community studies, we were struck by the relatively muted way in which many of our respondents differentiated these two groupings. Table 2.1 tabulates respondents' replies to the question 'what kind of people live round here?' To be sure, respondents did not tend to see their area as socially homogeneous, and in two locations, Chorlton and Ramsbottom, there was a strong consensus that the areas were socially mixed. There were, however, striking differences in the way people categorised such mixing, with some kind of distinction between locals and incomers being only one, by no means dominant, way of organising them.

Only in Ramsbottom was the distinction between locals and incomers much discussed, and indeed here it formed the dominant motif for talking about the local population. In Cheadle there was very little reference to such distinctions, while Chorlton and Wilmslow were intermediate between these two. Cheadle residents tended to see their area as homogeneous, with the major category used to understand both differentiation between residents and also things that respondents had in common, was age. This may be related to the fact that the entire area was built as an estate in the 1930s, and a few houses still occupied by their original residents.

Table 2.1 *Response to the question: 'What kind of people live round here?'*

Locale	See area as mixed (%)	Do not differentiate between local residents (%)	Distinguish locals/ incomers (%)	Distinguish ethnic groups (%)	Use age in describing local pop. (%)	Use occupation or class in describing local pop. (%)	Use attitude/ lifestyle in describing local pop. (%)
Cheadle	40	49	7	2	40	40	23
Wilmslow	49	49	33	4	20	71	22
Ramsbottom	66	28	53	2	17	68	6
Chorlton	81	17	19	10	19	70	17

Note:
Numbers sum to more than 100% since respondents could give multiple categories of people.

There was some kind of a sense of an original population, and subsequent generations of residents who had moved in more recently. However, respondents rarely drew strong social contrasts between the old and new residents:

> When we first moved in there were predominantly very old people, people that had bought the original houses, the house next door, number one, Mr Jarvis*, that is the original show house for the estate and he bought the house for £500 in 1930 whatever it was, he's 80 odd but he's a smashing bloke. The couple next door, well she's died now, the chap next door he's the same, he's 80 odd, and they were the original householders, same opposite, and we've noticed as we've been here longer, the elder people have basically died really and it is becoming a younger area if you like. I wouldn't say it's an area that people change a lot really, if a house goes up for sale it does generally go fairly quick. I would say it's an older community but I would say every year or so the average age is dropping so it's becoming younger. (C46)

> It's very mixed I think. What I found out when I moved in, which I didn't know beforehand, was that this particular estate was built between about 1935 and 1940, and they were houses built for rental, so some of the houses have been occupied by members of the same family for a very long time, so there's a mixed system, which I quite like in a way, between some houses which are owned and some which are still rented. Those that are still rented, a number of them, families are living in who are sons or daughters of the last generation, which is quite nice in a way. So I quite like the idea, that in a community, even if I were to leave tomorrow, there are people who've been here for a long time, and families that have been here for a long time. (C74)

Here the distinction between locals and incomers is rendered as a generational distinction, not fundamentally between different kinds of people, but as differentiated by age. Newcomers are the new generations which can legitimately replace the original residents. There were no clear geographical differences between the residences of the original families and the incomers, with the result that incomers were not seen as socially distinct, but as successor generations. Hence, just as the first generation moved to a new estate to better themselves, so new generations were comparable in choosing to move to the estate at a later point for the same reasons. An implicit, rarely stated, concomitant of this is the ethnic similarity of Cheadle residents, a group of homogeneous white residents in a city with significant ethnic diversity. This still powerful sense that there was an original 'community' entailed a sense of a place driven by time, related to an unusually powerful sense of nostalgia, which was much more marked than in the other three areas. This nostalgia had different components: in part it was linked to a widely shared sense that Cheadle had lost status. When asked what he liked and disliked about the area, one man recalled that:

I couldn't say there's anything I like about it, I don't really like it at all.

So it's different from where you were before?

Yes. It's changed beyond recognition really. You probably look back to when you were young and imagine it all right, but I think it's going downhill. ... (C101)

For one couple:

I'm sure we were happier, they were happier times. We don't like living in this age do we? It could be our age, you think when you look back times were happier, I don't know, but I do think life was nicer than it is now.

It's quite a common perception isn't it?

It's a bit dog eat dog now I find and in the days we're talking about you could walk out of this house and walk across the road to talk to somebody and go and visit them for reason, and leave your front door wide open, you can't do that these days. A lot of people our age are frightened of going out at night, this was never the case at one time. I mean the number of times my wife as a single person has walked through Manchester late at night, there was no fear at all of being accosted. You can't do that now. (C20)

Both these respondents recognise that their sense of nostalgia might not necessarily be a realistic account of social change, but might also be their own projection onto the past. This sense of personal ambivalence is of course a familiar narrative, akin to that of Hoggart's (1957) account of his childhood in Leeds, as well as Seabrook (1971). Blokland (2003) sees the development of nostalgia for 'a lost working class community' in an area of Rotterdam as related to its emergence as a fractured community (see also, Kearon 2001 for South Manchester), but in Cheadle, there is no explicit reference to the area as being historically working class. Table 2.2 shows that compared to residents in the other three locations, Cheadle respondents rarely talked about the occupation or class of people living locally, with the only common responses referring rather broadly to either the middle or working class. Several respondents used these terms interchangeably, implying relatively little sense of class as a significant divide (see further Savage et al. 2001).

This was all in marked contrast to the situation in Ramsbottom, where Table 2.1 shows that the majority of residents referred to the difference

Table 2.2   *Numbers of respondents' references to occupations and/or class in response to the question: 'What kind of people live round here?' (numerical counts)*

	Cheadle	Chorlton	Ramsbottom	Wilmslow
Media/cultural occupations	0	9	3	1
Professional occupations	4	20	7	7
'Professional'	3	17	8	14
Business people	0	4	4	12
Manager/ Administrator	2	0	8	11
Intermediate white collar occupations	5	0	7	0
'Middle class'	6	4	2	14
'Working people'	1	2	1	0
Manual occupations	9	5	5	0
'Working class'	5	7	6	0
Students	0	13	0	0
Unemployed	0	2	1	0

Notes:

Numbers do not equate to total interview numbers because not all respondents mentioned occupation or class, while others provided more than one category.

Terms such as 'middle class' and 'working class' include qualifying terms, such as 'lower middle class'.

between locals and incomers. The narratives of residents in Ramsbottom were marked by a powerful cultural polarity, between a group of 'born and bred' locals, (seen variously as old mill workers, residents of terraced housing, and pub-goers) and a group of predominantly middle-class commuters (who also were seen as an 'open' population, facing the countryside, the hills, wide open spaces, and able to gain easy access to the motorway system). Around this force field, multiple reinforcing dichotomies operated: between the 'social' and the 'natural', between the old and the new, between the fixed and the mobile, the working class and middle class. Whereas in Cheadle no other social categories were hung on to the differentiation between old and new residents, in Ramsbottom these terms carried huge cultural baggage. Joanne's testimony interestingly reveals the way that a commuter 'moralised' the local residents:

When I first moved to Ramsbottom it was a very ... it was the original sort of mill town and very dark and dirty – the shops closed at half past eleven because there were no customers around ... there are the locals born and bred and there's a lot of people like me, incomers really and truly.

Do those two groups get on together?

Well, I don't have any problems but perhaps the younger element that ... I know my friend's son who is about 18, he's ... he wasn't born there – when he has ... I think he has trouble in various pubs every now and again because he's a rich kid and an interloper and that sort of thing. I think ... I think there is a fairly local element that like to ... like to have a bit of a fumble every now and again.

The interesting reference to the 'original' town being 'dark and dirty', implicitly juxtaposes it with a 'new' town, now light and open. It is a boundary that is pervasive in part through its fluidity. Especially interesting is the invocation of an industrial working class, which is deemed to still convey authenticity to the local population, even though the industrial base has now almost disappeared. Here there are clear parallels with Edwards's (2000) account of nearby Bacup. For many Ramsbottom residents the old industrial base was still seen to explain the culture of the local residents:

I mean I think it's been a very working class area, there's all the mills around here and I think there's still a lot of industry, the mills are used for small industries now, so there's still quite a lot of what you might call the working class, which was where I came from, my father was a guard on the railways, very much a working class background. But I think in Ramsbottom, on this estate anyhow, there's a lot more people with more wealth I suppose, not real wealth but there's certainly a lot more finance coming into the town than ever did before. (R148)

We can see how differences between age groups, so powerful in Cheadle, are here incorporated into a narrative of industrial change and class divisions. R76, a self-employed craft worker saw:

two distinct areas. There's the old areas, the older people of Ramsbottom who have basically lived here all their lives, their parents live here, they've worked in the mills, there's those sort of people who tend to be the least prosperous people in Ramsbottom. The other people who come in onto the new estates who on a national sort of basis I would have thought you'd say they were reasonably prosperous, middle-class people.

The reference to 'those sort of people' indicates clearly enough the way that this discourse is one defined from outside – one critical of the old local culture itself. This is different to Cheadle, where residents could all place themselves in the generational account of change.

Would you say the type of people living here has changed over the years?

It has changed. Where I think 10 years ago there were mainly people who were born and bred in the village, there was quite a lot of mills in Ramsbottom at one time, there were a lot of millworkers, it had a culture all its own, that's virtually disappeared and it's become more and more people commuting to Manchester to work, less industrial work. It's become a little bit touristy with the steam railway coming through, so the shops are doing better and there's tourist type shops, which is an interesting development, they've built a Victorian station down there which is very, very nice, a replica of the previous one which I remember them knocking down, but it has produced wealth in the area. (R76)

Here we see the subtle association of the old 'with a culture all its own' against the new, signified not only by commuters but also by 'very, very nice' heritage buildings. The terms of the comparison between locals and the incomers are not neutral ones. This was especially clear in those interviews we carried out among incomers in terraced housing located close to the core of 'old' Ramsbottom, as Ronnie's testimony indicates.

Ronnie: an outsider's hostility to local culture

Ronnie (R28) was a trained gardener and manual worker who now self-employed and strongly resented the culture of manual workers. He was bought up nearby and had moved to Ramsbottom in the 1980s, though he had subsequently moved in and out of the town for a mixture of personal and work reasons. He had no qualms about voicing his antipathy to the locals.

> You won't change the people – the people leave a lot to be desired, some of them – the original Ramsbottom club, but ...

Why is that?

> Too clandestine, too common, too narrow. It ... it's pub and football and I detest both so I'm afraid I don't quite fit in, you know, so ... but basically the property was a good investment. ...

You said when you first moved here it had charm, what was it about it that had charm?

> It was just the quietness I think more than anything. The fact that you could park your car where you wanted, you could go for walks without having a million screaming kids kicking balls, throwing stuff all over and just general abuse. I suppose the last few years it's just a breakdown in all manner of things; respect, kids, etc., it's just ... it's abysmal, it's awful listening to it and it's always the kids and the girls are the worst of all – the language is just unreal. You never got that a few years ago, not to the same extent. I'm convinced no, I didn't, you know, because I used do a lot of walking outside at the front and you didn't get what you're getting now – the language it's just every day, during the day – it's not just when they're kicking people out the pub, it's all through the day – it's just ... it's awful ... Ramsbottom people are ... generally they won't spend much money on their homes as opposed to the football and drinking and fighting, etc. I may sound a bit scathing – I'm ... I don't mean to be it's just a fact – it's just the way they are. They are very earthy people, you know, very earthy people ...

What comes out of his account is the tension between the local population, seen in some ways as old, fixed, identified with pubs and football (though also as having become more dominant recently), and the potential of quietness and calm associated with a semi-rural location. We see an interesting association of the 'original' population as 'narrow', in conflict with his concern for using the open landscape. The evocation of locals as an earthy people, a form of 'partial connection' (Strathern 1991) of the social with the natural is an illuminating indication of this.

It is not incidental, then, that the idea of openness was frequently evoked as a powerful attraction of living in the area:

The people are very friendly, I like the area, you can't see it today with the mist but every window I look through I can see green, trees and that suits me (R90).

Any particular reason why Ramsbottom, is there anything that attracted you to this area?

The open spaces.

So that's something that you like about the area?

Yes.

Do you like the area in general?

Yes, just the openness, we couldn't have a dog at the other place, it was too closed in. So that was the reason.

Are those things that you still like about it?

Yes, it was a very good move. (R141)

Ramsbottom respondents exemplify several of the themes evident in the work of the post-war sociologists and anthropologists who emphasise the significance of the distinction between locals and incomers. However, there is one major difference. Incomers do not defer to the locals as being those with any kind of moral claim on place, in the way that older studies indicate they were generally prepared to do. In fact their way of framing the distinction between locals and incomers was highly congenial to incomers, since it defined the culture of locals as restricted, blinkered and outdated. There is, here, no sense of deference to the values of the long-term locals, no perception that older residents have some moral rights on the basis of their long-term residency. Indeed, rather, the reverse: it is those people who have made the decision to move to Ramsbottom because they appreciate its distinctive charms, its landscape, its vistas, who are better able to champion it. Unlike the 'narrow' locals who are there simply as a result of the accident of birth, they realise what is special about the town. That is why they moved there.

One can find traces of a similar account in Wilmslow, where there was a widely held view that there was an original 'old' market town, which had now been changed by suburban development. A widely shared focus for these concerns was the fate of Grove Street, the main shopping street in the old village, recently pedestrianised and increasingly marginalised as a shopping centre as large supermarkets opened on a nearby by-pass. As Table 2.1 indicates, around one third of respondents differentiated locals from incomers. However, the nature of this distinction was very different to that drawn in Ramsbottom. Rather than the focus being on 'locals' as the original population, in Wilmslow the emphasis was on the distinctive characteristics of the incomers:

> I would say there's a cross section of real Wilmslow people who have been here since the year dot. Born and bred here. There are I should say a *lot* of professional younger people going up the ladder and then they move on possibly to London ... or on to you know higher things. [*pause*] Yeah, I would say that's about it really. There's the ones that move and the ones that stay and stay and have stayed for many, many years. (W3)

This account slips between a view of locals as 'born and bred', the same term used frequently in Ramsbottom, to locals as being 'ones that stay', leaving the possibility that one can become local by moving in and staying put. What is of further significance is the critical tone used to understand the movers, those whose devotion to 'higher things' involves migration. One evocation of this critical take is through the idea of the 'executive ghetto'. For Stuart:

> I suppose I've had a number of moves and careers and you often end up living in what's known as executive ghettos and one of the problems of course is that if you are in an environment where there are a lot of people in your own professional ilk they are often moving and usually you find that your own social links are made through your wife, I'm sure that's a chauvinistic comment because there are many ladies who have professional careers, but quite often people tend to move because of the husband's work and often you therefore find the wife working part time or being a housewife and a mother and a lot of your social life is made through contacts at school or whatever. I leave the house in a morning often before seven and I tend to get home between six and seven, twelve hours a day, so there's not an opportunity during the week days to actually meet the neighbours. (W74)

Interestingly, therefore, whereas in Ramsbottom it was the locals who were seen to be restricted and limited, compared to the commuters who were able to appreciate the 'open countryside', in Wilmslow, it was the career spiralist who could be seen as limited by their devotion to their work and career. W21 presented a similarly critical view of the transient, middle class:

> It's a place where people move a lot. ... People are trying to move more. We were told by the Estate Agent that people in this area do tend to come from the south and just stay for a certain time. This neighbour here was moving out when we came in and there has been three lots of people been in there since. This side there was two that moved out, because we had a joke and said we must have BO, people always moving out.

For W2, this notion of a transient community is related to a sense of their passivity as they are 'shipped' by their companies to different areas, with the result that they ultimately lack 'roots'.

> I think it's a transient community and very much um er a place where people from accountancy and suchlike get shipped up here to work for a couple of years and then back to London again

and I've a lot of friends come and go that way. ... Yeah. Haven't really roots. Up from London and then down again.

We can see here how the 'transient spiralist' figures as a narrative foil in a rather similar way that the 'mill worker local' does in Ramsbottom. It defines a relationship between two types in such a way that one of the types has the moral upper hand. In contrast to Ramsbottom, locals are rarely associated with other social referents. There is an occasional reference to them being part of a 'Cheshire set', or having been long-term residents, but apart from this they do not stand out, in part since they have the same kind of jobs and incomes as other residents. It is thus possible for migrants to position themselves as allied to the locals when they become long-term residents, since they then differentiate themselves from the transient commuters. This tendency is enhanced by a further alliance between family and mobility which was mentioned by some respondents. Strathern (1981) and Edwards (2000) see the invocation of kinship as a central way that people established their sense of belonging. In Wilmslow, this idea was used as a means of justifying how one could move to the town and stay because it was appropriate to bring up families. An interesting exchange here is with W1:

It's funny you know ... they're different people you know you go back to the village days where it's their town and you're you've moved in here and it's our town anyway. And you still get that you know really. And um once you've been here a long time you get accepted as being one of them you know. ... I still hear these guys who were born and bred in Wilmslow and they're getting on a bit you know 50, 60 years old and when they were kids it was a village...

But it's changed a bit over time you would say?

Well it has because um there's still the family part which is this area um there's an awful lot of people who have moved here with jobs ... they don't stay here for ever. You know they could be here for five years then they work for ICI, Shell ... then they might go somewhere else then they go back.

Here we see a clear articulation of the theme of the distinctive nature of the born and bred locals. However these are not seen as families but as old men, but the 'family part' is comprised of the incomers who see the area as a good place to bring up children. Kinship is here invoked to justify how incomers can come to belong. We explore the point more fully in the next chapter, but here we simply note that this cultural opposition, in contrast to that in Ramsbottom, morally sanctions the locals over the transients, but only through broadening the definition of 'real' locals to include those who chose to move in and put down roots.

Chorlton, like Cheadle, has a weak cultural divide between locals and incomers. Initially this may appear to reflect the fact that it seems to have the weakest physical boundaries of the four areas, with its terraced housing blurring fairly seamlessly into other parts of the inner Manchester conurbation in the north and east. However, in fact, respondents did have a clear sense of Chorlton as a bounded place, marked by the natural boundaries of the River Mersey on two sides, an historic core, and a clear sense that it was different from other neighbouring inner city locations such as Rusholme, Whalley Range, and Withington (see Map 2.1).

Map 2.1 *Map of Greater Manchester locations*

Most respondents, as in Ramsbottom, saw the area as socially mixed. For a few respondents, this sense of mixing was related to the idea that there was a local working class:

Well, what I do like about it is it's very much a mix … in this immediate area, it does seem to be more professional people that are moving round, but just a stone's throw where you'll have students, you'll have people who are unemployed, etc., so it's a nice culmination of a mix, I think. And also you've got working-class people who have lived in this area for a long time who possibly, unfortunately, when they move out the people are different when they move in because they can't afford these properties because they've gone up a lot in price which is sad in a way because I think that keeps the colour of the community, but unfortunately, that's just the way it's going. So it's good in one way but in another way quite sad that you don't keep that local thing there. But yeah, it's a nice mix. (D23)

Yes, I think it's quite clearly 2 identifiable groups of essentially working-class, local people who have been born and brought-up here, most of whom are reaching retirement age now and their houses are being bought by people who can afford a £100,000 mortgage. And that's increasingly a lot of gay people, actually. An awful lot of gay couples. (D11)

Both these quotes indicate a juxtaposition of opposed populations. However, we see the subtle way in which the working class are not defined as having a distinct industrial base or culture – as in Ramsbottom – but essentially as aging and having inadequate resources to retain their presence. There is a sense in which affluent professionals are deemed to define the area, with the local working class a kind of residue which is 'unfortunately' in decline. Unlike Ramsbottom there is no sense that there was a discrete area of working-class residence, as the middle classes were moving into the very terraced houses that had formerly been lived in by manual workers. We can also see how the local working class is juxtaposed to students, professionals, and gay people, who were seen to embody chosen, 'elective' lifestyles and individual choices. This was especially marked through the common reference to students (see Table 2.2). A large number of respondents saw students as transient residents, living in rented housing and with scant regard for those around them (see also Kearon 2001). However, because being a student was a transitory state, it was possible for students to come to belong to the area, when they left university and became employed. Furthermore, because students could be defined as the transient outsiders, it was possible for relatively mobile professionals to define themselves as part of a more stable population. D64, a young administrator, who had recently finished a Masters degree, said that:

Yes, those are the two very distinct types that live here, there are lots and lots of social workers, my housemate's one of them, most of the group that when I initially moved here were students and social workers and residential care workers ... God it sounds like I'm stereotyping. The two groups that I noticed quite distinctly are the older people that are quite established and I just wonder half the time what they make of the community ... I think that students, because I was one myself, you rent properties for a year, in my case it's been longer but that's probably unusual, but you rent properties for a year and you know you're not going to stay so there's no point in making dramatic renovations so you have parties in your back garden and if it pisses off the neighbours you'll be moving out next year so it doesn't matter and I find that attitude quite selfish and I think it is a part of what goes on around here. (I mean it was) finals week and there were parties going on all around and it was just driving me crazy and I had to write my thesis, so there's the older generation gap, some of them are probably quite elderly, certainly well past retirement age and also very disadvantaged people that live very locally, you get used to people's faces. (D64)

Interesting that even a post-graduate was seeking to define herself against the 'selfish' undergraduates. In some respects this is a similar distinction to that drawn in Wilmslow, except that the transients were students rather than corporate spiralists (Kearon 2001). The kind of social mixing which was seen as significant in Chorlton was not one which tended to juxtapose social categories, such as locals and incomers. Rather, it was individuals who were seen to mix. This is rather similar to Robson and Butler's (2001) observation about middle-class residents in Telegraph Hill, London, who evoked an 'idea of the mix' that 'reside(d) in the way the interaction of individual (but overwhelmingly white and middle class) types – lefty/liberal, artistic/creative – enriches the social life of the hill'. To some extent, like Cheadle, this meant that age was an important signifier, often evoked through the ideas of 'yuppies' or young professionals:

> I would say a mixture. We were an aging population up to a couple of years ago on this little bit, but a load of yuppies moved in. You can't park your car any more, we did have two cars but I got rid of mine so we only have one. I believe a television presenter lives here, so I've been told. (D4)

> The weird thing is when I lived in the city centre appartment, you're literally on top of each other, you're living in the same building, but you didn't see anybody because they're all working long hours, they're all rich professionals, a lot of the time they're away during the week and it was just a weekend base, so you never saw anybody, you didn't really know anybody, whereas here you have a mix of different age groups, you have different sorts of people, like next door they're young professionals, this side it's a couple who've lived there all their lives, have teenage children, the house belongs to her mum. (D115)

In a sense, professionals in Chorlton were at least able to think that they lived among a diverse population, to confirm a liberal view of the benefits of diversity, and to repudiate a feeling that living in the city centre involved a homogeneous affluent lifestyle. The celebration of the diversity of lifestyles was common, especially with respect to sexuality, occupation, and leisure pursuits:

> It's quite a mixed place, and again particularly this bit of Chorlton. I mean take this road, probably 90% of the people on this road are not conventional in their jobs and therefore, I mean comparing it to where my parents live, for example and where I used to live when I was a kid, there's just such a mix. Once you get in it, if you think about moving anywhere else you think well, where would I go and why. ... Very mixed. There's a mixture of residents, owners and then these flats and next door down is rented by students. Next door he's first violin* with the Halle*; over there [name] is a cartographer* and a writer* and his wife runs a music school*; next door down is a builder and a market researcher*; next door down to that a Hare Krishna* and a solicitor* and his lodger; next door down to that used to be another musician and he's some highflying thing that stands in his back garden at eight o'clock in the morning yelling on his mobile phone, I don't know what he is; down this side, after the students there's a designer* and his wife and two kids, his wife was in BBC Television* in production and now she's moving into social work*; next door down to that used to be the catering manager from Lancashire Cricket Club*, and his wife who was in advertising* then went into teaching, now it's a pair of accountants*; over there on that side a bit

further down there's a Granada designer*. The mix of people, not even getting to the bend, I mean I know there's other streets that are full of lecturers for example, there's a lot of lecturers from various places round here, a lot of teachers and lecturers and that sort of people. Another architect in fact down there on that side. So very mixed. (D51)

Actually, this 'very mixed' population is comprised entirely of well-educated professionals and managers. There is a profound paradox at the heart of this liberal culture, which is that the celebration of diversity figures as a means of self-reinforcement, a form of self-congratulation for avoiding the narrowness of fixed lifestyles. While, at one level, difference is celebrated and welcomed, for instance with respect to diverse sexualities, family types and specific 'middle-class' occupations, this diversity also goes hand in hand with a liberal academic homogeneity. And indeed, alongside references to diversity, many respondents also reported their sense that the local population was rather uniform, defined in terms of their common cultural capital, and espousal of a particular set of urban professional values.

I find it very difficult actually to categorise them, but I would say that they usually have an academic background, not necessarily professional people but they've either been to university or are interested in education, that sort of area, although I can think of quite a few notable exceptions. But overall I've quite often thought that it's an area where most of the university and polytechnic staff live, so there seems to be a lot of contact with education. (D109)

I don't know, I think this corner of Chorlton is quite easy going, it seems to be quite arty almost, I think this part of Chorlton has that kind of feel to it, everybody's got their recycling boxes out. (D107)

What's quite interesting is that I don't see many people, for example, from ethnic minorities in this area at all, certainly in the areas that border here there are lots of people from ethnic minorities. ... If I had to sum up what kind of people live (here), I'd say trendy Guardian read types, but I don't know if I'm biased slightly in my impression of that because I go to the (name of café) for a coffee and for a meal or whatever and those sorts of types tend to go there. I mean I'm sure there is a massive mix but you do get the impression that it's very left wing, right on, trendy, I don't know why I have that impression but you do get that impression a lot. (D115)

Others reported more tersely a view of a uniform cultural set up, saying for instance that 'They seem to be a similar mindset, the people round here' (Susan), or 'I like the atmosphere, it's got a nice bohemian feel about it, it is a nice funky little area' (D16).

We can see, therefore, an intriguing liberal community where tolerance is premised on a kind of cultural uniformity. An interesting indication of this discourse is the references people made to the occupations or classes of people living in the area. Table 2.2 shows that despite the references to social mixing, the kind of occupations that local residents were seen to have were nearly all comprised of the professional middle class, with three quarters of references to people who either were likely to have university degrees, or were currently students. Especially interesting is the lack of any reference to managers living in the area, intermediate white-collar occupations or indeed to the 'middle class' as a whole. This is in contrast to Wilmslow, where the generic 'middle class' label was frequently proffered, along with profession and business people. In Chorlton, by contrast, there is a strong concern with mentioning specific types of professional occupation (as with D51, above) and a disdain for the term 'middle class' as descriptor of the local population. Presumably this label is seen as too staid. Indeed, the few respondents who used the term middle class to describe local inhabitants did so haltingly. D53 noted that, 'I mean I don't know if you can exactly label people middle class, working class, it's a very British way of labelling people isn't it, but if you did that, I would say it's a fair mixture of the two really'. The handful of references to working class residents allow people to indicate that there are other social groups than the professional middle class who live in the area. There is a sense in this discourse that professionals are individuals, somehow able to stand outside social relationships, and not a class in their own right (see Savage et al. 2001).

Thus the academically educated, professional middle class held sway, in the sense that they act as guarantors of morally legitimate differences. Here again, there is no sense of a past, historic, community that has moral rights on the area: rather the older working class residents, when they are seen at all, are seen mainly as residues. And, while there is no doubting their genuine embrace of diversity, one implication was to prevent difference being defined in terms of social categories, but rather in terms of individual lifestyles. Here there is a striking contrast with Ramsbottom.

Our four locations thus differ substantially, yet these are differences with some common threads. Fundamentally, although all four areas see a sense that there is a 'local' population, this is not seen to provide 'locals' with any moral claim on place. The fact that a particular population is of long standing residence is not deemed to provide them with any more rights than any other group who lives there, and in some places it gives them less. Even in Cheadle, the one place where the memory of long-term residents is most celebrated, the moral right of residence had given way to nostalgia. This is a very different politics to that found in Elias and Scotson (1965) where the 'established' could claim moral supremacy over the outsiders, or in Frankenberg's (1957) discussion of the category of 'strangers' in 'village on the border'.

Secondly, mobile transients were often held in disregard: especially corporate spiralists in Wilmslow and students in Chorlton. We see here a complex discursive opposition not between local and migrant, but between a group of 'elective locals', who chose to reside in the place on the one hand, and both transients and locals on the other. A common theme for these elective locals was their embrace of openness, whether this be linked to the pleasure of the open landscape and mobility as in Ramsbottom, the openness linked to different lifestyles premised on liberal professional culture as in Chorlton, or the openness of those who refuse to be corporate ciphers, as in Wilmslow.

Table 2.3 *Areas where respondents were brought up (percentages)*

	Cheadle	Chorlton	Ramsbottom	Wilmslow
Brought up locally	51	13	23	18
Brought up in Manchester area	26	19	17	11
Brought up in the north/mids	16	34	47	44
Brought up else-where in England	7	19	6	13
Brought up outside England	0	15	6	13

Note:
Local includes the neighbourhood, and adjacent villages and towns in the case of Ramsbottom and Wilmslow (e.g. Bury, Heywood for Ramsbottom, Macclesfield for Wilmslow).

In this sense, we can see a common discourse that subordinates both locals or incomers to an overarching narrative. This is premised on the valuation of a community of strangers: those who in Simmel's famous phrase 'come today and stay tomorrow'. These are the kind of people who have made a choice to live in a particular area and can thereby, through their agency, avoid the fixity which comes from the habit simply of living where one always lives, or following one's career slavishly so that one does not make a decision to place oneself anywhere. It articulates a view of 'elective belong-ing' in which those who have an account of why they live in a place, and can relate their residence to their choices and circumstances, are the most 'at home'. This theme is fundamental to the nature of contemporary local belonging: we elaborate on it throughout this book.

2.2 Belonging and attachment

In section 2.1 we showed how respondents repudiated the moral claims of both locals and transients, and how an ethics of 'elective belonging' was implicit in their accounts of place. Of course, many of our respondents were themselves 'locals'. Understanding their sense of belonging allows us to further elaborate the power of elective belonging. Table 2.3 reports the areas that residents had been brought up in, differentiating between those brought up in or close to their current address, the Manchester conurba-tion, neighbouring regions of England, other parts of England, and finally those from other nations (in which we include Scotland, Wales and Ireland). Table 2.3 shows that neither those brought up locally nor long distance migrants (defined as those brought up in distant regions of England, or in other nations) formed the major source of any local population.

The largest single group in all areas other than Cheadle were those brought up in neighbouring regions of England, namely the north, north-west and the midlands, all of which lie within 100 miles of Manchester. 'True' locals were

Table 2.4 *Location of kin (percentages)*

	All local	Any local	Any south	All south	All north	Any north	All Manchester	Any Manchester	N =
Ram (1)	13	8	–	18	44	15	13	–	39
Ram (2)	12	14	–	21	42	28	5	12	43
Cheadle (1)	48	2	–	2	16	10	13	13	31
Cheadle (2)	34	18	–	4	18	18	21	11	38
Wilmslow (1)	16	19	14	12	33	14	7	9	43
Wilmslow (2)	2	33	13	17	33	20	2	9	46
Chorlton (1)	9	2	25	11	40	9	20	2	35
Chorlton (2)	7	7	17	22	17	29	12	10	41

Notes:
(1) Parents and independent children (where applicable)
(2) Parents, independent children and siblings (where applicable)

a small minority of less than a quarter of the residents in all places except Cheadle, where they formed half the population. Even if we include as locals those brought up elsewhere in the Manchester conurbation, only in Cheadle does such a group form more than half the residents. However, there were even fewer cosmopolitan long-distance migrants. Only in Chorlton do such groups rise towards 20% of the whole, and among our sample as a whole, a mere 10% fall into this category. Almost as many people were brought up outside England as were brought up in the South of England, with the majority of these being Scots and Irish.

Table 2.4 reports the location of kin among our respondents. In both Ramsbottom and Cheadle there are no households where all non co-resident immediate family live in the South, though there are small numbers of such in Wilmslow and Chorlton. Only in Cheadle do a substantial proportion have all their immediate family living locally. However, it is the strength of regional family ties that stands out in all areas other than Cheadle. Around one third of households have all their immediate family living in the north – though not locally or in Manchester. Between one half and two-thirds have some immediate family members living in this kind of regional range. The remarkable weakness of Manchester family connections is striking in all four areas. None of the locations sees more than a handful of immediate family living in the Manchester area other than that which is very local to them. Respondents in three of the four locations are embedded in kin ties that stretch beyond purely local attachments and which show little sign of connection to Manchester, but which tend to link them on a wider spatial range. The dominant connections are not to England as a whole (though there are significant minorities in Wilmslow and Chorlton with southern connections) but with other parts of the north and midlands. In this respect, kinship articulates regional attachments.

Table 2.5 reports the relationship between people's sense of belonging and their geographical mobility. Here the important point is that in all areas except Ramsbottom 'locals' are more likely to feel that they do not belong than

Table 2.5 *Percentage of those brought up in different places who feel they belong in area of current residence (No. for relevant category in brackets)*

	Cheadle	Chorlton	Ramsbottom	Wilmslow
Brought up locally	45 (22)	50 (6)	81 (11)	36 (8)
Brought up in Manchester area	64 (11)	67 (9)	63 (8)	50 (5)
Brought up in the north/mids	43 (7)	63 (16)	50 (20)	79 (19)
Brought up else-where in England	0 (2)	56 (9)	33 (3)	20 (5)
Brought up outside England	(0)	43 (7)	67 (3)	50 (6)
Total 'belonging'	48 (42)	58 (47)	60 (45)	60 (43)
Total who are emphatic in stating they do not belong	10 (42)	11 (47)	11 (45)	9 (43)

Notes:
Local includes the neighbourhood, and adjacent villages and towns in the case of Ramsbottom and Wilmslow (e.g. Bury, Heywood and Rossendale for Ramsbottom, Macclesfield and Bramhall for Wilmslow).

'Belonging' indicates those saying they belong, including those who say they belong now, but did not initially. All ambivalent responses are counted as not belonging.

incomers. Just as we have seen that discourses of residence tend to be premised on assumptions of elective belonging, so those who live in their original area of inhabitation tend to be less comfortable. By contrast, in all four areas, migrants from Manchester tend to feel that they belong, and middle distance migrants from neighbouring regions are strong 'belongers' in Chorlton and (especially) Wilmslow. In all four areas with the partial exception of Chorlton, long-distance migrants do not feel they belong. Middle distance, regional, migrants appear distinctive in finding it relatively common to claim 'belong-ingness', compared to both born and bred locals and long distance migrants. Feeling at home does not appear as a property of being brought up in an area.

Of course, the meaning of belonging varies. Nearly everyone was able to talk about what it meant to belong, the exception being one person in Cheadle who said that he had never thought about it before. For locals, belonging often meant familiarity linked to upbringing and routine. Such accounts were often terse and not amenable to discursive elaboration.

So what things do you like about living in this area now?

I feel safe somehow, this is me, I'm home. (C26)

Yes, I have always lived here. I feel safe here. I know it. (D55),

These kind of responses were found among the 'locals' in all four areas. Stuart, from Wilmslow, was unusually articulate on this point:

Fundamentally I am of this area: I wasn't physically born here ... but I have lived here in Wilmslow from the age of 18 months ... but the forebears on my mother's side, they have been in (the area) for generations ... I feel very much at home here and I think I always have done so ... well you know what it is like if you grow up in an area and you find all its hidey-holes, corners, advantages, disadvantages, you become one with it. (W20)

The idea of belonging as familiarity is central to existential renderings of the meaning of place and community, as well as Bourdieu's conception of habitus. However, most locals were clear that this kind of familiarity is often not enough to convey a full and assertive sense of belonging. Rather, people felt that 'their place' had been transformed so that they were no longer fully at home. Even though W20 was emphatic that he still belonged to Wilmslow, he was critical of the loss of its local council, and lamenting that the high street had become 'Globesville' as it had lost its independent shops. Other Wilmslow locals felt more disenchanted, with some of the older professionals lamenting the rise of youth culture and the loss of its traditional gentlemanly status (see Savage et al. 2004a). There was a general sense from all the four areas that reporting a sense of familiarity was not enough to stop you feeling an outsider. Jane's story is a particularly striking example.

Jane: the local stigma of a single mother

Jane (D110) was an unemployed single mother, living in a small terraced house rented from a Housing Association in Chorlton. Jane had left school at 16 and worked at odd jobs, mainly as a shop assistant, and after a period bringing up her son, was training to be a nurse. Currently she had suspended her studies to look after her demanding son. She said that 'probably because I've grown up round here, I feel comfortable', and also that she enjoyed the local amenities. Nonetheless, she also reported a sense that 'I shouldn't really be living here'.

I feel privileged to live here because I know what the demand is for people to live round here. There was a house for sale and it's gone within weeks. But I feel as though I should have a good job. There are some snobs round here, my parents are a bit snobbish, I've been brought up a bit of a snob but I can't really say I am because I'm not in that position socially. I can feel it inside and I'm working towards it.

Do you feel as though people look down on you?

Yes there have been people looking down on me, like 'she doesn't seem to be working, how can she afford to live here?' ... you're judging all the time, as soon as you say you're a single parent they say how are you coping, have you got any money.

Do you think people in the pubs and shops know who you are and judge you in those terms?

Yes at first they judged me and were a little bit harsh on me, but then they get used to you being around the area and the more they can trust you. It is the first thing they judge you on, your social class.

Jane indicates how the social mixing celebrated in Chorlton is premised on relatively high incomes, and those lacking such resources cannot fall back on a sense that they are a different category of people (as they could in Ramsbottom).

It is revealing that of only three people in Chorlton who clearly felt they did not belong to the area, two were locally brought up. Most other locals in Chorlton viewed the transformation of the area detachedly, either seeing the emergence of cafés and shops as nothing to do with them, or as a sign that the area had deteriorated.

Therefore, although locals frequently had a sense of familiarity or safety in an area, this did not necessarily translate into a sense of belonging. Cheadle is a particularly interesting example here. Well over half the residents in Cheadle had been brought up within a mile of their current house, and even those coming from Manchester had rarely moved more than four miles from their birthplace. The result was a group of residents strongly embedded with kin: two-thirds of the sample had either their parents or the majority of their non-resident children living close by, at most within a 15-minute car journey. Yet, although this degree of local family connection is similar to that found by Young and Wilmott (1957) in Bethnal Green in the 1950s and in other working class 'community studies' such as Hoggart (1957) and Roberts (1971), it did not convey the kind of attachment to place that might be seen as implicit in this invocation of a stable community, as Stuart's testimony starkly indicates.

Stuart: the homelessness of the locally raised

Stuart (C13) was working as a manager for a small plastic moulding company*, having previously worked in similar jobs in other parts of the world. In between times he had also been involved in his wife's design business*. He had enjoyed highs and lows, at one time having the finances to send two of his children to private school, but had recently fallen on harder times, and his current position, working for a friend's firm, involved very hard work for little financial reward. He had previously lived in a grand house, but had lived in his current three bedroom semi-detached house for eight years. It became clear in the course of the interview that the house had actually belonged to his family since it was built in the 1930s: indeed he had been brought up in it. He was not happy about his decision to move back to his own childhood house.

I realised it was a mistake because it's like not moving forward, but moving back. I've always said to my wife that it was a bad move on my part, I didn't give it a lot of thought, but we'd spent a lot of money on the house because, at the end of the day, with respect to my mum, it's an old lady's house, so we gutted it, literally. So moving back to Cheadle, Cheadle's changed, like everywhere else, it isn't that I've never been away, I've lived abroad. I had a fantastic childhood here, but it's changed, it was a beautiful area at one time, there was a load of wide-open spaces, yes it probably was looking through rose tinted glasses.

But you feel like it's gone down?

Yes, it's lost the villagey feel. We still call it the village, Cheadle village, but anybody that's moved in here 15 years ago calls it the village. Everybody knew everybody, ... because my parents come from a two up two down environment, it was still neighbours over the fence. The lady who unfortunately has now died, but moved away and retired, I used to call her aunty. I could wander into her house, my mum and her always had a cup of tea at 11 o'clock in the morning, it was the old values and that's how I was brought up. That's changed, everybody keeps themselves to themselves now. In my teenage years I used to go drinking in Cheadle, I would never drink in Cheadle now. ...

The next question is would you be sorry to leave this area?

No. I suppose it's where you're going to, I wouldn't be sorry if it was going down, but no, I feel as though I could move anywhere in the world.

And do you feel part of the community here?

No. I think that's what I think I was trying to explain before. I know everybody, or my mother knew everybody in this drive, it's weird because it's unusual as all the old neighbours had died, and I've not bothered to get to know new neighbours. That may be my fault, we keep ourselves to ourselves, we have very good neighbours either side, I probably know four families in this drive, whereas at one time when I was a kid, I knew everybody. It's probably quite unusual, because I'm literally living where I grew up.

Stuart is essentially relating his inability to account for moving back to his parental home. While aware that his decision is related to family loyalty and a sense of childhood attachment to Cheadle, his decision to move back to his home does not allow him to present himself as a forward looking individual, able to decide his place in the world. His nostalgia is related to his sense of guilt for not moving elsewhere, for not choosing somewhere to live. 'Staying put' is a badge of failure. To be an individual requires you to move away from the place you happen to be born and brought up, so that you can claim your own place as a marker of your achievement in life and your conscious decisions. We see here a narrative of the individual that is stymied, in Stuart's own eyes, because of the difficulty of linking self-development to a move back to his childhood home.

Stuart's account of his disappointment at moving back to his birthplace is extreme, but other locals report the same sense. C17 had moved away from the area to Carlisle, then moved back, and also articulated a sense of shame:

Well we used to live in (name), I think since we've moved away and come back. I think there's more crime, the streets are dirtier, it's just generally more run down I think. I think it's a lot to do with things like the out of town shopping centres, I mean you can go up Cheadle high street now and there's not many shops, a lot of them have closed down, everybody goes up to the out of town shopping areas, yes we've noticed a big difference. (C17)

There was another sense that because Cheadle had not changed much, it was a mark of personal failure that one was still living here. Similar sentiments were evident in Chorlton. When Edith (D68) was asked, 'you said you came from Chorlton originally, have you always lived around the Chorlton area?', she replied, 'I've lived overseas for 2 years, but apart from that yes I've always lived in Chorlton, not much to say for really is it, but still'. In both Chorlton and Cheadle, there was a pervasive sense for locals that immobility was a mark of failure. This was not true, however, in Ramsbottom, where local residents emphatically claimed their pride in the town, as Joe indicates.

Joe: the pride of a born and bred local

Joe (R48) was a middle-aged manual worker who prouldy proclaimed 'I've always lived in Ramsbottom, always. I wouldn't move out of Ramsbottom even if I won the lottery'. He elaborated this by saying that the great virtue of the town was:

> Well, I like walking and I've got a dog but the dog's knackered. I can go walking. There's hills outside and Moors, so I'm off up there.

Joe was characteristic in disliking change to the town, reporting that the town was taking:

> A direction that I don't like but it's progress they call it.

> *And what sort of direction do you think it's going in?*

> It's being more of a suburb of Manchester because there's a massive estate up there because I used to go ... it was a farm and I used to go there because my mate worked there and now there's about 500 houses on it.

When asked if he belonged, Joe answered emphatically, 'yeah, definitely', before qualifying this by saying that he belonged to 'the local community, yeah, but not the community as a whole'. In response to further questioning about why he felt part of the community he answered: 'Probably because I've been here that long. Nothing special, just because I've been here that long'.

> *And would you be sorry to leave this area?*

> I don't think I would leave. I love this area, but like I said, I don't think I would.

> *What kind of people do you think live in this area?*

> Working class, except for all these new estates, they're all commuters.

> *Sort of commuters and white-collar workers?*

> I could be wrong, but I think that's what they are

Joe's case is revealing because his familiarity was associated with a clear sense of pride in belonging to Ramsbottom. This was possible because of the spatial separation of the commuters

---

> from the old town, his ability to draw upon categorical distinctions (that he was 'working class') to sustain his sense of attachment, and also by his ability to draw upon the same discourse of the 'open' country that was widely used by incomers. He was thus able to connect to discourses of elective belonging and link his sense of belonging to a class identity, in a way that was not possible in the other areas.

Several other men shared Joe's sentiments. R54 noted firmly that 'well I'm not leaving, but I would be sorry to leave'. In explaining why he felt he belonged to the community he explicitly related this to his union and industrial activity:

> Besides this job I do some work for the [named trade union], I'm the branch secretary in Ramsbottom, so I've about ten factories, so I'm involved with most of the factories in the area, so that's how I know people and I also use the pubs in the locality.

These accounts are typical of these local residents. While critical of changes to the town, they were able to retain a sense of moral ownership in part through the use of the language of class, and in part through their ability to share in discourse of rural openness of the countryside. They were able to draw upon the rural location of the town as a resource which entitled them to belong, even while lamenting many changes to the town itself, which they saw as being spoiled by the rise of tourism, the closure of old shops and the rise of shops geared towards trippers, and the dereliction of local planning. R41 said she liked living in Ramsbottom because:

> First of all it is familiar. I think as a person I like being part of a community where I am known and where I know, to some people that is not important. I like the place and I think it is a beautiful valley because the trees soften it and on our doorstep we can go to the hills and it has the advantage of being near urban centres like Manchester where there is culture, the theatres, etc. It is good. (R41)

Conclusion

In this chapter we have traced the problems of maintaining even a weak view of residential space as the territory of a local, born and bred community. Attachment to place is detached from historical communal roots in that place. It is important to resist any nostalgic current, still evident in communitarian thought and urban sociology, to defend the idea of an historically rooted local community, however precarious this may be perceived to be.

We have traced this argument in several ways. Firstly, in all areas other than Cheadle, 'local' people are now a small minority of the population. Secondly, although locals usually report a sense of familiarity, this does not convey a sense that they belong. The issues here can be related to the modern dilemma of development traced by Berman (1983). Insofar as a place stays much the same as when people were brought up, as in Cheadle, then it is a mark of failure to continue to live there. Insofar as the place changes and develops, as in Chorlton, Ramsbottom, and Wilmslow, then people feel that 'their' place has been lost, spoilt. It is not possible to retain the best of both worlds. The modern individual has to move, and by choosing a place to live they endeavour to confirm a sense of who they are. This is a process which defines residential space as a habitus for social groups to form, cohere, and act.

We have examined a powerful discourse of 'elective belonging' that is articulated in three out of the four areas. This is in some respects an elastic discourse, since we have seen how different kinds of social divisions are mapped within its terms in Wilmslow, Chorlton and Ramsbottom. It implies a view of residential attachment that articulates a distinctive ethics of belonging that has nothing to do with the claims of history. It repudiates the claims of locals trapped in the past and also the transients who are here today and gone tomorrow. Rather, it is premised on the values of those who come today and stay tomorrow, who make a choice to live somewhere and make 'a go of it'.

A recognition of this ethics of 'elective belonging' offers the potential for rethinking our understanding of contemporary local belonging. We saw in Chapter 1 the difficulty of juxtaposing the global and the local, with the implication that the kind of eclipse of the local we have traced here necessarily involves the rise of global, cosmopolitan, attachments. Unlike Castells, we do not see local attachments as historical residues, defensively constructed in opposition to global processes. Rather, we see elective belonging as embodying attachments that permit various kinds of global connections to be drawn. Fixed places thus play crucial roles within globalising processes. They become sites for new kinds of solidarities among people who chose to live in particular places, and whose deep concern about where they live is unlikely to be overlain with extraneous concerns arising from knowledge of others who have historically lived in the place. A new potential for collective action is made possible.

Notes

1 This line of thinking spawned a major research profile on the significance of the middle classes in rural social relations which continues to this day. For discussion, see Newby (1980), Urry (1995), Cloke et al. (1997). It also had a major impact on cultural studies, through the incorporation of this theme in the early work of the Centre for Contemporary Cultural Studies, with its interest in the imaginary local working-class community (see Hall et al. 1975).

2 Perhaps the best known being Stacey et al.'s (1975) second study of Banbury.

3 This more fluid rendering of boundaries between locals and outsiders can be seen in more recent sociology, such as Crow and Summers (2002) and Southerton (2002).

3

Parenting, Education and Elective Belonging

In the last chapter we identified how belonging is defined not as an attribute of being born and bred in a place, but when a chosen place of residence is congruent with one's life story. In this chapter we explore the role that mothering and child-rearing plays in this achievement of elective belonging. We show how mothering can become a means of both attaching women – and indirectly, men – to place and a means of sedimenting different kinds of gendered cultures of place. We start by focusing on how the regional incomer mothers talk about the way that their children locate them, how they become a means for performing belonging. We show how this process generates detached social networks, rather than close social ties with neighbours. In the second part of this chapter we turn to consider how education acts as a distinctive field (Ball et al. 1995; Ball 2002, and Butler and Robson 2003) and how parents buy into distinctive locations in the educational field through their choice of residence. We show further subtle differences in the way that parents articulate their relationship with their children. In Wilmslow, a culture of 'family first' permeates, with mothers in particular being expected to sacrifice their interests for their family, but in Chorlton, with its liberal values and relative gender equality, educational choice poses more problems to local parents. We also trace these patterns of engagement in the educational field through participation in parent teacher associations in our four areas, indicating how narratives of participation relate to embeddedness in the locale and the habitus of each area which is related to the gendering of family practices.

3.1 Mothering and belonging

Although residents in all four areas talked variously about the people living close to them in terms of their age, class, occupation, lifestyle and occasionally their ethnicity and sexuality, they rarely spoke overtly about their household organisation, for instance in terms of being 'conventional' nuclear families or more unconventional. This is despite the fact, as we indicated in Chapter 1, our four areas differ significantly in their domestic organisation, with Wilmslow being characterised by conventional, male dominated, nuclear households, but Chorlton having relatively egalitarian gender relations, at least as far as income levels are concerned. These differences tap into well-attested geographical variations in gender relations (see Duncan and 2003). In part this lack of overt reference reflected a strong resentment, even in Wilmslow, to the idea that women should be housewives and homemakers.

In Wilmslow, there were only three full time 'housewives' (out of 28 women interviewed) in our sample, one of whom was now retired. These expressed considerable discontent with their situation. W3, the wife of a musician in a local orchestra, now stays at home to bring up the children. When asked if she feels she belongs to Wilmslow, she answered enigmatically:

Oh there's a question [laughs]. Sometimes I do, sometimes I don't.

Right

Sometimes I feel like an imposter. Maybe that's something to do with recent experiences in life though. And sometimes not.

Such unease with the housewifely habitus is not unusual, and was often voiced by women who had put their careers 'on hold', such as Susan.

Susan: the reluctant dependent wife and mother

Susan (W5) was married to a chief executive with three daughters (aged 14, 17 and 20), and had moved five times to different parts of the country. She was struck by the 'unfriendliness' of Wilmslow. When asked if she felt she belonged to the area, the answer was a crisp 'very definitely not'. Although trained as a nurse and having worked as nurse trainer and as consultant, she had abandoned her career and currently worked part time. While supportive of her husband's career, at various points in the interview, resentments about the inequalities between them surfaced. 'I'm at the bottom and he's at the top. Very sad, but that is actually right'.

The decision to move to the town was based on instrumental calculations of schooling quality, and compared to previous residences she was struck by the lack of feeling and warmth.

Yes, generally detached. There isn't a sense of community ... I had thought originally that Wilmslow was more of an entire town of its own, but in fact it's not. It's consists largely of people who have moved up from the South [] themselves um and those that have lived here for a very very long time ... Also most women of my age are ... [pause] it's not, yeah I think most people go back to work um may be there isn't such things going on.

In Wilmslow, there continued to be some arenas in which women were formally treated as secondary to men, especially with respect to membership rights of women in some – mainly golf – clubs. Women frequently protested at these situations:

Yes, I hate the male chauvinist bit of it. Very much so. They get away with murder at times. ... Certain days we can't play. We can't play on Saturdays and because times are changing so much, I mean half the men there are retired and not working so the whole things is ridiculous really. (W59)

Those women who were able to define their engagement primarily through their motherly involvement were generally much less antagonistic, as Liz indicates.

Liz: The comforts of mothering

Liz (W88) was married to a senior manager. Her attachment to Wilmslow was oriented around her children – with her first response in reply to being questioned about why she lived in the area being 'just a nice area to bring up the children'. A university graduate, she had taken on a part-time pharmacist's job while her husband worked as a GP. Her loyalty to the area was considerable 'all my friends are here, our social life's here. I couldn't imagine living anywhere else'. Her social life revolved around sports clubs, which welcomed her children and encouraged a family atmosphere. She normally played tennis once or twice a week, and had made lots of friends through it.

I like playing tennis, it's nice for the children, I want them to get into tennis, I'd rather them play sports, rather than go shopping and doing other things, I always feel that my childhood was good because I played lots of sport, I played golf all the time, so I want the same for my children, I want them to cycle down there and meet their friends.

And would you say you felt attached to other members of the club?

Attached to other members? Some of my friends play, I suppose the one I'm attached to, I'm attached to because I live nearby and their children go to the same school, so it's terribly incestuous, tends to be the same friends that do everything together.

So it's a network?

Yes, I have friends at school, I'd see them at the tennis club, they'd come round for dinner, I go out for lunch.

When asked why she joined a leisure complex she reported:

It's lovely, it's just very relaxing, it's a great stress reliever for my husband, he works very hard, so it's nice to go and keep fit there, it's nice for the children to go and see other children, I like the children to be active and fit and swim and I quite like the fact that I can go and lounge around the pool, whereas the local leisure centre is just go, have a swim and come out again, whereas there you can relax and have the afternoon there with the children and they're quite happy, they have children to play with, there's a playground, it's nice.

So you can spend more time there?

Yes, it's just a really nice thing to do, it's a nice retreat you know we work hard to earn the money you might as well enjoy it.

Table 3.1 *Respondents with children and age of children*

Area	% with children up to 18yrs in F/T education	% with only children over 18 yrs	% with only pre-school children	% without children
Wilmslow N = 44	45	51	2	2
Cheadle N = 43	40	37	9	14
Chorlton N = 47	27	8	8	55
Ramsbottom N = 47	34	32	17	17

Liz's story, compared to W59, shows that if the housewife's role can be inscribed as a motherly one it could in certain circumstances be more easily endorsed. Mothering provides a means by which gender relationships were 'retraditionalised' (Adkins 2002) around conventional assumptions of male dominance, though in covert ways. This is an especially important process since, as Table 3.1 shows, only in Chorlton – where the conventional nuclear family was less strong – do less than half the households have co-resident children. The experience of bringing up children, and more specifically, mothering, was a key means by which gender relations were reinscribed, not explicitly around the relationships between men and women – which were largely implict and rarely a topic for discussion – but around child-rearing. Mothering 'naturalised' gender and household relationships, so deflecting them from the minds of both men and women as issues for comment.

Mothering is a fluid state, one that demands the performance of appropriate activities on the behalf of children, ones that can never be said to be finally fulfilled. It is therefore a key device inviting women with children to chose to 'put down roots' through their mothering practices, which thereby reinforces the process of elective belonging itself with its disdain for locals and transients. Incoming mothers thereby talk about their children as a resource in narrating their belonging to their place of residence (see Brannen and O'Brien 1996). R135 provided us with a detailed explanation of why she now 'feels part of a community' in the area, where relationships around her young daughter structure her account:

I really like living here yes. I wouldn't want to move and Pete's just got a new job up in Bolton* and I suppose it would be easier to say alright we'll move and go, but having once been bitten doing that it seems a bit silly to do that. And after eight years, especially having Molly, there's a good school at the end of the road, we've got a lot of friends now who live locally so it would be a shame to move from here now, it's a nice area.

So you've made friends actually here?

Yes, because we didn't know anybody when we came up here, and with having Molly I've also got quite a lot of friends now who have small children from groups around here, like Tumble Tots which is an activity thing for small children to go to, I've met a lot of women through that, and Molly has a lot of friends her own age. I guess it's mainly to do with the people that you know.

W25 focuses more on how having children has enabled her to feel as if she belongs to a community:

Yes, I do now, or else I wouldn't have stayed as long really because I'm originally from Merseyside so ...

Right. What makes you feel you belong?

Yes, I've got a lot of friends – lot of contacts.

Right, right. Do you feel part of a community?

Yeah, Yeah, I think since I've had the children especially because ... I mean, I was working full time before so not as much then but I think that now people know that I'm sort of a sitting duck ... I've met a lot of people at the Mums and Toddlers groups – they tend to come round with their kids and vice versa really.

We have a sense here of how these women perform elective belonging through their mothering activities with children. In Chorlton D12, who had moved from another area in Manchester, identifies how social contacts generated through her daughter had provided her with a network of other mothers to socialise with:

Yeah, she goes to a local nursery 3 days a week because I'm working those 3 days, and we've started going to a music class, locally, on Friday mornings, and she goes to the occasional mother and tots group. Whilst I was on maternity leave we went to an NCT organised Monday morning group and that's where I met most of the sort of mother and baby lot

So you met them initially at the NCT but you still keep together and meet up, that sort of thing?

Yeah. There's a lot of under five's in Chorlton with quite active social lives as well.

And what would you do with your mother and baby social life?

We usually meet on a Thursday either morning or afternoon and arrange to do something like go to the park or ... a local play group, that sort of thing, and sometimes we just pop round to each other's houses ... I suppose in that I've become friendly with a lot of the mother and toddler mothers, so yes, I suppose it has.

Do you ever see them out of mother and toddler mode? Do you ever see them to go out for a meal on your own, that sort of thing?

Yeah, we try to arrange things so that it's just like a girls night.

And what sort of things would you do there?

There's quite a regular night out at one of the pubs, The Beech, which I used to go to but I've fallen off a bit now. We go out for curries, things like that.

In these discourses, schools become the focal point of social networks around children and become important in achieving a sense of belonging and 'community'. This mode of talking was most frequently identified in Wilmslow and least noticeable in Cheadle. W108 in Wilmslow identifies the role that children and schools play in helping her achieve a sense of community

I think it's just a funny thing. I quite like it in many ways, but I can't imagine spending the rest of my life here even though I've always said I wouldn't move. So yes, I think part of the community in that when you have a young child at a primary school you do get involved, you feel part of that community, not maybe the community at large, not so much so, but particularly with children at primary school, playing football and things like that. So in that way you do.

This reference to 'that' community, rather than the 'community at large', tellingly indicates that it is only particular social networks that are invoked here. In Chorlton, D44 identified the role of the school and children in bringing people together:

I don't know about community, we obviously all live together, you know the people in this street, you know a few people further out, but having said that, the top of the road I don't know anybody, there's no great community spirit. What brings us together more than anything else I would think would be the girls school.

Some mothers imagine the impact this will have in time on their social networks and attachment to place, so in talking of her physical isolation in a quiet part of Ramsbottom, R114 highlighted how her young son would enable her to become more socially involved and achieve a sense of belonging:

David starts school in September and I think that's better, he's at play group already and already you pick out a few mums and you get chatting with other people and I think sometimes you've to be in an area quite a while before you start meeting people and I think once he goes to school it will be different again, he's getting friends round here and there'll be PTA and all sorts of things, so I'll get roped into all sorts then.

In Cheadle C91 drew on children and schools as resources with which to articulate a feeling of partial and equivocal belonging:

I don't know it's hard to say. In a way I suppose, I mean my daughter goes to school, so there's like a community feeling from school, but apart from that, well it's OK here, just within this road.

So do you feel part of the community here would you say?

Well again, more so now, I think it's very easy when there's just the two of you to just get involved in doing just what the two of you want to do, but when you've got children you get involved more. So more and more so getting involved in things that are going on in the school.

Again we see a reference here to a partial community 'from school' which is seen as distinct from a broader community in which C91 is not involved. Yet, just as mothering changes as children age, so the networks it invokes are transient. It was widely recognised that the relationships formed specifically around child-rearing and schooling could be transitory and superficial, as D47 highlights. When asked if she had enduring friendships from contacts made with children's, friend's parents:

I don't think so, not friends that have lasted. People you meet when the children are babies you don't necessarily have that much in common and don't keep in touch.

Yet, it was also noted that there was the potential for these relationships to become deeper and longer-lasting, but that for this to happen there needed to be more of a connection than just children, which would not be enough alone to sustain the relationship, as W1 explains:

> There were many more of them (friends) ... they've dropped off actually I mean ... whilst the children were at the same school ... was the one, this one here. Course we started going to these um functions you know parents teachers and I got to know the people and then we might go for a meal and for a drink or to each other's houses um but when they leave the school, they left the school and the wives weren't meeting at the school to pick them up it kind of dropped off a little bit. Some we kept some we didn't. But um you'd have to then make the effort to actually make contact to go out again. Whereas when they're talking in the school it gets mentioned doesn't it? What you doing Friday night or ... so I think ... but an awful lot of people but there's still two or three that we see.

In all these narratives, women are seen to be 'naturally' preoccupied with the business of child rearing. R13 and W14 talk of how their partners have made friends through their children:

> Yes, Claire has. Claire tends to make more friends because she works part time now, she had a full-time job, she works part time and on Thursday and Friday she's off so she tends to take Danielle to play groups, she tends to take her to coffee mornings and things like that and she's built up relationships with other ladies via Danielle really. I have not met anybody through Danielle as such that because it's just never come about.

> I think we do now, yes, particularly Alison because she is at home with the children, well two of them are at school and one of them isn't, she is at home and she has built up a good network of friends around the area, so I think yes she certainly feels she belongs there, I am very comfortable there, I work quite long hours so I suppose I am not as integrated into the local community as she is, but we know the neighbours very well and there are friends around ...

In all of our areas both those with and without children drew on children to articulate ideas of belonging, or not belonging and to narrate their relationship to their place of residence. We see, however, that the kind of belonging invoked is a conditional one which is often registered as being apart from other, deeper and more communal forms of attachment. Indeed, it is by examining the narratives of those respondents who didn't have children that we see the important role that children play in enabling respondents to achieve a sense of belonging. In Ramsbottom R82 indicates how not having children distances him from any community involvement.

> Oh no, definitely not. Next door we get on well with and people across the way we know, but further away than that I haven't got a clue. It's quite close around here, the immediate ones ... but further away than that no, I don't get involved in any community facilities, I'm not sure there are any, there probably is if you've got kids and they go to school.

Whereas in Chorlton D43 and D55, highlighted how not having children made achieving a sense of community more difficult:

> Well no, probably not in that we don't go to church and we don't have kids, so in that way we're not part of the community, because I think that's how you get into a community by joining things, so that doesn't really apply to us. We know all our neighbours and stuff, we know all the shop-keepers in each road.

> I think it is because I don't have family and don't have children. With children you belong quicker with school and things like that but as far as I can I feel I belong.

For W7, our only Wilmslow respondent without children, there is still a need to draw upon children narratively to articulate why she feels comfortable where she lives, even if in this case it is the 'lack' of children that ensures a fit between residence and life situation, and despite the fact that it is clear from this narrative there is no real sense of belonging or community:

> The majority of people around here are middle-aged to elderly, so they're not with children – which we can't stand … but the fact of the matter is I travel so much that I tend to find it's a state of mind that for me has dispelled because I spend so much time away from home living in other places.

D50 and D68 provide us with an interesting contrast, as it appears that for some women in Chorlton child-rearing can threaten feelings of belonging. Here there seems to be a tension between the life situation of the respondent and their cultural imaginary of 'vibrant' Chorlton, to such an extent that moving house is being considered:

> It is really vibrant the centre of Chorlton so we like that a lot. There are a couple of aspects about it that have niggled me since we have been here. Partly this road, we really like this road, the neighbours are really nice, nearly all the people that we got on well with have moved out of Chorlton and gone elsewhere. The new influx of people have been mainly young couples and there are no children this end of the street which is a shame now that we have kids. You feel like it would be nice to have other children round. They have to go quite a long way to play with neigh-bours and there is a kind of difference which bugs me a bit, people are not very friendly. They are all into their work and have quite a lot of money and are not really interested in stopping and hav-ing a chat. Keep themselves to themselves. They are not as friendly as they used to be. (D50)

> We've been looking around, probably to Glossop somewhere like that and I've got a daughter that lives there and it's quite nice round there.

> *So your talking about a move to somewhere more rural really?*

> Yes.

> *And away from the town?*

> Yes because I mean she's 10 and I can't let her out on her own, not that I would, in this day and age I don't think I would, whereas my other children, she's going to high school this year and our

other children we did let go on there own, but I don't think I'd let her go on her own, it's just getting far too busy and there's just far too much going on, yes I'd like to know that she's safe if she walked out the front door, I mean I think the furthest she's ever been on her own was to do some homework, so she went to the corner just up there, but that's it … when we lived in the terraced house and my other children were young. You see really apart from Helen from across the road who has 2 children, there aren't any other children her age along this road.

In all these cases we can see that having a sense of community, or feeling that you belong are not inherent qualities of living in a particular locality, but rather have to be worked at, have to be achieved, a process to which child-rearing is central.

3.2 Educational choice

Other studies have pointed to the significance of schooling as a means of securing the loyalty of migrants to particular places. In the 1960s middle-class spiralists would often cite the nature of local schooling as a reason for staying put even if the opportunity to move arose (Pahl and Pahl 1971). However, while this earlier generation of spiralists largely took the quality and nature of local schooling as a given over which they had little control, many parents, and especially mothers, saw it as important to be active in generating the 'right kind' of local schooling. For this reason, elective belonging involved becoming incorporated into local environments, which tied residents into different positions within the educational field in our four areas. Processes of educational attainment are ever more crucial for affecting people's life chances (see Marshall et al. 1997; Savage 2000) are hence localised, in ways which have been explored by Ball et al. (1995) Ball (2002) and Butler and Robson (2003b). Ball et al. (1995) identify how class specific circuits of schooling operate in London, with middle-class 'cosmopolitans' rather than working-class 'locals' being the most active choosers of schools for their children in the education marketplace. This argument is developed by Butler and Robson (2003b) who argue that locality and educational provision are key to mapping the habitus of middle-class life in inner London, the crucial point being 'how the immediate locality of residence enables access to a wider locality of educational provision' (2003b: 7). Here, we develop this argument further by considering the important role that schools and schooling play in the achievement of elective belonging.

Schools and schooling were issues raised by most respondents with children, but were particularly resonant refrains in the more 'cultured' middle-class areas of Wilmslow and Chorlton. Respondents talked about the mode of schooling to articulate and embody the comfort or lack of comfort felt living in their chosen areas, with the result that schools and schooling was one of the key motivators to move or to stay in a particular location. In Wilmslow the striking feature in terms of school selection was the use of independent schooling with 55% (see Table 3.2) of the sample sending their children to independent schools, or a mixture of independent

Table 3.2 *Respondents with children in education and mode of schooling*

Area	State (%)	Independent (%)	Mix of state and independent (%)
Wilmslow N = 20	45	40	15
Cheadle N = 17	94	0	6
Chorlton N = 13	85	0	15
Ramsbottom N = 16	88	0	13

and state schooling.[1] This is much higher than the national figure of 7% (*Social Trends 31* 2001) or the regional figure for the north-west of 5% (*Regional Trends 36* 2001). In all of the other areas state schooling is the dominant mode of education, although both Chorlton and Ramsbottom have a significant minority who use a mixture of state and independent forms of education.

In Wilmslow this use of independent education was seen by many as the local 'norm'. It was important to secure the 'best' for their children, and to have control over their children's education in any possible way – by buying into private schools, by being involved in their schooling, and by intervening in the provision of local schooling. This is an example of Ball's (2002: 128) identification of how value systems are constructed, amended and influenced within families, social networks or local communities, as part of 'what people like us, in this place, do'. He shows that appropriate attitudes towards parenting and schooling, are formed and maintained in particular social contexts. Importantly, in this instance it is not always that the schools are physically located in Wilmslow – since in fact many of the favoured private schools are located some distance away, often in South Manchester – but rather that Wilmslow is the kind of place where the values and standards of independent schooling 'set the tone'.

Sarah: the values of private schooling

Sarah (W98) was from one of the most affluent households in our sample. She was herself a teacher in a private prep school, and was preoccupied by getting the best education for her children.

... like the fact that you can find like-minded people with the same experiences. My husband and I both have university degrees and research, so we're a fairly academic sort of family, the schooling is very good, the secondary schooling, there's a tremendous choice. Both boys have gone to ... we have educated to eleven in state schools and then gone to the private system after that, mainly because Andrew came up here at 11 and went to a Grammar school, having done two years with a scholarship as a chorister in London in a private school, and we were so delighted with it that our second boy has just done his first year. Although I didn't want to be in the position of paying for school education, it's hard once you've seen a school of that calibre not to look at it. My daughter's gone through a local fee paying school, but with a scholarship, I think she feels short changed that she hasn't gone to a city school, but I'm still convinced that for her it was the right decision, she's not as booky, she's clever but not as academic as the other two, she loves her music and her sport, and is permanently running on a timetable that's not school days. So with four children I found that it's made my life simpler, I just pick her up within five minutes and I couldn't have done that, she would have had to forfeit some of those things. So I think for any family there's every possible option open to them. Certainly the families that we have a lot to do with have sent their children to the state school and are also delighted with it, my children begged not to go there, they felt that if they tried to work …

Sarah highlights how not using independent schools affects feelings of belonging, and uses a complex set of legitimation devices to justify her decision.

This reflects findings from other studies on the middle classes and educational choice, as Ball (2002) has suggested consumer choice in the education marketed market such as the decision as to whether to educate privately or within the state system can provoke conflict and struggle for parents over values and principles. Consistent with this we found that middle-class parents could be inconsistent, contradictory and prone to legitimating past and future actions. Social practices are informed by value systems, but people are often involved in what Zanten and Veleda term 'ethical bricolage' (cited in Ball 2002: 114) a contradictory complex cobbling together of values and principles to justify the educational choices made. At the heart of this and central to the decision-making is putting the 'family first' (W108):

It's been a funny thing to deal with really. One thing I think we've found here different from where we lived before is that a lot of children go to independent schools, which sort of changes the balance for your own children. It's alright now. There is a peer group.

And was it an active decision to send them to state schools?

Well I mean you know, if they went to independent schools we wouldn't be able to go on holiday in the same way, I suppose you take the decision to live in a different house. I don't know you just maybe do different things. Also for me it's the principle. It's difficult when you don't know who you're sort of talking to (*laughter*). It's just the way really I suppose things evolve.

W62 who used education in the independent sector for his first three children but whose youngest attended a local state school, explains his use of state education for her child and in so doing reinforces how significant education is for Wilmslow respondents with children, and the role parents play in it. This is an important point for it is the high level of emphasis placed on education, and parental involvement in it that is a key feature of the habitus of these Wilmslow respondents, and it is this that facilitates the feeling that their chosen place of residence is congruent with their life stories and situation.

Why did you not send him to private school?

James tried a selective state foundation grammar school and did not get in. But he is making his way and the school is developing. He has got 9 GCSEs. This is typical of Wilmslow. It is the norm. I think there are kids who get none, of course there are, there is a spectrum but within our circles Alistair has got I think 10 A stars, William his brother has 10 A stars as well and will go on and get 4 As at A. He is not quite up to that but will get As and Bs. I work in Stalybridge* and they are lucky if they get 5 Cs but they have other skills. But Wilmslow is that level. I think it is the kind of area where parents push a lot. They are very keen that their children succeed.

Examining the narratives of those respondents who had made a very deliberate choice to use state schools, it is clear that such parents thought that they could intervene more effectively through becoming involved in their state education rather than simply through spending in the private sector. W51 is committed to state education, but for this commitment to sit easily with his practical sense of habitus it requires 'working' at and a high level of parental involvement and intervention.

Yes, we're very committed to the state system and in fact so committed that when I came here and found that the school needed equipment I became a governor, or was invited to become a governor, and I'm now chair of governors.

So you're quite committed to that side of it?

Yeah, we were both brought up in state schools and went on to university and have a very strong commitment to state education, and wanted the children to actually experience the same, all be it in somewhat different and difficult circumstances …

You mentioned you were governor of the school, that's not a club as such obviously but it's a committee that you're involved in, what made you join that?

Well, I was driven primarily by the need for improvement in the school at that time and the fact that if we did and were going to send our children there then some active involvement in it was going to be necessary, but also I was driven by the fact that I've always tended to commit some time particularly to education for a long time having been chairman of governors of the primary school that my children attended.

This narrative of involvement was typical of Wilmslow, in particular the edge of instrumentalism that pervaded this talk of social involvement. We can also see how this degree of parental participation echoes that found by Vincent (2001) in her 'Little Polities' study which identified three forms of parental intervention, high, intermediate and low, where for the high cohort 'having a relationship with the school overtly demonstrating your concern about your child's education, was "what people like us do"' (Vincent 2001: 349). In Vincent's study this high cohort were the more affluent, higher educated and generally public sector professionals, in our case this high level of parental intervention was evident for private sector workers too, particularly if they were using the state education system. Thus, intervention and involvement are seen as being an expression of good parenting but there is also a need to register with the school that you are a 'good' parent (for the implications of this for PTA involvement, see Bagnall et al. 2003). This intervention is a way to subject the school to surveillance and Vincent characterises this group of high involvement parents who acted in this way as 'risk managers' and certainly in the extract of W51 we can see evidence of this as he talks of the need 'for improvement in the school at that time and the fact that if we did and were going to send our children there then some active involvement in it was going to be necessary'.

Thus, we can see the ways and the extent to which parents are willing to intervene and involve themselves with the school in order to achieve the desired results for their children. However, not all respondents do make the right choices to allow them to feel at ease. W35 is an interesting counterpoint here, where it is difficult to elect to belong to an area that does not live up to your expectations:

Obviously in a cheaper area you would get more rooms, more space, and I'm bitterly disappointed with the education here, I hadn't done my homework properly.

Why is that?

They are crummy schools even though it's a very posh area. I said bitterly because I look at all the houses around some of them are 3 and 4 hundred thousand pounds, in the road, and I go into the local state school, which is literally across the road, from me ... and I'm not at all impressed.

Is that where your daughter is?

Yes I've got a little girl but she doesn't go there.

But she does go to school.

She has just started school. So I'm not impressed with the Conservative council, although I'm not Labour. I'm not impressed with the services on offer, I'm not impressed with the schooling, I wasn't impressed with the lack of nursery education. So it seems to be pay for it or sell ... It's my own fault, there's a Catholic church down the road and I'm obviously a Roman Catholic and I intended to send her to a Catholic school, and I went down and saw a building next to the church and thought it was the school, it wasn't, it was the parish hall and the actual Catholic school is miles away. It hadn't struck me that I was in a different diocese, until after we had moved. I am used to one diocese with Roman Catholic schools on every corner. There are none down there. She's at a private prep, and the other Catholic school ... I'm not really impressed with that one either.

Chorlton presents a very different picture to Wilmslow. Unlike Wilmslow, it was not seen as a 'natural' place to raise children. Its dominant liberal and cosmopolitan ethos was not well equipped to deal with a culture of 'family first', especially because of its gendered connotations. A few respondents found ways of linking their perception of Chorlton with its schooling if they were seen as reflective of the area's 'mix'. As D25, a manager with the Local Authority, put it:

> Yeah, I generally like the area. It's got good schools for the kids, and as I say, it's got a nice mixture of people. It's got a nice mixture of cultures as well, so it's not a stereotype area, you've got a nice mixture.

A few others were able to identify their own personal involvement and understanding of particular schools as reasons why they were happy with the interplay between schooling and the local area. D98, a teacher, noted that:

> It's also handy because the schools are very good, I particularly rate the high school, where I was a governor, and particularly the junior school that two of the three boys still go to is very good. So for those sorts of reasons really. ... Yes, I mean Chorlton actually is a nice cosmopolitan mix, it's got a small group of students, obviously a fairly comfortable mix then of people with children and not, so it supports a fairly nice night life as well.

But here it is important to note that his own high level of parental intervention, and his own cultural and educational capital as a teacher, linked to his role as a governor, were crucial to making a success of his children's education:

> Yes I'm a governor to the junior school where two of my three boys still are and I was a governor of a high school, for a term, but found that I couldn't do all of that very well, particularly with the marriage split up, so rather than trying to limp on doing something badly, I gave up the high school governorship and retained the junior school one ...

> *So what do you enjoy about that?*

> Well I suppose being a teacher as well meant that you actually made a contribution in a different way. Also it was good to be on the governing body of the school where your children were. ... But it was very much a conscious decision, because I'm an LEA governor so I'm representing the Labour council on the governing body, to put something back in to the school that my kids were getting so much out of. Also because I was a teacher I thought that perhaps I could put a dimension in which many governors couldn't do.

However, in the main, the issue of local schooling was a key aspect of the liberal conundrum identified in Chapter 2. Social mixing is fine in principle, but is premised on mixing between 'people like us'. Faced with the reality of schools with real social mixing, problems arose, and provided a challenge to the relationship between the choice of residential location, the biographical construction of self and the imaginary vision of place. The lack of fit between habitus and educational provision led some of our Chorlton respondents with children to feel less at ease, and have less of a sense of comfort in place. Indeed for some this sense of discomfort was enough to make them contemplate moving. The perceived inadequacy of secondary educational provision in the area was for some a crucial issue:

> Well we like Flixton and Urmston, round there. Well Trafford if we do stay put somewhere for schools, although the primary schools have a good reputation round here the secondary schools are pretty poor, it's quite a widely reported thing the drift, as kids get to nine or ten everyone leaves and goes back to Didsbury or goes into Trafford. (D107)

Kerry, who works in the media, originally from Scotland but who had spent time working in London provides an illuminating reflexive and articulate account of the difficulties faced by mothers like her, who feel they are living in the 'right' place but are now having this challenged because of the educational choices they are faced with. We can see here how our work echoes the findings of Ball (2002) and Butler and Robson (2003b) and the link they identify between housing and education markets. These parents with high stocks of cultural capital are faced with a dilemma, whether to live in a diverse area, or to move somewhere with 'better' educational provision. Their political and moral values are challenged by a need to make the 'best' educational choice for their child. There is a clear tension between their liberal values and 'family first', with its gendered assumptions, as Kerry indicates.

Kerry: the contradictions of liberal parenting

Kerry (D27) was a succesful media professional, who liked living in Chorlton, but found herself in a schooling dilemma.

> ... because we decided to move house ... I mean, our children are both at primary school in Chorlton the local comprehensive is on the up, but it hasn't got a very good reputation, so we were quite concerned about that and we were thinking about alternatives.

And what kind of things do you like now about living in Chorlton?

> Well, we've thought about this a lot because we were researching other areas. We love the diversity of the people who live here. I mean, many of our children's friends parents have become our friends and many of those people are lesbian couples and now I respect the way they live and they have become really good friends of ours regardless of their sexuality, that's not an issue, and I like the fact that my children are growing up knowing children with same sex parents and not seeing that as peculiar in any way. I also like the fact that

---

there's a very good racial mix in Chorlton. I mean, that's important to us because we've got mixed race children and we don't want them to be in a very small minority. It is a good racial mix, it's not just Afro-Caribbean, it's Asian, Hindu, Sikh, Moslem, there's also quite a lot of people who originally came from Arab countries, and Chilean, so it's very mixed, so that we like a lot. … Chorlton centre itself doesn't look to be in such good shape but then the property prices are going up and I think people are beginning to feel a lot better about the comprehensive school. I mean, that is the big, big issue for people living in Chorlton and you will find a lot of people on sort of middle to high incomes deciding to move away from Chorlton once their children approach secondary school age because they're very concerned about the comprehensive school here, and if you compare the GCSE results with other schools results in the Trafford/Cheshire area, they are lagging behind in a big way.

Do you know any parents who use private schools here?

One or two people I know use private, that's not so common. I think what you tend to get are parents put their children into Chorlton state primary and then they get extra coaching so that they pass the 11+ for the Trafford grammars and some of them might look at city grammar schools but that's a very sensitive subject because you get this sort of dilemma because people choose to live in Chorlton because it's pretty liberal and they come to this stage of oh God, we're not happy about the comprehensive and do we feel comfortable about going back on our principles and sending them to private school. So yes, a lot of them opt for other areas because it's easier.

Later in the interview, Kerry also uses education as a mechanism through which to identify the pervasiveness of the class system.

I don't think that's changed at all, and even at state primary schools in Chorlton, you can pick up the middle-class parents because they will know the head teacher, they'll be on very friendly terms with the head teacher because they'll make it their business to know the head teacher and it's all about confidence, it's all about expectations and it's all about asserting your rights. Of course, it's very, very class based.

Thus, for some of our Chorlton residents the fit between habitus and residential location is under stress as they try and reconcile competing and sometimes contradictory values, perhaps echoing the private/state choice dilemma for our Wilmslow respondents. However, in Wilmslow it is perceived that this dilemma can be overcome by parental intervention and involvement, whereas in Chorlton the nature of the problem is perceived to be too great for such a solution. Rather, in Chorlton, the issue of schooling becomes 'individualised', in terms of the dilemma it is deemed to present to parents, and the reliance on a strategy of either moving or staying. There is no dominant sense in Chorlton of a 'norm', or agreement over what 'like-minded people' do.

Ramsbottom parents are intermediate between Wilmslow and Chorlton for here there is far less dialogue about schooling except to express a general sense of happiness with it. Just as we have seen in Chapter 2 that Ramsbottom most conforms to the community studies model of tensions between insiders and outsiders, so its residents subscribe most clearly to the model that educational provision is a given over which parents have little control. It is an important factor in assessing the quality of the local environment, but does not prove to be all pervasive. These feelings perhaps also reflect the lesser degree of cultural capital available to the respondents, most of whom have achieved middle-class jobs not so much through educational attainment but more through promotion within large organisations. Education is presented as one factor among many in assessing the quality of place.

> Just the quieter area really, we've moved from ... and we went on the East Lancs (railway) years ago and like it here, but we never really thought we'd end up here. Then as time was getting on and my eldest daughter was coming up to thinking of high school, the one that we was near was really going downhill and we thought that while she'd still got a couple of years at primary school we'd start looking at moving. So I suppose yes the schools was a big factor, plus looking at the secondary school which had a good reputation, and we just liked this area. (R158)

For many others like R141 and R149 it was a positive if un-looked for benefit of living there:

> The schools have been very good, we didn't really know before we moved into the area. (R141)

> *So what brought you to this house and the area?*

> The fields. There's fields at the back. We lived as the crow flies less than half a mile from here, but it was up a cul-de-sac where apart from one family everybody else's kids had grown up and left home, the children didn't have anywhere to play, so we decided we'd move here for the children. Everybody else that's moved in has kids and there's fields and woods ... No, the kids are very settled in school now and I wouldn't want to disrupt them. The local secondary school is very good, they're happy here and have friends. I'm a wanderer but I can't expect them to be. (R149)

In Cheadle, talk around schooling and educational choice was generally less salient, but as Reay and Lucey (2003) have identified discussions around choice often mask the fact that choice is a marker of economic privilege and the more distant parents are from economic necessity the more choice is possible. In Cheadle many of our respondents did not have the economic or cultural capital to make choices over schooling, and in general didn't articulate schooling as a problem, as Bourdieu has identified 'the lack of capital intensifies the feeling of finitude: it chains one to a place' (1999c: 127). Thus, for our less affluent and mobile sample in Cheadle educational choice was less of an option, and provoked much less debate, with a more passive acceptance that the local schools were 'OK' or even good.

> *So they go to local schools?*

> Oh yes. ... There's certain little things, you know, educational wise they are quite good. The curriculum and stuff are quite good, you know they take them out and physics and stuff they have always been fairly good at. I have no problems about that. (C70)

However, there were some who countered this 'feeling of finitude' such as C97, an export administrator, married to a 'Council' worker with two children and a relatively low joint income of under £20,000. C97 expresses a sense of dissatisfaction with the schooling, and a desire to be able to have more educational choice, and potentially make use of independent schooling, or move house, while at the same time she clearly demonstrates an awareness of the impact of a lack of economic capital on choice:

> I like this particular road, it's nice and quiet and I like the neighbours. We've never had any trouble round here. We don't really dislike anything particularly, I don't think the schools are very good. I've got two children at one school, but then I think that generally education is not good, I think at the moment they've been making an effort to change things, I can see that my eldest daughter's doing a bit more work than the youngest one. But generally I'm quite happy living here.

Later in the interview there was a clear acknowledgement of how more money would improve her 'choices'

> Well if we could afford to move to a better area and a better house with better schools then I'd do it, definitely, I would say that we are not in a brilliant area, but if we could go up we would, I'm not saying this is the end, I'm dead happy here, but if our income suddenly increased to such an extent where we could move then we would.

> *And would that make you a different class?*

> Yes, you'd be climbing up. I don't know, I mean there's places where I wouldn't move to, we just want the best, and we wouldn't move to an area where there were children I wouldn't want them to mix with, I like them to mix with children whose parents have the same interests and things like that.

Rather like Ramsbottom respondents, the quality of local schools can be salient, but can be partitioned from their sense of place more easily than among Wilmslow and Chorlton residents. However, for some of the younger professionals living in Cheadle schooling was also a more salient issue, and often there was an ambivalence expressed at the perceived quality of educational provision. As C32, a computer software consultant who was one of the most economically affluent respondents in the area stated:

> It concerns me, yeah. I try to find out a bit more about just how … what the schools are like here and talking again to the children who … people … neighbours seem happy with the school. I'd just like to know a bit more about that. I've no reason to think it's bad or that there's a problem but it's certainly a factor for where I'd want to live. Directors at work have … some of them have deliberately chosen their area according to a very good State School, …

We can identify a relationship between elective belonging and educational choice and provision, and that this can be connected to the extent to which educational options are more or less congruent with the habitus of the

Table 3.3   *Respondents involved with PTA and type of involvement*

Area	Superficial involvement1 (%)	Intermediate involvement (%)	Deep involvement (%)	Parents involved (%)
Wilmslow	25	13	63	80
Cheadle	67	17	17	35
Chorlton	57	14	29	54
Ramsbottom	11	67	22	56

respondents and/or their cultural values and imaginary construction of place. Educational access and provision can make people feel more or less comfortable in place, and it is this 'comfort' or discomfort which is crucial to the 'dialectic of positions and dispositions' as people move between different kinds of physical locations. In Wilmslow there is perceived to be a fit between respondents's habitus and the fields of education and housing, although this can lead to movement within the field of education, for example the choice of the state or independent sector. In Chorlton, a challenge is posed to elective belonging for those with children because the strong cultural imaginary construction and investment in Chorlton as a cosmopolitan site of liberal diversity, does not always fit with the perceived inadequacy of the available educational provision, and the habitus of respondents who value education. There is a tension and lack of fit between the housing and educational fields which leads some respondents to consider moving. Educational access and provision is much less of a feature of elective belonging in Cheadle and in Ramsbottom education provision is less prominent as a feature of elective belonging. Thus, the extent to which educational provision matters is related to how much education and cultural capital are part of the respondent's habitus.

The extent to which these processes become related to social action is made manifest by considering the extent of involvement with Parent Teacher Associations (PTA) in each of our areas (see also Bagnall et al. 2003). Table 3.3 shows that a high number of Wilmslow respondents (80%) with school age children are or have recently been involved to some degree with the local PTA.[2] This is quite different to the picture that emerges in Cheadle, where only 35% of our respondents or their partners are involved with the PTA. Ramsbottom and Chorlton occupy intermediate positions between Wilmslow and Cheadle in terms of PTA participation.[3] Table 3.3 also shows that 63% of our Wilmslow respondents claim to be deeply involved, such as being on the PTA committee, or regularly attending committee meetings.

These findings can be related to the work of Vincent (2001) and Vincent and Martin (2002) on the possession and deployment of 'parental voice'.[4] Their work considers the varying reactions and interventions by parents on a range of educational issues including PTA membership and involvement. The form of 'parents' social spaces shape their voice' which 'expresses the deeper classification of social space' (2002: 113). In the case of Wilmslow, we see that a 'high' level of participation in the PTA, is in accord with and reflective of the habitus of the respondents for whom high levels of educational, economic and cultural capital are the norm. We would suggest that such a level of participation, and the form of social capital it generates, enables a fit between social and spatial location and so is another means to elect to belong. While in Cheadle lower levels of participation, and strength of parental voice reflects a habitus more focused on everyday survival and getting by. Ramsbottom parents are intermediate between these two. For these respondents PTA membership is not vital for achieving belonging in the same way as it is in Wilmslow for it is not what draws them to live in this location. Similarly, in Chorlton while for more than half of the respondents with children some form of participation in the PTA is seen as being as the norm, this tends to be on a superficial rather than a deep level.

Bourdieu argues that 'individuals who move into a new space must fulfil the conditions that that space tacitly require of its occupants' (1999c: 128). Certain spaces require certain types of economic, cultural and social capital. We argue that 'doing' the PTA is one means for people in Wilmslow to acquire the necessary capital to 'belong' because it is seen to generate 'like-minded' (W98) networks of people who also share similar kinds of habitus. Liz encapsulates this in the following comments:

What sort of people got involved with the PTA?

Very middle class, professionals, management that sort of thing, but with the same ideals about bringing up children, interested in their children's education and just with a similar lifestyle to what we have ... go out and have a meal with a friend, but generally no, I go to a lot of PTA meetings and things like that and he has a lot of evening meetings, nights on call of stints working in the emergency centre, so he works quite hard.

Cheadle provides us with an important contrast here, for performing locally-based parenthood takes a quite different form to Wilmslow, with attitudes towards the PTA startlingly different, as we see with C101 and C17:

Have you ever been involved in PTAs?

Oh god no, they should all be shot. ... (C101)

Can I just ask you, through your children at school, are you involved in any parents associations or anything like that?

No not at the moment, not involved at all.

Is it something you might do in the future?

I don't think so, I think the people who are attracted to it don't attract me basically. (C17)

It is important to note the degree of *instrumentalism* that pervades the narratives of social involvement in Wilmslow. For example, PTA membership is narrated as a mechanism through which to access and build social networks. This way of talking was particularly prominent among our incoming but 'staying' Wilmslow residents. W13 moved to Wilmslow with her partner from Tunbridge Wells and joined the PTA:

partly to meet people, partly to help fundraising for the school, and it's quite a good way of finding out what's going on as well.

And would you see those friends away from the PTA or would it be mainly school events?

It's mainly at school events but there'll be one or two …, it's all such a network round here, there'll be people at the PTA and people at other things. (W13)

Susan joined the PTA:

To make friends … I have always been involved … it is a mechanism of meeting people and becoming part of something because you don't have that feeling of belonging in the area when you come into it and it's much quicker to become part of something and also it gives you a close-ness to your children. Considering that school takes up a lot of their time in life so you're actu-ally sharing that … I've got a lot of friends from it. Well friends and acquaintances, more acquaintances probably than close friends. (W5)

These extracts indicate the way in which the connections to other parents generate 'weak ties' (Granovetter 1973) which are vital in providing access to social networks in the area. Frazer (1999) has also drawn attention to the idea that loose ties of acquaintanceship and friendship can be important both for individuals and their social outcomes. Involvement can also play an important role in securing extra knowledge or 'cultural capital' about the education of children (Reay, 2000, Bourdieu, 1977,1998, 1999c). The narrative from W12 below illustrates the complex inter-relationship between the building of social and cultural capital:

I went (to the PTA) because I know that you find out a lot about the school and how things work and to meet other mums that I perhaps don't meet at the school gates and things like that. Just the interaction and to be part of it really and I like to know what's going on. … Well I've not com-mitted myself to being totally involved in it yet because well partly because Matthew has only just started school and I've only just started my college work and I don't know how that's going to … you know I wouldn't like to say I'll be the secretary or something when I don't know how much work will be involved in other things. I'm intending to go to all the meetings if I can, as many as I can, and sort of take it from there … the headmistress chats to you as if she knows you … they make you very welcome … playschool as well … I didn't feel as though I was completely new to it at all really … familiar faces dotted around the circle so I didn't feel as though I was completely new to it at all really.

Ball (2002) sees this kind of social capital as allowing access to the kind of 'hot' (rather than cold, i.e. documentary) information that enables children to succeed within the education system. This type of knowledge is highly valued and as we can see here mothers often seek to build and draw upon networks of other mothers to provide this 'hot' first hand information (Ball and Vincent, 1998). This way of talking about involvement with the PTA, and networks around children was less prevalent in the other areas, although echoes of it could be heard from some of the younger professionals with young children at nursery or school, who were newer to the areas and less embedded than most in terms of family and residential networks.

This kind of parental intervention was normally defined as a mother's role, though these assumptions were often left implicit (see further Bourdieu, 1998: 68, cited in Reay 2000 and Ball 2002). In our research women, particularly but not exclusively from Wilmslow, did play a key role in this process, as W34 highlights:

Parent Teacher Associations? Things to do with school, anything like that?

Carolyn is a member of the Parent Teacher Association. That is the closest connection with the school. She is more directly involved with the school and establishing connections with the school before Rebecca went there than I have.

This is further elaborated by W69 who with her partner co-owns a textile company, for whom child and school-based associational involvement is seen as a constituent of married life:

and I've just started to learn bridge which is not the easiest but I'm learning and then I've done during my married life lots of school PTA committees.

Did you used to be on the PTA?

Yes, I was Chairman of the PTA at the Girls Grammar school and I then became a parent governor, I was on all the other school committee's that the children were at and I was on the synagogue committee and I was a magistrate and then I became a Samaritan and I do talking newspaper, bits and pieces. I do feel strongly that one should actually put something into the community, especially if you live like we do.

However, we have to be careful here to avoid constructing middle-class attitudes and practices as normative (Reay 2000). Certainly not all our Wilmslow mothers were deeply involved, or enamoured with the PTA. Yet, as the following extract shows, W27 felt the need to provide a narrative of legitimation based around 'time' and previous voluntary group participation to justify her non-involvement:

Do the schools you send your children to have the equivalent of PTAs, and do you belong to them?

No. I run a mile. I just haven't got the time in my life at the moment for it. It tends to be basically the mothers that have nothing better to do I think, they don't work or they do voluntary work or something like that. I'd rather just give £10 extra a term or something to be honest with you, I think the faffing about, I did quite a bit of this fundraising and stalls and whatever when I was in the NCT, because I was fairly active in that, and it quite honestly bores me, it seems so trivial,

I know it sounds awful, but to raise £50 after you've spent months planning something, organising it and having meetings about it. To me I just don't want to do it.

Here, we can see how this echoes the findings of Vincent and Ball who identified how in narratives around child-care, mothers are required to navigate their way through 'very potent and very immediate normatives of "good mothering"' (2001: 649). To achieve this mothers engage in and deploy 'legitimation talk' and 'emotional work' and through these forms of talk actively manage guilts and fears. In the extract above not having the 'time' is used to legitimate the lack of PTA involvement, but the respondent is keen to highlight 'good' mothering practices such as involvement with the NCT.[5] We can identify the moral tale (Ribbens et al. 2000) that is being told here: that despite not being involved in the PTA, this respondent is a 'good mother'.

Conclusion

We have seen how narratives around mothering, child-rearing and schooling were key in articulating respondents' relationship to place, and how the cultural meaning of place, cultural values concerning education, and the economic and cultural capital available to respondents played a key role in their ability to achieve a sense of belonging. In Wilmslow sociation relating to children was reflective of a habitus based around diffuse networks, weak ties and 'getting ahead' (Granovetter 1973). In Cheadle people were more embedded in the locality, with stronger links to the area through residence, family, leisure and work, sociation was framed by these existing ties, and we identified a habitus based on the power of 'strong ties' and 'getting by' (Bagnall et al. 2003). Ramsbottom occupied a more intermediate position, with sociation linked to the degree of embeddeddness in the area, thus in Ramsbottom it is the in-comers rather than the 'locals' who are most likely to draw on children as being key to sociation. In the case of Chorlton fewer people had children, and children were less a part of the cultural imaginary, and at times for those with children this led to a sense of discomfort and thoughts of moving. However, for others with children, there was some similarity to patterns identified in Wilmslow but key differences were that the sociation was not as heavily gendered, and the edge of instrumentalism that pervaded many of the Wilmslow narratives was not as evident.

Notes

1 The norm here was for children to be educated in the state sector at primary level, and for the independent sector to be used at secondary level.

2 Respondents with children who had now left home or were at University also demonstrated similar levels of membership and involvement with PTAs.

3 It is important to note here as Power et al. (2003) have identified, that schools vary in organisational culture and ethos and that this has a significant bearing on parental choices and children's experiences. While we acknowledge that this could be an important factor in parental participation, as we did not study the schools directly, we cannot specifically identify the influence of schools. But the important aspect for us is how parents used social involvement around school as a resource to narrate belonging.

4 This concept is derived from the work of Hirschmann cited in Vincent and Martin and is defined as 'any attempt at all to change rather than escape from an objectionable state of affairs' (2002: 30).

5 Natural Childbirth Trust.

4

Suburbia and the Aura of Place

Stereotypes of contemporary suburban life invoke the idea of detachment and an instrumental relationship with place. Classic studies of middle-class migrants, from C. Wright Mills (1951) and W.H. Whyte (1957) in post-war America, to Colin Bell (1968) and Ray and Jan Pahl (1971) in Britain, evoke the idea of the rootless, mobile, and instrumental suburbanites. In more recent American studies, such as that of Bellah et al. (1996) and Baumgartner (1991), suburban life is seen as entailing morally distant relations with neighbours and a retreat from developed modes of civic engagement. Mike Davis invokes the suburban communities of Los Angeles as invoking new kinds of privatised withdrawl, a tendency most manifest in the spread of 'gated communities' in the US but with parallels in England (Wynne 1996). The image of the anonymous suburb has become a mainstay of American fiction, being a central motif of the struggles against pointlessness which preoccupy characters in the work of Richard Ford and John Updike. Similar images are invoked in films such as Sam Mendes's 'American Beauty'.

There is a different view which does not subscribe to the idea that suburban life is soulless and detached. Silverstone's (1997) collection emphasises the utopian possibilities of suburban life, pointing to the way that in the British context suburbia has been a wellspring of popular culture. It is not incidental that so many pop icons, ranging from John Lennon to David Bowie, hail from suburban origins. In this chapter we develop this argument regarding the magical qualities of suburbia through our analysis of the aura of place in the minds of our respondents. We develop our account of the tensions of elective belonging by building on the widespread recognition that globalising processes involve a comparative frame of reference (e.g. Robertson 1992). Particular places are highly meaningful, and residents do not see themselves as living in 'placeless' environments, but in sites which are highly emotionally charged. Even where people's attachment to place seems largely instrumental, we excavate more complex symbolic meanings of place.

This chapter begins by examining the complex tensions surrounding neighbouring. We show that there are subtle processes leading to both involvement and withdrawl from neighbours that are not amenable to simple arguments regarding increasing privatism. In the second part of the chapter we show how most respondents have highly charged senses of the symbolic importance of place to them. People's instrumental relationship to residence is overlain by more intricate emotional attachments which involve placing their areas of residence in a wider symbolic geography. The last part of the chapter shows how certain areas are defined in the minds of their residents in terms of their imaginary connections with other symbolically powerful sites. These imagined places define their place as copies of, or renderings of specific other places. We therefore emphasise that rather than residential places being faceless or anonymous, they are emotionally highly charged and have distinct meanings which can only be understood in terms of relationships between places.

4.1 Neighbouring and respectful distance

The tension between space (as fixed location) and place (as meaningful territory) has a long history, which Casey (1997) traces back to the ancient Greeks. Most recent accounts are indebted to Henri Lefebvre's (1991) brilliant analysis. For Lefebvre, capitalism generates abstract space, as commodification entails the parcelisation of land and the use of abstract measures to define space, so leading to the stripping out of qualitative judgements of space in favour of quantitative measures (see Harvey 1983, 1985). Yet this stripping out of place into empty spaces allows the potential for people to redefine and colonise spaces in myriad ways (see also de Certeau 1984). This emphasis – that abstract space can be subverted by representational practices championing the politics of spatial particularity – has been elaborated by Shields (1991) and Hetherington (1997) who emphasise that modernity moralises place, through the generation of diverse place myths, utopias and heterotopias. This tension is best rendered through Walter Benjamin's concept of aura, especially when placed in the broader context of Bourdieu's recognition of the territoriality of distinction (see Savage 1995; Gilloch 1996).

Benjamin (1973) argues that the development of mechanical reproducibility challenges the aura of cultural objects that previously were unique in time and space, leading to a new cultural politics not premised on the distance of audiences from auratic cultural products. Aura is not simply eclipsed in an age of mechanical reproduction but is displaced. People seek aura in those arenas where it cannot be mass reproduced, leading to an oscillation between distance and nearness. Places come to play a particularly role in this dialectical relationship. The experience of places involves a 'transitivity', a mobility, which evades representation (Caygill 1998). Global communications allow the mobility of the imagination (Appadurai 1996). Yet the continued aura of place necessitates a comparative frame in which the distinctiveness of places is defined with respect to other places, in the way that Benjamin plays off Berlin against Naples, Moscow and Paris (Buck-Morss 1989; Gilloch 1996; Caygill 1998). Therefore, rather than globalisation proliferating generic images and symbols, such as those of the globe, we see it as organising a comparative auratic politics of place, as unique places jostle for attention. However, as Benjamin insists, seeking out these auratic places is ultimately self-defeating and undermining. If the distance that creates space between the viewer and the auratic object is overcome, then the object is no longer truly auratic. But when the auratic object remains distant, viewers seek to get closer. There is an unstable oscillation between belonging, distance and aura.

This dialectical tension between distance and propinquity allows us to develop a theoretical account of 'elective belonging' as a core feature of contemporary attachment to place. Belonging is not that of an individual to a fixed community rooted in place, but rather, one in which the place becomes valuable to the individual:

I like the life that I have created for myself here. Not so much Wilmslow it's my life in Wilmslow because it is a pleasant place to live, people are generally polite we don't have a lot of hassle. I would guess if you went to live somewhere nearer a bigger conurbation … you could have more problems. (W33)

So do you feel you belong in Ramsbottom?

It belongs to me. I don't feel an outsider to a degree, probably because I don't … I think I tend to float above it, you know … you know, I sometimes hear of political situations that the youngsters tell me about and I think, you know, are we living in the same world but then again, you know, being sort of middle aged and boring you tend to be slightly cotton woolified sometimes, don't you? (R21, Joanne)

Well as you can tell I'm a southerner. I've lived in the North West for 11 years. I feel very comfortable here but I'm an outsider. I don't want to go back to London, so I suppose I'm a bit of a hybrid, really. I am an outsider, I mean, the newsagent is of the older generation, Mr. Bond*, and there's a line of people every morning buying newspapers, all of whom he addresses by their first name, all in their sixties, and they all know each other and I dread to think what those poor people think about the likes of us horrendous people but we have a cleaner who's of that group of people and she is extremely friendly and we get on very well with her. (D13)

This is a similar account of community to that which parents discussed in Chapter 3 when evoking belonging to a particular network (of parents), rather than a community more generally. It is possible to feel you belong while recognising that you remain an outsider. There may be a community of locals 'out there', queuing up for the newspaper, drinking in the pubs, but one can let them do this and not feel constrained to join in or have much to do with them. Belonging is here dependent on being semi-detached from place, with the result that one need not get too drawn into an environment in which there is little personal control or individuality. This is a similar relationship to neighbourhood that Blokland (2003: 162) discusses in her study of Hillesluis, Rotterdam, where for a few residents 'although their practical neighbourhood use is low … the neighbourhood is one of their means for arranging their lifestyle'. Belonging becomes detached from local involvement:

I think Chorlton differs. I think ... yeah, I feel part of the community without being involved in the community. Apart from school and the kids, and I wouldn't say on this road at least that we mix a lot with neighbours, but we know a lot of people to let on to and to talk to on the street. None of us have got family in Chorlton, so we feel comfortable without sort of being in someone's pocket. (D25)

The ethics of neighbouring indicates the tensions here. Although people can chose where they might live, they cannot readily pick their neighbours, and there is a danger that one's neighbours colour (in a literal way) one's environment. Massey and Denton (1988) have examined the increasing ethnic segregation of American suburbs at the very same time that overt processes of racial discrimination are reduced. With the exception of a very few of the most wealthy residents in Wilmslow who lived in detached houses and sought to retreat entirely behind their (mostly electronically controlled) gates, neighbouring involves managing proximity. This is different from becoming over-involved with one's neighbours, in that it entails maintaining proper distance from them, yet it does require constructing the right kinds of ties. Very few respondents sought to make any kind of moral distinctions between 'good' and 'bad' neighbours, and in addition there was little sense of any kind of shared destiny, through sharing a common history or set of values with them. As one Wilmslow respondent put it:

In order to be part of a community you have to have some shared history, some shared feelings something that binds you together and I haven't been there long enough to establish that. I think I might be in a little community with my immediate neighbours. ... So literally I know these three or four neighbours around me. The ones down the road I don't. Not in the true sense of community. Not in the sense that I belong to a Catholic community or I belong to a community here, that there was a shared understanding a shared history. (W35)

Only in Ramsbottom and to a lesser extent Wilmslow, which we have seen are characterised by a recognised differentiation between locals and incomers, were some neighbours characterised as being long-term residents with distinctive kinds of local knowledge:

'The good old days' they're all gone! And yet we lived next door to an old lady in Bank Road* who had been born and bred here and whose parents owned the shop on Grove Street and she remembers before, remembered the 'rec' (recreation ground) being built on Main Road and it was a real village community then. (W2)

Although Cheadle has a large number of people who have lived in the area for many years, people rarely mention this when discussing their neighbours. Only one respondent here made any mention of such a neighbour, reporting of one 'gentleman', that he:

was 92 this chap ... but he was very active you know very active in the brain and very active kind of chap you know. And he'd lived in Cheadle since 1930.

And he could have told you a lot. [*laughs*]

[*laughs*] He'd had told you *everything*. Yeah, marvellous 'cos he'd have told you he remembers when it was fields here you know … he was a fantastic chap. (C4)

The form of neighbouring reported is different from that conjured up by historians of early and mid-20th Century cities, which was concerned with monitoring and policing the moral worth of local residents (see, famously, Roberts 1971 on working-class Salford). After all, admitting to having dubious neighbours reflects badly on one's own choice of residence. By contrast, a few people did feel that they were ostracised by some 'snobbish' neighbours: 'the only thing is sometimes I don't fit in, because there's a lot of businessmen and policemen and I'm just an old run of the mill worker' reported one man (R147). More common was the concern to identify one's neighbours as 'people like us'. A few respondents, especially in Wilmslow, put this in an instrumental way:

we do have a variety of neighbours and there's actually quite a nice feel and I think it's much more important for my wife rather than myself and this is probably the first home that we've moved to where she has had 100% of the choice, most times when I move house I look at it as a business decision in terms of the cost, the amenities, the mortgage, the different aspects of the environment, schooling, housing, community and so on and I tend to take the lead being the managerial component of the relationship, but this is the first time she's really chosen and she is, probably more than any other house we've lived in, most comfortable here because of the whole package of the location and neighbours. (W74)

This is an unusually articulate sense of the construction of neighbours as part of the 'whole package' which one might buy into when choosing an 'appropriate' place to live. Wilmslow respondents were indeed much more preoccupied with the occupations and status of their neighbours than elsewhere, testifying to a recognition of the power of neighbours to define the area – especially worrying when one has no direct control over who can move in. More commonly, this was expressed in rather different terms, as a sense of people being pleased that 'people like us' were living around them:

The people on this estate are generally a lot of people like us, middle class with young families who moved to the area because it was a nice place to live, the schools are good …, my parents were reasonably well off working class and desperately keen that we should be well educated, so we were, and we've both got reasonable jobs with reasonable amounts of money coming in, and we've moved into a nice neighbourhood and all the people that you know are similar to yourself. (R138)

The dominant mode of neighbouring found in all four areas is a variant of that discussed by Abrams in the 1970s (see Bulmer 1986). Abrams shows that neighbouring existed as a public activity, where crossing boundaries and becoming too interventionist runs the risk of causing bad feeling and tension. This theme is expressed among our respondents in terms of common refrains around the need for respectful distance.

Yes, as you can see, we're in a cul-de-sac and everybody keeps their own distance, it's quite an advantage I think that everybody watches everybody's house without being overly neighbourly so you've got that balance ... I much prefer it as it is, I like to be friendly with people, I like people to speak and it's nice that we have got those people there if there's a problem, but I think it would be a nuisance having them constantly on the doorstep, and likewise if I was constantly on theirs. (C21)

Once every blue moon, it's not very often (that a neighbour would call), she's not continuously knocking on the door. It's not that kind of neighbour relationship where we're in each other's houses. (C34, Edward)

It would be kind of more by arrangement, unless you went round and they just kind of invited you in for a drink as a consequence of you popping round to ask them something. So as I say, it's not in and out of each other's pockets, but if we were to go round then it wouldn't be unheard of to be invited in for a drink and a couple of hours of chatting. It would usually be by prior arrangement. (C38)

But we're not the sort of people and it's not the sort of road where people are in and out of each other's houses all the time. You would talk to everybody on the street, but go in by invite most of the time, unless it's just literally popping in to borrow something that you know somebody's got. Or like the architect down the road, Nigel, we know him really well, and when we were having trouble with the building and the builder and I knew what he was doing was wrong, I just went down to see Nigel and said will you come and have a look at his job and he came up straight away and told me what I thought but in proper technical terms and then I could tell the builder properly and make him take me seriously. (D51)

A number of these idioms, notably the concern 'not to live in one another's pockets' have a long history. However, it is important to see them as rhetorical devices as much as a description of how neighbouring works. Table 4.1 shows that especially in Cheadle and Ramsbottom, both areas where the discourse of 'respectful distance' was strongly held, there was significant neighbouring activity reported. Half of these respondents reported that neighbours popped in, on a regular basis, without advance notice, and the range of services and support was considerable, ranging well beyond the common concern to keep a look out on houses when people were away. Many elderly residents had neighbours popping in to do shopping or chat with them, with some reporting being given vegetables from back gardens, as well as home-made cakes. When it became known that one resident had visited prisoners, neighbours sought her out to talk about relatives who they knew in prison. It was very common to give Christmas cards to neighbours.

Because neighbouring was generally construed as a public activity, there were favoured ways in which neighbours tended to meet each other. Except

Table 4.1   *Neighbouring practices (percentages)*

	Cheadle	Chorlton	Ramsbottom	Wilmslow
N 'popping in'	49	19	47	33
N socialising in public	21	4	17	2
N visiting each others' houses socially	0	2	17	22

Note:

Popping in = number who reported neighbours dropping round without notice.

Socialising in public = going out with neighbours to a 'public venue' such as pub, club, church or restaurant.

in Wilmslow it was unusual to invite neighbours to each other's houses for a social visit, which would run the risk of embarrassment or imposing expectations of return invites.

> I'm not one for going in for a coffee and I don't have people in here for coffee, I like the neighbours just to say good morning and hello over the garden fence, and that's what it's like here, so I suppose that's why I like it. They're all quite a bit older than us actually, in fact there's very few children in this road. (C97)

> We don't live in each other's pockets.

> *You pass the time of day?*

> Oh yes. We know everyone and we get on with everyone but we don't live in each other's pockets. We have been to parties next door but never been to parties in other houses but we do go to parties elsewhere. (R42)

There are subtle exceptions. Among men, drinking with neighbours at the pub or social club was common, especially in Cheadle. It was quite popular to socialise across the garden fence, which for several respondents extended to inviting neighbours to barbecues in the summer. Neighbouring children visited each other's houses, and sociability around picking up neighbours' children from school and babysitting was common. Having neighbours around on special occasions, notably Christmas or New Year, also helped establish that at other times of the year the home was out of limits.

The only exception to the general rule that house visiting was off limits to neighbours was in Wilmslow (see Table 4.1). This was related to the strongly gender segregated roles in the area, since it was always women who catered for neighbours, and not infrequently it was other women who were invited in. Elsewhere, especially in Ramsbottom, neighbours spoke about how the growing numbers of women working affected the culture of dropping in to one's neighbour, since one no longer expected to find anyone in.

There was a widely articulated view that respondents could be closer and more friendly with their neighbours if they chose to be. This account was articulated in several ways. One was that the particular geography of their road made a difference to their neighbouring, the main implication being that in more favourable architectural situations (e.g. a cul-de-sac) they would be more friendly with their neighbours. Sometimes this took a nostalgic form, which projected 'real' neighbouring as something which happened in the past. Seen in this light, such accounts become ways of endorsing one's neighbours without interacting intensely with them now.

This neighbouring ethic was particularly strong in Cheadle, but could be found in all four areas. However there was also evidence that it was being challenged by a different mode of neighbouring, which was especially common in Chorlton and to some extent Ramsbottom. Here neighbouring was an extension of friendship, so that neighbouring as a distinct public activity became less important. Chorlton is interesting in that it is the least neighbourly of the four places (see Table 4.1) with fewer neighbours 'popping in' than anywhere else and low levels of public and domestic sociability with neighbours. And yet many respondents commented favourably about its friendliness and neighbourliness. The reason for this apparent discrepancy is that it was friends who happened to live locally who replaced neighbours in the minds of the residents. An instructive exchange on this point runs as follows:

How frequently do neighbours drop in without telephoning and just turn up, does that happen at all?

On this street?

Well within the area, they don't have to be next door neighbours, but it could be in the street.

It's a rarity, but if they want to borrow anything or they need any help or they want to pop in for anything then they will do, so it's probably every couple of weeks that someone will probably need or want something, or want to ask you something, so it's probably every couple of weeks we get a call from somebody.

(Partner) But in terms of Anne-Marie and Paul who are two streets away and Zoe and Emma, it depends how close you draw the neighbours.

So if it goes a bit wider you've got friends cum neighbours that will pop in?

Oh yes, daily.

Right, and they're friends who were friends before they moved here that now are almost neighbours?

They happen to be neighbours but primarily are friends. (D14)

The last phrase is the key one here. Friendship is the central relationship, but this does not exclude being a neighbour. Indeed, elective belonging involves choosing a place to live amongst your own kind, with the result that having local friends becomes an endorsement of one's place of residence.

How frequently do friends and neighbours drop round to your house without notice?

Friends will pop round, tap on the window if they are going to the pubs or if they are passing, but not neighbours. It is pretty much each to his own. (D34)

A particularly interesting example of this comes from a young female craft worker:

How frequently would neighbours drop in for a chat, does that ever happen?

Do you mean immediate neighbours?

Well fairly immediate, not necessarily friends.

You see a lot of my friends just happen to live round here, I have quite a lot of people popping in but they're within a 5 minute walking distance, the people like the guy downstairs from here, he's very shy, but I'm on speaking terms with all those three lots of people, they wouldn't say pop in but if I see them I'd stop and say hi. (D93)

Being a neighbour does not mean that one cannot become a friend, but in this case the neighbouring relationship becomes redefined:

Next door we're very good friends with and I would say at least once a week we have a chat, he will pop round or we'll talk over the back garden, that sort of thing. So that's pretty constant really. With other neighbours it's often a passing in the street thing, not actually a popping round thing. (D53)

In some cases, respondents did become close to neighbours, but in this case the relationship was changed into friendship. As this happened, it stopped being primarily a public role and involved inviting neighbours into the house:

Yes, because I've got very friendly neighbours. For my birthday, my 40th birthday, I've got three siblings and those siblings and partners … so there were three neighbours who I felt comfortable with … so I would say that I've got friends as neighbours. (D11)

This orientation to neighbouring had a number of practical implications. Rather than leaving keys with neighbours, as was common in the other areas, keys might be left with friends living a few minutes walk away, and these friends might also be charged with looking after the house when respondents went away. It meant that the distancing common amongst neighbours was not applied to friends, with common conviviality taking place in the domestic house. However this rendering of neighbourliness as friendliness means also that one can ignore immediate neighbours for day to day practical reasons, leading to social exclusiveness as one deals with one's local friends rather than one's neighbours. The lack of contact between Chorlton respondents living close by but in separate social worlds is indeed remarkable, being more marked than that found in the other three areas, and echoes Butler and Robson's (2003) arguments about the 'tectonic' relationships they uncovered in gentrifying areas of London.

4.2 The meaning of place

Earlier community studies saw people's involvement in their neighbourhood and local social life as central to understanding their engagement and commitment to place. However, among our sample, respondents were keen to keep emotional distance from their neighbours, yet were often highly committed to their place of residence. Indeed, nearly all residents presented emotionally charged accounts of their relationship to place. An indication is that only five respondents, all from Cheadle or Wilmslow, claimed that they could live anywhere. A University lecturer from Cheadle commented:

I don't really feel any attachments, my attachment is to the stability of having the house that I like and a wife and child that I love and a job that I enjoy.

So place isn't that important?

No, if you shifted all of those, then in theory you could shift them practically anywhere. (C38)

Deidre: non-attachment to place

Deidre (W7) worked for a large financial institution, and spent much of her working life travelling around the UK providing training courses run out of corporate hotels. Married to an older man, she identified as a private person with few social ties, her account of why she came to live in Wilmslow emphasised, indeed almost reveled in, the functional reasons underlying her choice.

How did you come to live here?

I don't think there was any particular reason for coming here other than my husband and I got married, and we wanted something that was close to motorways which it is, literally 5 minutes or half an hour depending on the traffic, 5 minutes from the motorways. It's on the doorstep of the airport. It's close to my parents; they live in Altrincham*. It's a desirable area. We thought when we bought the house that the chances are that if there would be an improvement in house prices here would be as good as anywhere. Close to the city centre in terms of being close enough to be convenient, far enough away.

And indeed, Deidre expressed her sense of rootlessness through talking about moving house and was clear that she did not belong to the community.

I spend so much time away from home living in other places. So I don't have the emotional tie either to the property or to the community. I think if you live somewhere and you spend

---

everyday there, by definition you'll see more of the people around, and I don't because they're working. I hear them mowing the garden and I think, oh, next door are out doing the garden, but that's really the extent of it. So, no, I don't have a sense of community. I'm aware of its existence because my friend across the road, I say friend because I know her slightly more than I know other people, is head of the committee for a party that I work for.

Here again we see this sense of detachment, spoken about almost with pride. She refused to see herself as having an emotional relationship with place. Pride in living in the area became primarily an issue of defending the price of her housing.

Are you proud of living in the area?

Proud is probably a difficult word for me. I don't really have that sort of feeling. I'm conscious that it's desirable. I'm very conscious that it's regarded as a desirable area when people say: 'Oh, you live in Wilmslow, do you?'. So I suppose the answer to that is possibly yes. But it's for different reasons because what I think to myself is, oh well, good. As long as it's a desirable area that means that the house prices will be going up. ... In fact, it's more to do with the money than it has to do with social perception, and that's what I'm conscious about; I would hate the area to go down and lose the value of the house. I mean, because I paid £50,000 for it which is probably worth better part of £300,000. I would be gutted, yes, if Wilmslow went down in status and I lost the inherent value because I need that if I want to move. But it's not really the social aspect.

Deidre insisted that she could easily move elsewhere.

Would you be sorry to leave this area?

Yes and no. Yes, I would be sorry to leave the area in that I've been happy here. No, because having travelled round all sorts of parts of the country, I know there are very beautiful places within the country where I am quite sure I could be equally as happy. It's different from generation to generation. My mum comes from Bristol. It's a beautiful place, got everything you could possibly want because I've often said I'm looking to move, and you wouldn't move from here and I've said: 'Well, yes I would', because I know this isn't it; the only place I could be happy. And so I think it has a lot do with your lifestyle to start with as to how you feel about a place, and mine is so fluid.

Deidre's story is not exceptional. Stuart, an air traffic controller at Manchester airport, also reported:

I'm pretty adaptable really. I've moved around, ever since I started work I've always moved around the country because the job is mobile and therefore if you've got to go you move on. And possibly because we don't get so very closely involved in the local community it makes it that much easier to move on. (W42)

Such respondents appear to exemplify the 'transience' which we have identified in Chapter 2 as being the object of derision by many respondents. They exemplify an apparently close relationship between instrumentalism, detachment, mobility and the irrelevance of place. Yet even for these five, things were not quite so straightforward as they made out. Deidre had actually been brought up a few miles away, and recognised that she was a northerner. She was involved in various local charities and organisations, and regularly visited her parents who lived a few miles away. To some extent she was ashamed of coming from Manchester, and was 'conscious of the fact that Manchester has a very negative image socially'.

In fact, the vast majority of respondents combined instrumental with emotional relationships with place, whereby they established personally salient connections to place through comparing the qualities of various places they knew and which mattered to them. Peter's case is an instructive example.

Peter: achieved attachment to place

Peter (W51) was a senior Director for one of the area's largest multinational firms. Brought up in a working-class family from Birmingham, he graduated from Manchester University, from whence he joined his current firm and moved round the country as he climbed the corporate ladder. Peter combines his hectic work life with a very strong commitment to Wilmslow, and he displays a clear sense of ease and comfort in his residential surroundings.

> The nice thing about Wilmslow is that we've got a strong group of friends. We've got a good social circle, which is outside of work, not really anything to do with work, which is good. So that was a very positive point sort of very early to coming up here. Things that we also like about it was that we bought the house very close to the town centre here, that's worked very well for the kids as they've grown up and become more independent they've been able to walk in. It's a good point of communication sort of by British Rail both for me and my family, so for me for work in terms of travelling either by air or by rail then the facilities are pretty good BR or whatever it's called now not withstanding. We're also fresh air sort of people, so and my wife is a North Walean, so actually access to the Lake District and the Peak District and North Wales is very important to us.

While he was pleased that Wilmslow was a convenient place to live, Peter also expresses emotional attachments ranging some way from Wilmslow, stretching out to Wales and the Lake District. While recognising himself as a transient, he is entirely at ease with living in the area.

> Well, we have no reason to move away while I'm working here, like we could move to another part of Cheshire but we don't feel the need to do that, we're very comfortable where we are.

Peter was involved with many aspects of the social and cultural life available in the area. He had been governor of the local comprehensive school. He ate out regularly with his wife and friends, and visited local pubs on a weekly basis. He joined the local golf club, and had played badminton regularly in the past. He was an active member of the local church. He also had emotional links to the north, which play a key role in rooting him in Wilmslow. In his case, they were based on attending Manchester University.

> Well, when I did my degree in Manchester sort of nearly 30 years ago it was actually a beautiful city and somehow or other in the last 20 years the local planning authority has gone absolutely wild and destroyed a lot of its beauty. A lot of the lovely buildings are still there but not in the sort of number or quality that were.

Peter's case shows how an instrumental orientation towards place invoked a cultural geography which placed him amidst various personal reference points.

Rather than a concern with the quality and nature of local ties and personal relationships, it is this ability to place oneself in an imaginary landscape which is central to people's sense of belonging. One indication is the resonance of people's 'arrival stories', their accounts of how they came to live in their current residence. These were partly functional accounts presented in terms of the demands of job and family, but they also invoked occasions for musing and personal reflection, whereby respondents talked of their own lives as implicated in the choice of places to live.

For many respondents in Wilmslow and Ramsbottom, these stories focused on the convenience of these areas compared to other adjacent sites:

> We moved here in June 1990, so we've been there 7 years. Why Wilmslow? Because I was a deputy at the time and we had been married a number of years we had been married 8 or 9 years I think. I was desperate for a child and I wanted to find a good area, because we lived in north Manchester, in Prestwich, which was going down hill quite rapidly I thought. I worked on the other side of Manchester, and my husband at that time was working in Warrington, so it was a matter of finding another good area. Quite snobbish, I know it sounds awful, but a good area, a good school and that was reasonable for travelling to Wilmslow at the time. We drove all over the place. Quite literally went all round Manchester and kept coming back to Wilmslow. So that's why we started looking in Wilmslow. (W35)

> We've been here since March 1996. We moved here, I'm from Clitheroe* originally, and I was working in Blackburn and my partner was working in Manchester, so it was somewhere that was nice to live that was mid-way between the two, so that was the reason for choosing Ramsbottom initially … I think it was a case of looking at the map and thinking that looks about mid-way between the two, we actually looked at Bolton, but preferred this side, so decided to look round here in earnest. (R97)

These accounts see respondents looking for a 'good', 'nice' area between key busy sites of work and kin, but with little interest in the specific qualities of the place itself. Ramsbottom and Wilmslow are seen as 'empty' places, to be filled by busy people juggling their commitments.

Well basically a nicer area, we wanted to move further out into the country like everybody does in Manchester. Chorlton was ideal for where we were both working and we could nip into Manchester and go for meals, we probably had a better social life then because it was so easy after work and things to go back into town. But again, your lifestyle changes really, we became more traditional, wanting to move out. (W27)

As we saw in Chapter 3, Wilmslow's 'emptiness' was primarily to be filled by families and children. In Ramsbottom, however, there was more interest in how the town's empty, 'nice' rural space could be used for relaxation.

The reason we moved here, my husband is originally from Mossley* and I'm from down south and when we got married I didn't really want to be too close to all his family and friends, I'm very friendly with them, but I didn't want to be an outsider, so I used to live in Sale, and Eric lived with me before we got married. For Eric it has to be somewhere with hills because he's a keen moun-tain cyclist, so it just so happened I was working and had to come to Ramsbottom one day and we were looking for houses anywhere really, and I drove round and thought it was a nice place, quick to get to Manchester, so we ended up seeing this house and came here. (R59)

There were very different kinds of arrival stories in Cheadle and Chorlton, which did not position these two places as nice spaces for leisure and family. Rather, both these places were already 'full' of resonances in the minds of their arriving residents. Most people moving into these two areas knew a great deal about them beforehand, and respondents did not think they were moving to a generically 'nice' area. In Cheadle, the strength of existing family ties was important. Even for those who had moved into the area without having kin already in the area, there was usually a clear sense of the 'pecking order' of the area within a local status and housing hierarchy. This was also linked to how much respondents could afford (interestingly, the cost of housing was rarely voiced as a reason for living in any of the other three locations, except for some Wilmslow residents who wanted to live in a high price area). Arrival stories here tended to be terse, and placed their arrival in the context of its status position in the local housing market, 'it was a move away from Stockport, I suppose really to a slightly more exclu-sive area' (C136).

Before we lived in Wythenshawe on a council estate and we were in business, we had a couple of … shops on the estate and we sold them and with the money we had left after we'd paid all the bills and the income tax we decided to move out, it was better for the kids to get off the estate. I'm not a snob, by any means, but it was better to get the kids off the estate. We've been back since, to the estate, and we're glad we did make a move. (C55)

Chorlton incomers were different again. They were unusually reflexive and 'knowing' about why they wanted to move to the area, with only a few respondents saying they moved there by chance. Although the convenience of the site for getting around Manchester was important, the focus was usually on Chorlton's own positive features.

I wanted to live within about half a mile of a green space, I used to do a lot of running, and where I lived before was in Rusholme, and it was near a few parks, so I was looking around that area and round here. This area is near to green bits but also not too far to cycle to the university which I had a lot of work at. So it was ease of access into town but also to be near to green bits. (D11)

Yeah, we've lived here about 3½ years, and I grew up in South Manchester anyway ... and when we got together we decided first to live in Stretford because it was cheap but convenient, but really we'd always fancied living here, partly because of the style of the houses that we liked and partly because of what the neighbourhood is like and what there is around here: plenty of pubs, restaurants, shops, all sorts of interesting places to go. (D12)

I decided to move when I could, to a bigger house and I knew this was a good road in some ways, it's very close to town. I used to go in the pubs down the end of the road and socialise a bit, and as I said I've a friend who used to live in one of the houses opposite. (D52)

Like the Cheadle residents, the knowledge deployed here is very local, but rather than relying either on perceptions of a fixed status hierarchy of areas, or on family connections, the emphasis is on knowledge gleaned from individual experience and contacts, or to adapt Ball's (2002) terminology, 'hot', rather than 'cold' information. Indeed, contact through friends often led residents to move to Chorlton. D70 came to the area due to:

My work. At that time I was a schoolteacher and got a job at a school in the area, but I knew the area because I'm actually locally born. I was born in Altrincham*, so I knew Manchester, came to Manchester as a child, and I got a job in the area ... first of all I was living in walking distance from where I taught and then I had some friends who lived in Chorlton and I came to live near to them and still within close distance of my work.

Arrival stories of this kind are testimonies to power. The stories of Chorlton residents are rich with the power gleaned not by economic resources, so much as information derived from contacts and experience. The power of cultural capital to provide confidence in individual judgements is evident here, and knowledge derived from the social capital of ties and connections allows Chorlton residents to exactly pick out where they want to live. The arrival stories of Cheadle residents, by contrast, exemplify a less reflexive concern to move to a 'better' area, drawing mainly upon received ideas of the standing of the area amongst nearby neighbourhoods rather than specific, personally acquired knowledge.

To some extent the arrival stories of residents in Wilmslow and Ramsbottom are of those with high amounts of economic capital. This may explain their lesser concern with the intrinsic qualities of those places. In Wilmslow, furthermore, the significance of gender divisions is all too apparent.

Most women had little say in deciding to move to the area. This lack of power often extended to the choice of where to live, with women turning their initial journey to an area selected by their husband as a kind of mystery story, as was certainly true for W3 who talked of moving to Wilmslow from the north-east of England following the relocation of her husband's job:

He had come down here in the April. We sold our house and actually moved in August, so he'd been down here, he'd been here in the April and he had decided I think on about three rows in Bramhall and parts of Wilsmlow and that's why it took me so long to find somewhere because in 1972 the property was selling very, very quickly and of course by the time he came home with the brochures and came back they'd gone, so it was a very much last minute, it was absolutely the night before he was [starting] the last possible day he could get a house ... he rang me and said I've got one ... it was totally strange to me and I kept getting these local papers and saying, well what's wrong with that one, you know. I was getting pretty desperate ... He was very cunning because Manchester to me is Manchester but he was very cute because he brought me across the A68 across to Carlisle down the M6 and in via Knutsford ... so I mean I got a very, very favourable impression of the entire place.

W21 told a similar story, remembering exactly her first trip to the area, also planned by her husband to avoid going to Wilmslow via Manchester itself:

When we first came in, I always remember, we came in the Altrincham Road, there, and we stopped at the bottom, there were no flats there then, and there was only a few houses on the front. Beyond the houses into the first road and we did that just to get the feel of the place and I said right away 'I like this' and then we looked at the house one of these cheaper houses, which is really what we wanted, we didn't want an expensive house at first, but we saw the house and when my husband came down the stairs, the stairhead, he bumped his head on it and I thought this is no good he's going to knock himself every morning, so that was out. I circled around the area, Bramhall, Alderley Edge, because we knew someone at Alderley Edge, he was a friend at a church we went to who used to live up here and she referred us to her mother who lived in Alderley Edge.

These evocative accounts of the contingency of arrival were never made by people moving to Chorlton or Cheadle. They all knew the place before moving to the area, and had no striking first impressions when they actually moved in. Women in other locations who moved to places with little control over their move presented their story in much more direct terms. 'I was living in Didsbury with my husband and when my marriage broke up I was looking for somewhere that I could afford'. (D47)

4.3 Networks and the cultural imaginary

We have argued that arrival stories differentiate 'full' from 'empty' places, where both gained their meaning from comparisons which respondents

Table 4.2 *Percentage of respondents referring to London in various ways*

Respondent mentions in connection with	Cheadle	Chorlton	Ramsbottom	Wilmslow
Has worked/lived there	5	17	13	36
Work links	12	4	6	24
Family connections	7	26	11	33
Friends there	5	21	4	9
Leisure trips	5	13	15	29
All personal links (1–5 above)	16	45	28	71
Evaluative/comparative	26	53	15	20
No references	49	30	23	18

Note:
All personal links total less than rows 1–5 because some respondents have different types of personal links

made with other places salient to them. Comparisons between places are not only made on the basis of the practical importance of places for work, family and leisure, but also rely on a complex set of symbolic signifiers of place. Magical places possess intrinsic significance as a hallowed site of cultural practice, the kind of aura that functional sites lacked. Both Chorlton and Ramsbottom are magical sites, related to a cultural geography which linked them respectively to a cosmopolitan idiom centred on London, and a northern countryside. These two places were specifically situated so that their residents could imagine themselves as attached to certain lifestyles through their choice of residence.

When we asked respondents about their sense of belonging, and their feelings about their local place of residence, we were not expecting them to refer to London, nearly 200 miles away. None of our questions specifically asked how respondents used or contacted with London. Table 4.2 shows, however, that London has remarkable power, with over half mentioning the city at some point during their interview. For residents of Chorlton and Wilmslow, well over two-thirds of respondents mentioned London. A relatively high proportion of Wilmslow respondents had either worked at some point in London, had family living there, had work links with London requiring them to visit it on a regular basis, or visited London for leisure purposes. They rarely made evaluative comments about the city, however, or drew comparisons between Wilmslow and parts of London. By contrast, well over half of Chorlton respondents mentioned London in an evaluative way during the course of their interview, and for many it was a highly charged cultural signifier. One third mentioned London more frequently than any other place except Manchester.

For some, these are minor asides:

I've no desire to move to London or anything like that to be honest. (D109, Susan)

So do you feel like you belong here?

In the respect that its a bit like living in London where in this area anything goes, it's very tolerant. There's a big gay community, a big lesbian community and its very tolerant. (D14)

We liked it (Chorlton) a lot. It seemed the only part of Manchester that we really had any affection for. We were not that enamoured with property and different areas of Manchester. The ones we liked we could not afford and Chorlton seemed like a good compromise, not even a compromise because it is ideal in many respects, it is close to the city centre, really handy for getting out of Manchester, near to the motorways and we love Beech Road with all the shops down there. Like a little village, very like a London suburb, so it just seemed right. (D50)

For a sizeable minority of respondents, the comparison is to a specific location within London, with Chorlton's appeal resting on its similarity to (or difference from) what has happened in parts of London:

In what ways do you think the area is changing for the good or bad? Do you see it as changing in positive or negative ways at all?

Well, it's becoming more affluent. It's generating what I would think of as a Hampstead effect: literally in this maybe square mile here there are some very interesting shops at the end of our street but they're becoming fairly esoteric … and I know people who live in Hampstead who complain that they can't buy a newspaper anywhere. (D13)

In what ways do you think this area has changed? Do you think Chorlton is changing much?

Yes I have definitely seen what I think is really exciting development. Its having the shops, not all stuff I would be interested in but you look and think its different, quite continental. You have your café bars and things. One is just beginning to put live music on and you think that's town centre stuff and you see Derby Road* advertised in national papers. This is the Carnaby Street of Manchester. It is difficult to get housing here, students and people would love to live here. (D34)

What is it about it that you like?

I don't want to sound pretentious, but it had an element of being quite a nice place to live, it had an element of Camdeness about it without being Islington but it is fast becoming Islington which is a shame really. When we bought the house we bought originally it was an odd road round here because a lot of the houses were owned by the same guy and he rented them so a lot of people have lived there since the War but then it was gradually … we had two cars and it was never a problem but more and more it became a problem. I like Chorlton. It is one of those very difficult things to define about why you like certain areas. We thought about moving to London because my girlfriend had completed a course in London. (D20)

As the last of these quotes indicates, in some cases respondents had lived in, or had connections with London, and their fascination was rooted in their own experience. But those who had been brought up in London were not, usually, those who mentioned London particularly frequently. The reasons for the salience of London lies more in the symbolic importance of London seen as an imagined cosmopolitan space, so that the positioning of Chorlton in particular (and Manchester in general) depended on replicating it. In this way, global cosmopolitan identities were asserted on the basis of specific imaginary connections with a leading world city (on which see Hannerz 1996; Beck 2002; Urry 2002).

What about Manchester itself, do you think Manchester is changing, or changed in the time that you've been here?

Yes, definitely, I think in the 80s it was so trendy and with the music scene and stuff I don't think there is that any more, but it's associated in people's minds like students love to come to Manchester because they think it is a hip happening place, apart from London, but I think it's moved on from that, I think it's gone a lot more cosmopolitan in as much as all the different types of bars that have opened and it's not just beer, beer or drugs, drugs, it's tried to go more 'cosmo' you know with having all the bars with café seats outside, which is great if you want to sit on Deansgate and breathe in the fumes, but no I do think they're good, I think it has gone more cosmopolitan. (D89)

The evocation of London is interesting in view of Hannerz's (1996: 128) arguments that only a few global cities, such as London, are able to generate a global appeal as 'durable sources of a new culture'. Chorlton residents, however, remained ambivalent. They were aware that Manchester in general, or Chorlton in particular, cannot legitimately claim London's degree of cultural distinction, precisely because insofar as Chorlton is attractive as a copy of an urban original, it cannot claim ultimate authenticty. References to London were agonistic and ambivalent, veering between championing their area as comparable, before recognising its ultimate inferiority. The respondents thereby – haltingly – recognise that the cosmopolitanism they identify is in fact not spatially mobile but is ultimately characterised by the urban space of 'truly' global cities. This recognition represents in a nutshell the complexities of Chorlton's cosmopolitan identities. While respondents may hanker after cosmopolitanism, their realistic claims to it are limited by Manchester's social, political and cultural subordination to London:

In what ways do you think the area is changing?

I think it is becoming more trendy. Round the corner we have two wine bars that have opened in the last few years, two expensive clothes shops, very good for young people and just various things. Lots of restaurants.

Do you think it is good or bad?

Yes I like it, it reminds me of London and places I lived in. In a way I would quite like to be living in London. I can't afford that, but that type of feel about it, I would like it to be a bit more cosmopolitan.

If you move, where would you like to move to?

Well my ideal sort of place would be somewhere by the sea that is fairly town-like, somewhere like Brighton, sort of London with the sea, or somewhere where the architecture is really nice, Cambridge or Oxford. (D47)

Susan related a revealing story. When asked if she was proud of living in the area, she replied:

I find proud a bit difficult, because I don't feel particularly proud of it, but I do feel at home here to some extent, although I'm actually a hybrid because my mum was from Lancashire but my dad was a Cockney and I feel a strange affinity to London if I go down to London, which I don't in a way feel for Manchester. I feel as if I'm going home when I go to London and I don't get that here, but I like living here and I feel at home here.

With the choice of a Lancashire or a London identity, London wins out. We see how cosmopolitan yearnings were articulated by residents who actually had very localised frames of references, reporting how they had come to live in the area as a result of specific personal connections. These 'northern cosmopolitans' exhibit both highly localised knowledge, and have cultural imaginations that stretch out to more cosmopolitan places. Their attachment to London becomes understandable as a means of mediating the tension between their local rootedness and their cultural aspirations, as Steve intriguingly reveals:

Steve: the tensions of northern cosmopolitanism

Steve (D20) was a university graduate, highly reflexive and articulate, and very active in Manchester's music scene, where he drew upon the contacts his partner had built up from her job in the music industry. He worked as a jobbing builder in the exhibition industry, embraces the values of manual labour and exemplifies a kind of 'muscular northern cosmoplitanism' that is critical of the more intellectualised forms of cosmopolitanism, which he sees as embracing a bland kind of 'niceness'.

People are becoming, you are getting solicitors moving here and there are wine bars, it is like Fulham in the 1960s, it is becoming gentrified and becoming gentrified very quickly. What was nice about it is that you get people who have lived here for a while who moved here because they were, particularly this street is very typical, biggish houses, who bought them in the 1960s when everyone wanted to live in open-plan type housing.

People like the guy next door works with pottery* and the guy who used to have the house next door was a painter* but now it is all getting a bit nice and I am not good with nice. I would rather not have people coming round and looking at the front garden and think it is tatty, which it is. Then it is the way I get, for years I have had because of the nature of the work I do I am quite often covered in crap, and it is that being treated as a moron because you work with your hands I don't especially enjoy. It doesn't bother me but I find it slightly sad and the people who are moving in, being a professional is seen somehow as more interesting than making pottery*.

Steve distances himself from the gentrification that he sees around him, yet also embraces Chorlton as a place where he continues to want to live. Steve was a gregarious and sociable man, involved in the local pub scene, as well as the cricket team. He instructively revealed his own ambiguities about whether he belonged.

> I feel part of the community. Belonging here, I have a different sort of concept of the community. The walk to the pub from here, if I do it any time of the day or night I would bump into two or three people to speak to or at least to say hello to or acknowledge. Yes, I do feel I belong, I feel part of the community but I am not sure I belong. In terms of living here I do feel I belong.
>
> Steve's ambivalence was also linked also to his identification as a Liverpudlian. For Steve, Liverpool exemplified more unpretentious, working-class values, in contrast to Manchester, which had neither the true cosmopolitanism of London, or the straightforward, 'in-your-faceness' of Liverpool. Again we see the instability of northern cosmopolitanism, in Steve's case not only through the reference to London, but by the additional comparison with Liverpool.
>
> *Do you like living in Manchester?*
>
> Yes, but I don't feel in any way that I am a Mancunian. I am from Liverpool but I would rather live in Manchester than in Liverpool. I find Manchester a very bland place. I find it … has always been a counter-jumping city. … The architecture, there is nothing, it is rather pretentious, rather tacky and tasteless Victoriana. It is very new. The problem is that it is trying to compete with London while the good thing about Liverpool is that it is itself. Manchester is desperate for everyone's approval. Manchester has a massive inferiority complex, it really wants to be London and it betrays it by resenting so much.

To understand Chorlton residents' sense of place it is important to understand their identification with London as cultural centre. This was very distinctive. Residents in the other three locations were much more emotionally withdrawn from the capital. The few Cheadle residents who made evaluative comments about London were derogatory, complaining about its crime rates (C98), its scruffiness (C71) and its crowds (C20). References to London were articulated predominantly within the frame of a kind of local patriotism dedicated to championing the claims of Manchester in competition with London:

> So yes, I think things are on the up and up and I suppose the attitude of Manchester itself is improving, at one time we used to be the underdogs to some of the larger cities, especially London, but now we compete on an even scale, we do quite well. (C79)

Or, more disparaging, 'I mean London is virtually owned by the Arabs now isn't it?' (C20). Wilmslow residents were also fairly critical of London. In part the fact that they visited the city regularly led them to a less positive account of it, and most evaluative references about the city dwelled on its traffic problems. This predominantly negative evaluation of London was in part related to the antipathy towards transients that we have explored in Chapter 2. These were sometimes seen as by-products of London:

Would you say that you felt you belonged in Wilmslow?

Yes and no. Yes I probably do. But the way it's changing it's almost becoming a suburb of London, where a lot of offices are opening up, solicitors offices, lawyers offices, computer companies, they like it because it's got a nice atmosphere and they're taking over totally and changing it, just like when you travel round one of the London suburbs. I think it's because of the comments I made earlier, because it's near to the airport, because it's easy to get into London on the main line from Wilmslow. (W93)

Ramsbottom residents saw London as largely irrelevant to them. Insofar as London figured, it was as a figure of insult. One respondent objected to *The Times* newspaper on the grounds that 'their Life Style and magazine stuff is so self-centred, inward looking London Sloane Square, I can't read that' (R37). Ramsbottom respondents had a very different cultural imaginary, not one that looked south to the metropolis of London, but one that looked north. Drawing upon the idea of Ramsbottom as an open space positioned between 'busy' spaces, theirs was an imagination that sought contact and validation through evoking the Yorkshire Dales, the Lake District, and Scotland. For many respondents Ramsbottom represented a miniature, achievable access point to this vista, located sufficiently in the hills, but within easy access of motorways. Well over half went walking in the local area, ranging from strolling with the dog to long hiking holidays. For some people, living in Ramsbottom was directly related to their interest in hiking, so that their residence was an exemplification of their single-minded lifestyles.

Bernie: hankering after the northern hills

Bernie (R80) was an IT professional, but he did not relish his work which was a means to an end. His main passion in life was hill walking, an interest he shared with his wife. He had extensive mountaineering experience and was currently completing the Scottish Munros. His arrival story was concerned how moving to Ramsbottom allowed him to be 'at one' with his overwhelming life interest.

Well basically we were looking all over the place for houses and we wandered out in this direction, being depressed with what we'd seen in the way of houses that were already built, and we found this estate being constructed. We wanted to get further out into the hills having previously lived in Whitefield, we're both walkers so we used to spend all our time coming up here on the bus to walk over the hills at the back. At about the same time as we moved here I got a driving licence and we've never walked up the hills again! It was really somewhere in the hills and this was an area that we'd frequently walked in and we quite liked the area.

When Bernard was asked if he planned to continue to live in the area, he replied:

> That's contentious! We're both happy living here but we would like on retirement to probably move closer to the big hills, the Scottish mountains or something like that.

Further, it became clear that Bernard's Ramsbottom location fitted his devotion to mountain landscapes:

> I had been on holidays in various areas of the country with my parents on … holidays, and they had a tendency to go to the west coast of Wales or south-west England. When I was at school I went on an Easter holiday into the Lake District which converted me into a Lake District fan.

How old were you then?

> I'd be 13 I think. That stayed with me until basically when I was probably 18 and had a job, I invested in a summer holiday in Scotland because my father had been recommending it so much and instantly turned me into a convert for the Scottish highlands, but I only ever knew one area of them because it was the area you could get to by train, that was Glencoe and Ben Nevis area. Then about eight or nine years ago I got a driving licence and we were over in Switzerland and somebody joined me on an ascent of one of the big summits, well invited me along for an ascent, and after I'd done it he suggested that I might actually enjoy the Swiss Alpine Club. That really opened up the Scottish highlands because they go all over the place and then you start thinking about where to go when you're not going with them.

Bernard exemplified the kind of detachment which is a key component of elective belonging. He had little connection with Ramsbottom itself.

Do you feel you belong here, do you feel part of the community?

> No not particularly, I don't think I could, I don't think I would feel part of the community particularly anywhere, because my lifestyle doesn't involve me in items in the close area.

Why is that?

> Well I'm away from the town all day at work and our weekends are spent either with friends up and down the country or we spend a lot of time in the Scottish highlands walking, so we do an awful lot of mileage travelling away at weekends. Apart from that all our friends who come to see us here are staying with us for the weekend so you're still in a very insular block. I mean I love the place, but I don't regard myself as being part of the community.

Bernard's narrative indicates a form of belonging premised on distance from the local community and organised around the power of a distinctive imaginary geography. He does not have much to do with people living in Ramsbottom, and has an arrival story testifying to his ignorance of the area. Yet he is now at home in the town, because it can act as a cultural signifier for his beloved northern countryside itself.

Undoubtedly, Bernard's story is unusual, but his general sentiments are not uncommon. Ronnie, who we met in Chapter 2 voicing his hostility to the Ramsbottom 'locals' also waxed lyrical about his ideal place:

Mmm, North Yorkshire. Oh, I love North Yorkshire, yeah.

On the moors?

No, not on the moors, no, I like rolling hills, valleys. I like ... I like ... when I say I like peace and quiet, yes, but I like to see houses and shops; I can't live on a moor and I like people around but my type of people – is that awful – a more ... a much quieter and more serene way of life with a lot less traffic blasting through – just the type of place ... settled. Grassington – absolutely beautiful. Where you can step out your door and you can look at fields but, yeah, the little towns there or the little villages there, you know. (R28)

R13 wanted to open a guest house in the Yorkshire Dales 'because I feel at home with the Yorkshire Dales, I like that, I feel that by the time I get to say 45, 50 I'm going to well and truly have had enough with education and it's something that I think I could make a good job out of'. Many other respondents talked about their movement to Ramsbottom in terms of their possibility of conveniently living out this kind of rural vision:

it's on the edge of hills, there's plenty of countryside, you can go for walks from the door without having to take the car. (R138)

Within 2 minutes you are within what I would call countryside, even if you're not deep in countryside, you're not actually miles into the moors like you would be in North Yorkshire, but there's greenery around, there's plenty of things to see. (R78)

We love it. I can look anywhere and there's hills ... obviously we've seen it through the seasons, in the spring it's a beautiful picture, in the summer it's gorgeous with the sun, autumn all the trees change colour and it's perfect, and when the snow's on them all it's like a postcard, it's just beautiful. (R67)

The appeal of the rural is a familiar theme in British culture (Miller 1995; Urry 1995; Cloke et al. 1996; Matless 1998). However, what stands out from our interviews is the extent to which this rural landscape is defined in specifically northern terms. Ramsbottom respondents clearly have northern mountain landscapes in mind when thinking about place and have little sympathy for the southern English pastoral idyll (see on this distinctive kind of appeal, Samuel's (1998) account of his childhood spent in similar mountain landscapes as well as Cosgrove et al. 1996). Very few respondents spoke with any interest in, or knowledge of, southern English rural landscapes. Those few exceptions whose idea of the countryside was more southern oriented felt much less at home in Ramsbottom. R81 was a young consultant originally from Cheshire, who had been to an elite southern university. She made no bones about her preference for living in south

Table 4.3   *Strength and orientation of place identifications*

Key spatial references	Cheadle	Chorlton	Ramsbottom	Wilmslow
London	Weak, negative	Strong, positive	Weak, negative	Moderate, negative
Northern countryside	Absent	Absent	Strong, positive	Weak, positive
Cheshire countryside	Weak, positive	Absent	Absent	Moderate, positive

Manchester should she have the chance, a view which was related to her attraction to its rural landscape:

> I suppose I don't like it's image really, when you say you live in Ramsbottom everyone sniggers and says I wonder what that's like. I suppose I'm slightly biased because I originally come from Cheshire, so I know south Manchester better, and I suppose if I was going to live anywhere in Manchester I'd like to live somewhere south, Hale or somewhere like that, it's got a different feel about it from Ramsbottom. (R81)

She went on to report that she liked:

> Cheshire ... but that's the side of Manchester that I know best, and the countryside, I have always felt that there was nowhere as pretty as Cheshire, Lancashire is nice but it's a totally different sort of feeling and landscape, like it was in the north-east, I don't think you could describe it as pretty but it's interesting.

Chorlton respondents on the whole, have little interest in rural imagery, and when they do show an interest, this tended to be gentrified towns, such as Settle and Hebden Bridge. Table 4.3 summarises the salience of spatial identifications between the four places. Chorlton and Ramsbottom are distinctive in having very clear connections to others. Cheadle and Wilmslow, by contrast, have no overwhelming orientations to one place, being more functional.

In Wilmslow the strongest imaginary associations are with ideas of the Cheshire village, yet these were not as strongly marked as the equivalent feelings in Ramsbottom for the Northern countryside. This is partly due to the way that Cheshire itself represents ambivalent regional imagery, since it evokes a 'southern English' pastoral in a northern location. Although one third of respondents spoke fondly of Cheshire, the idea it evoked was rather vague, and because it lacked specificity, it tended to lack real resonance:

> Yes. I would say (I belong to) Cheshire and also that is central to you know you can go up to Scotland or down to London and it just feels quite central and you can get to the Lake District, Peak District and the country bits are around as well. (W3)

There was also a sense that Cheshire's distinctiveness was being eroded by the urban growth of Manchester. In addition, the really 'pretty' iconic

Cheshire villages existed near to Wilmslow, with the result that Wilmslow itself could not compete with these:

I liked here after I'd seen it. I had seen Prestbury, I looked at Prestbury, but ... there's not a lot in Prestbury when you get down to look. It's very chocolate boxey and pretty, but there's not a lot there. Wilmslow had a little bit more. It was a nice walk with the pram from here into the centre to do the shopping and it wasn't too big. (W3)

Another point of comparison was the small village of Alderley Edge, three miles away but more authentically part of Cheshire's sandstone landscape:

Well a friend of ours who also came from Bradford, lived in Sale and so he said look come over one Sunday and I will take you on a 12 mile radius of Manchester and of course he took us to Alderley Edge, showing us the high point – mind you we are used to higher points than that in Yorkshire, I don't know I remember we came over one or two weekends looking at places and finally came here. Because in those days it was rather nice. (W10)

Unlike Ramsbottom residents, who could define their empty place as gateway to the northern hills, Wilmslow respondents could only see their place as a useful, convenient base to get to landscapes which were actually some distance away. Thus, Wilmslow residents were strong enthusiasts for the Lake District and North Wales (where several households had second homes), yet while they explained that it was easy get to these places on the motorway from Wilmslow, they could not credibly claim Wilmslow as part of such landscapes. Unlike the Ramsbottom residents, their place could not be both simultaneously empty and magical. It is this which perhaps explains that despite its affluence, several respondents commented on the soulless character of the town.

Conclusion

Within the tradition of community studies, belonging involves attachment to what is near to you. It involves knowing other people in the area, being socially active in the neighbourhood, being embedded in ties of kin, and understanding local traditions and customs. We have not come across much evidence of this kind of belonging. People's relationships with neighbours are organised around an ethic of respectful distance. Rather, belonging does not require people to get involved in the local community, but rather evokes attachments to distant places. The concept of elective belonging is our way of making sense of this kind of relationship to place. It deliberately avoids polarising immobile locals against rootless cosmopolitans. Elective belonging exists in a tension between an instrumental and functional orientation to place on the one hand, and powerful, emotional and auratic yearnings on the other. Such emotional attachments, we emphasise, need not be conferred by a history of long residence, or by being born and bred in a particular area, but are related to people mapping their own biography through identifying places dear to them. In this way, people can feel 'at home' even when they have little or no contact with other local residents, and little or no history of residence in the area.

We have also shown that this general process works differently across our four locations. Ramsbottom and Wilmslow are empty places, defined as 'nice' spaces, sites conveniently located between other active spaces of work and kin. They testify to the power of economic capital, with wealthy residents seeking a 'nice' place, with their relative lack of cultural capital entailing a lesser interest in the innate qualities of place. Cheadle and Chorlton, however, are full spaces, with respondents often moving to the area because they are already embedded in social ties based in these locations. In Chorlton this testifies to the power of cultural capital (and its overlaps with social capital), while in Cheadle the social capital of kin and proximity are pre-eminent.

Cutting against this axis, we differentiated the magical places of Ramsbottom and Chorlton from the functional ones of Wilmslow and Cheadle. Ramsbottom is both empty and magical because its rural character serves as a kind of gatepost to a northern hilly landscape. This is a possible reason why rural places might be so generally attractive to middle-class residents in the UK (see generally Cloke et al. 1993; Phillips et al. 1995; Urry 1995). They encapsulate two of the desired characteristics of elective belonging: they are empty places which do not require people to get involved if they do not wish to, yet they are also magical and possess aura. Chorlton, by contrast is magical, but is also full, and draws a rather selective kind of resident well endowed with cultural and social capital.

Wilmslow is the closest of our places to being an anonymous suburb. It has some hallmarks of being a rather soulless, functional place. Although its residents often identify with Cheshire, their feelings are far less marked than equivalent feelings in Ramsbottom for the northern countryside and Chorlton for London cosmopolitanism. Although an exceptionally wealthy area, it has a more muted sense of belonging, especially for women and older men (see Savage et al. 2004a). Nonetheless, even here, most residents spoke fondly and evocatively of their networked sense of place. In Cheadle, by contrast, people's comparisons were less emotional and more based on the idea of a fixed hierarchy of places in which Cheadle represented a higher status than other neighbouring areas.

Our case study locations map out the spatial co-ordinates of a broadly defined 'northern middle class'. Just as we chose our locations to represent particular mixes of capital, so we can see how these differences are related to subtle ways in which place is conceived and related to other places. But this should not distract us from the commonalities evident among all these places. In every area, we see a population predominantly raised in the north of England, with a strong sense of identity with various aspects of the northern life. With the exception of London's appeal to Chorlton residents, they have little attachment to the symbols or icons of southern England, and considerable attachment to the countryside and urban spaces of the North.

We can conclude by noting that these northern attachments, important though they are, do not generate a strong sense of regional identity. As we have seen, northern identities are dependent and derivative of southern ones, a process we have seen most powerfully illustrated by the Chorlton middle class who ultimately accept the cultural writ of London cosmopolitanism. Northern identities are different from northern English identities. Most respondents saw Scotland and Wales as part of the north, notably in the way that Ramsbottom residents appealed to the Scottish hills in a similar manner to their evocation of the Yorkshire Dales. However, the fact that both these nations see themselves as autonomous from the north of England reduces the cultural resources available for mobilisation by the northern English. Finally, regional identities are themselves strongly disorganised between alternative sources of support: county, city and region. In particular there is a fundamental rift between those who look to the countryside and those who look to the city of Manchester. In all four locations, Manchester was the closest major city, and we can understand better the nature of elective belonging by examining more fully the complex relationships which residents have with the city itself. This is the subject of the next chapter.

5

The Ambivalence of Urban Identity: 'Manchester, so much to answer for'

By 2005, for the first time ever, the majority of the world's population is expected to live in cities, yet the prospect for urban life is subject to intense debate. One influential school has argued that cities are becoming fractured through suburbanisation and the decentralisation of employment the rise of networked technologies which depend less on physical proximity, and the privatisation of urban public space (Sennett 1998). Los Angeles is often seen as the template for this kind of 'post-modern urbanism' (Davis 1984; Soja 1989; Dear 2000). Such spaces are the basis for an urban sociology premised on the significance of mobility and networks, which develops an 'urban theory based on the transhuman rather than the human, the distanciated rather than the proximate, the displaced rather than the placed, and the intransitive rather than the transitive' (Amin and Thrift 2002: 5).

A second view insists on the continued significance of central urban space. This alternative view has several components. One argument is that in a flexible economy, the existence of a 'creative milieu' based on the face-to-face contacts (Tornquist 1983, Hall 1998) remains crucial for economic development.[1] Hall (1998: 964) argues that even in the current period, marked by the advance of information technology which allows unprecedented mechanisms for spatial dispersal, 'the likelihood ... is that in an age when the injection of technology produces cultural renaissance, cities and especially urban cores will retain their attraction for a wide range of activities that require face-to-face contact for production, or consumption, or both'. Patrick Le Gales (2002) has developed this argument in the European context by claiming that the relative decline of the nation state has given more potential to cities to act as key 'players'. The vision of urban dystopia presented in American cities, and the LA school in particular, is not transferable to Europe where there has been more sustained concern to retain and indeed regenerate the urban public realm.

In this chapter we address these two different views of urban life by examining the agonistic and ambivalent relationship that our respondents had to the city of Manchester. In drawing out this complex relationship, we extend our argument that the meaning of place and belonging is defined not in terms of face-to-face community but in terms of their networked relationships with other locations. Whereas we showed in Chapter 4 that residents in our four locations looked to different places that were important to them, here we examine their forced relationship to their main urban centre. Like it or not, they all had to live in the shadow of Manchester as the city which defined and placed them and to this extent they remained centred on the city, despite the attempts of some residents to break free from it. By assessing the nature of their relationship to the city itself, and its role in their imaginations, we build on the argument that people's connections – both imagined and lived – to other places, are fundamental to their sense of belonging.

We are interested here in how our respondents report the significance of the city in their daily lives and imaginations. Our research has some parallels with Taylor et al.'s (1996) study of everyday life and what they term 'local structures of feeling' in Manchester and Sheffield, with the exception that our research strategy involves placing respondents accounts in their local neighbourhood context (in a similar manner to Buck et al. 2002 and Butler and Robson 2003a for London). The analysis draws upon our coding of every reference that respondents make to their use of Manchester, whether this concerns their commuting to work, their shopping, or their leisure. In most cases we probed our questioning in these areas to ask respondents what use they made of the city centre, so our information is comprehensive. We make particular use of questions we asked at the end of the interview where we asked respondents explicitly to reflect on how they thought the city was changing, and how much use they made of the city.

5.1 Manchester as civic project

As we will see, people talked about Manchester in many ways, but there is one revealing point of congruence about how they did not talk about the city. There is very little sense that the city was (or should be) a community with shared values and concerns. There are few traces of the historic vision that the city was a civic community characterised by self-governance and cultural and political autonomy. Such a vision of the city as collective entity has a long history, which can be traced back to the freedoms and institutions of medieval city-states (Poggi 1978). This concern also informed modern urban planning and governance, manifested for instance in Victorian schemes for civic improvement, and the expansion of urban welfare during much of the 20th Century. Of course, even during the 19th Century it is possible to detect pressures towards more centralised modes of governance, and since 1945 and especially since 1980, these have led to a dramatic restructuring of urban governance which has given increasing influence to centralised authorities, powerful interest groups, and has reduced the salience of public forum for decision-making (Stoker 1998; Monbiot 2000). Nevertheless, Le Gales continues to see this Weberian view of the city as justified in view of the 'loosening grip' of the nation state. Le Gales argues that 'the medium sized European city model … shows capacities for adaptation and resistance … for diversity structured by institutions, and for generating public authorities worried about social exclusion processes and as much concerned with culture and integration as with economic development' (2002: 275–6). However true this may be for key political actors at the urban level, this certainly does not filter down to local residents and impart in them a sense that they are part of an urban community. Indeed, it is remarkable that when asked how Manchester was changing, virtually no one talked about its public housing policies, its welfare services, its schools or any other aspect of its local governance. There was very limited discussion of its changing economic base, and very few people mentioned anything to do with urban politics at all.

This having been said, a few traces of a more communal orientation to the city is evident among a few elderly residents who were stirred to comment, usually critically, on the local authority. D63 was a Conservative supporter who mounted a critique of the Labour council's policies:

> I don't think it's the councillors that are wrong, it's the order of priorities that are wrong, mind you they've got things like rent rebate, rent rebate is the council's problem, it's not the government's problem, it's local isn't it, I think an enormous amount of money is spent on social security, which should be in my opinion a government thing, so like people said we want more local involvement and so on, this is the argument of Liverpool, we don't want the government telling us this, we don't want the government telling us that, we want to do it ourselves, but they've not got the bloody brains to do it.

D63 was pretty much the lone one in arguing for local autonomy in urban governance. A handful of other respondents criticised aspects of council policy, and there was some residual feeling against Graham Stringer, Labour leader of the Council in the 1980s who presided over its switch from 'new left' resistance to an endorsement of consumer-oriented commercial urban redevelopment strategies (Quilley 1998, 2002). Yet even the specific question we asked respondents about what they thought about their local council rarely engaged respondents who mainly made comments about the quality of very local services, such as rubbish collection, parks, or schools. For the vast majority of respondents, Manchester was not a community, but a series of physical interventions in the built environment. These physical forms were certainly 'read' for their social implications, but there was little sense of urban public realm above and beyond them, as John's testimony indicates.

John: reading the urban cues

John (D98) was a somewhat jaded teacher, and long term Labour Party activist. He had come to Manchester from the South 30 years before, and loved the city. It is striking how he related his concern with issues of poverty to specific kinds of physical urban developments.

I like Manchester, I've liked Manchester almost from the day I came back in 1969. I think it is changing. In terms of the city itself, I was only talking to somebody about this today, there was an article by Sophie Grigson in the *Independent*, who'd come back to Manchester to go to a restaurant in town and she was talking about how Manchester seemed to have been transformed since the bombing. I would dispute that, I think Manchester has been transformed but I think it's been a much longer process, it goes back probably to the early eighties when there was the development agencies that took over parts of the city. But you can certainly see that Manchester's much more lively than it was, even ten years ago, there's obviously the Castlefield development,[2] there's the gay village, there's just a feeling that there's more prosperity about, the wine bars and the café bars, which I think are a welcome trend. The city itself I love, it's a city I know very well from my student days, it's a marvellous jumping off point for large parts of the country, within a couple of hours you can be in the lakes or Merseyside or going south. So yes I think it has changed. One of the things that worries me slightly politically is the increasing poverty in certain parts of the city, and the fact that certainly there did seem to be a trend of more and more people before the Labour Government got elected of not voting, of becoming people who've just fallen off the register and I don't think that's just the poll tax.

John cares about the city. However even though he is a political activist he has little direct knowledge of how people in the city are faring. Instead he relies for cues from the media and from his reading of physical developments, 'the wine bars and café bars'. Visual markers become synechdoches for urban well being more generally. Although he is aware of the 'down side' of poverty, this is evoked in an abstract way, which could apply in any large city.

Only one respondent, an employee with the Benefits Agency, mentioned any kind of knowledge about the city gleaned from discussion with other people:

Well I've been very impressed with the changes in Manchester. Having always worked in and around Manchester, I've got a very good knowledge of the area and areas like Castlefield and G-Mex, all those sorts of areas, I've seen improve dramatically over the last ten years. I think Manchester's a lot cleaner and smarter than it used to be, despite the bomb going off, some people would argue it's done us a favour really to get rid of part of the Arndale Centre. But I think generally they seem to have finally got a grip on it. I think the dangers are that now some of the areas are starting to decline around Manchester. … There's been huge changes around Hulme. *I also talk to the police and all sorts of other people* and Hulme itself is a far better area, but the problems have been moved on. I still visit some of the rougher areas and you can see the problems, nobody seems to be tackling drugs, and that is killing off some of the estates totally. It impacts on a lot of people's lives and I think if you could improve certain areas it would keep them at bay. (C21, italics ours)

C21 was the only respondent who referred to conversations, in this case, with the police, in talking about how the city had changed. Even so, he is also preoccupied by intervention in the physical infrastructure, the development of Castlefield and G-Mex, as markers of change. Some respondents are explicit about their reliance on such cues because of their lack of any other knowledge:

> Yes, I think there are some changes taking place. I can only probably talk about the way it looks and feels, not so intimately … I mean I think when you go into Manchester in the evenings, it seems very lively, there's a lot of people about and I like that, you drive through and say, they're all out in their shirtsleeves these kids and it's freezing. (C102)

C70 tries to talk about changes to the city's prosperity, but his account becomes vague and unspecific:

> I think its on an up really … there seems to be a lot of work about obviously because the way the economy is, it's, things have tended to get cheaper, you know … I think people are earning a lot less, you know what I mean … people are earning less for what they were doing originally.

What we see, in short, is the difficulty for most respondents in sustaining intelligence about the city that does not fall back on their individual perceptions of change, primarily drawing on visual cues, their reading of the urban infrastructure. This is testimony to a city largely stripped out from any kind of collective knowledge or awareness. Few respondents have the involvement in civic organisations which allows them to develop an awareness of city life. During the period of liberal governance in the Victorian period and into the 20th Century a range of civic urban institutions, such as charities, the church and its related institutions, local government, political parties and trade unions generated their own knowledge and awareness of urban conditions as part of their public activities (Morris 1990; Kidd 1993; Rose 1996; Joyce 2003). Such institutions, all of which had different kinds of stake in governing these cities, established the role of the expert middle classes in defining and addressing urban problems. Thereby significant groups of the middle classes generated knowledge of urban conditions which superseded the casual visual regard and which not infrequently developed personal knowledge of the cities' inhabitants (for instance through the routines of house visits and church activity). As Poovey (1995), Yeo (1996) and Joyce (2003) show, the development of statistics and other kinds of social science has its roots in such endeavours. Among our respondents there was little evidence of any kind of involvement in civic associations organised on a Manchester wide basis, with the partial exception of the few members of political parties and church related groups. Most associations that were organised on a city-wide basis were based around hobbies or leisure pursuits which allowed enthusiasts from all over the city to come together and permitted members to develop what Bellah et al. (1996) call 'lifestyle enclaves' which removed them from other issues of local concern. What we see is the 'hollowing out' of the kinds of urban knowledge routinely generated by the middle classes in earlier generations and the increasing significance of visual impressions generated by a reading of the physical infrastructure. There were few effective devices to allow

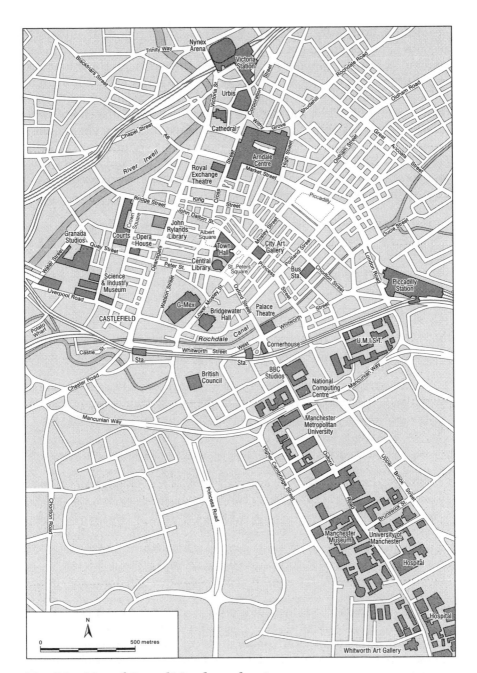

Map 5.1 *Map of Central Manchester locations*

people to generate intelligence on the city other than through individualised casual perception.

How then, do we understand the role of visual cues in urban interpretation? Lynch (1960) relates the power of urban images to the way that people draw upon urban cues in navigating their way round the city, and his account has been drawn upon by Jameson (1991) in his concern with new kinds of cognitive mapping in fragmented post-modern conditions. Our respondents indicate that the power of the visual resides less in its functionality, in the sense that people use visual cues pragmatically to guide them round urban sites, and more in the way that particular sites – which may be only rarely seen – are symbolically powerful and can be mobilised to convey specific kinds of meaning. Following the arguments of Kracauer (1995) and Benjamin (1973) we see the shattering of any sense of urban solidarity, and specific, unconnected, sites surface as key images of the city. The city becomes its buildings:

> I don't identify with Manchester, it is a dreary place. Its character is one that whatever they seem to do with Manchester, I think it was good it was blown up, unfortunate that people got hurt, but Manchester is odd bits. When you drive up Oxford Road the different style of buildings is huge and you think, Oh we never get anything right. You compare Manchester and Bristol. Bristol is an extraordinary place. ... (W62)

The buildings of Manchester stand in for Manchester, so that the reflection that Manchester never gets anything right is triggered off by its architecture. The same kind of response is evident among those who like the city:

> I love (Manchester). Much more than London. I'm really rude about London. I wouldn't have stayed here so long, I came here without any idea of what it was like and at the time I just wanted to be somewhere different where I didn't know anybody, so it served its purpose. But I love it. I think everything about it is great.

> *And do you think it's changing?*

> I suppose it's changing, but I think the things that I like about it are still very much the same. I like the compactness of it as a city, I like the buildings, people are often very rude about the way that Manchester looks, and yet if you look at it it's got the most fantastic buildings. We got married in the Town Hall which is absolutely gorgeous, the John Ryland's library and all of these places are wonderful and I think we've got the advantage now of the changes that are happening are making it a really big shopping centre and we're getting all of these quite posh shops in, so I think that's superb, it's sort of upping its status a bit. (D52)

The everyday spectacle of the city is used as a basis for the imagination of that city, and powerful battles take place to define the meaning of particular urban sites. There are clearly some sites which elicit remarkably uniform views. A particularly common refrain concerns the universally disliked Arndale Centre, built as a shopping centre in the heart of Manchester in the 1960s as a beacon of modern planning, now taken to represent its failure as well as the loss of 'old' Manchester. Many of our respondents concurred with Gardner and Sheppard's (1989: 126) description of such developments, 'Bleak, windswept, grey concrete wastelands ... brutal urban landscape'. Not a single respondent had any affection for the Arndale:

Well, I do have strong feelings, on, you know, the shopping centre, the Arndale: I think that's dreadful. (W68)

I can't stand the Arndale Centre. It is disgusting. I know it is an awful thing to say but if they had just parked the car (with the bomb) on the other side. It is a horrible place, especially if you knew what was there. It was lovely, little alleyways, shops, there was character. (D55)

Oh I don't love the Arndale centre but I don't know many people that do, but King Street, although I wouldn't necessarily go to Armani or whatever it's nice to have them there to look through the windows and then go and get the equivalent in Top Shop for half the price. (D64)

But when they put that monstrosity up the Manchester Arndale Centre that was the end of the city centre, it's horrible. (D68)

There is also a striking preoccupation with dirt as the visual sign of moral failure and more general problems with the city (see 'classically' Wilson and Kelling 1982). For some respondents, dirt becomes a key signifier of urban change:

But if you go and have a run round that area now, it's not in the same class at all, it's dirty. You see little things like sidewalks and grass verges, they don't seem to be tended like they used to be tended. I can remember as a schoolboy playing marbles in the gutter and the gutters were always swept clean. It just seems to have deteriorated generally and certainly become dirtier, what's made It like that I don't really know, whether it's councils or whether it's environment I don't really know. (C17)

On a couple of occasions last year I've just been extremely sad with it. It seems dirtier than it ever was. (R135)

I have never seen such a dirty area as Cheetham Hill was. I have never seen paper and rubbish and it was horrible. I can't say anything about any other areas, I don't know them. (R63)

I think it's also unfortunately, that one: it generally gives you the impression of being dirty and whether it's litter or what, there is a lot of it about. (W51)

Visual perceptions such as this are organised into powerful motifs and play a vital role in encouraging evaluations of the effectiveness of the urban redevelopment of Manchester. Since Manchester exists in the minds of its residents as a visual infrastructure, rather than as a 'community', the grandeur of high prestige projects of urban redevelopment, such as the Bridgewater Hall, the post-bomb development of Corporation Street, the new housing in Hulme and Moss Side, are indeed designed by developers to impress those who pass by (rather than those who necessarily live or work in them) as a means of persuading people that the city is becoming more prosperous (on these developments see Williams 2002 and more generally Mellor 2002).

Table **5.1** *Respondents use of Manchester's urban space*
(% of respondents)

Activity	Cheadle	Chorlton	Ramsbottom	Wilmslow	All
Commutes regularly	9	23	17	31	37 (20%)
Occasional commute			6	7	6 (4%)
Used to commute	2	2	6	13	11 (6%)
Shops regularly	19	40	19	17	44 (24%)
Shops 'specially'	7	9	43	31	41 (23%)
Never shops	14	51	38	52	97 (53%)

Note:

Commutes regularly: either respondent or partner commutes to city centre, or Trafford park, or Oxford Road universities or hospitals.

Occasional commute: main workplace elsewhere, but occasional meetings in city, or irregular commuting to city office once a week or less.

Used to commute: either respondent or partner used to commute.

Shops regularly: either city center is most frequent venue for certain kinds of shopping (e.g. clothes or books), or shopping more than 3–4 times per year.

Shops 'specially': only shops for presents or special occasions, twice a year or less.

> Its changing a lot, I think there is a lot more money around than even two years ago, you see places like Moss Side and I guess that in a couple of years someone that hasn't been there for four years won't even recognise it, they are rebuilding everything, renovating so many buildings, also in the city the fact that the northern quarter of Manchester is becoming more trendy and the people are living in the city, coming back to the city, all the developments they have done in Castlefield. (D33)

5.2 The centrality of Manchester: working and shopping

During the 20th Century, cities had a clear urban core and hinterland, with employment and services mainly being located at the centres, and residential areas being located in the suburbs. Over the past 40 years there is a well-documented trend towards the decentralisation of employment away from urban cores (Harrington 1990). This trend towards decentralisation is clearly evident among our respondents. Only 24% of the households in which we interviewed had some kind of commuting relationship with the city, whereby respondents commuted either to the city centre, the adjoining Trafford Park industrial estate, or the Oxford Road corridor where the hospitals and universities are clustered. This figure rose to 30% if those who used to commute but are now retired are included.

The strongest commuting relationship was found in the most affluent area, Wilmslow, where half the residents either do, or used to, commute. Certainly, many respondents in Wilmslow saw changes to commuting patterns as an important way of understanding the meaning of their residential area. W20 recalled the days when Wilmslow was a dormitory suburb of Manchester. Wilmslow, he observed was:

> physically separate yes (from Manchester), but on the other hand everybody's father, so to speak, worked in Manchester and you were, you know, either an accountant or a solicitor or whatever

you were – a cotton merchant and … and you lived up in Wilmslow or Alderley (Edge) if you were a little better off. After all, Alderley, as you probably know when the railway went out there they gave lifetime tickets to people, didn't they, to encourage them just to go and live there.

His wife concurred:

The interesting thing though, the days of our youth when we were living here, all the profession … well, semi-professional, professional people worked in Manchester. I mean, my father worked in Manchester always and anybody saying 'going into town' that meant going into Manchester. But now people are working out here. People living here, just as many of them are … don't go into Manchester at all.

Archie's historical eye was unusual but the view that 'Wilmslow was a dormitory town' was echoed by other respondents. W62 went on to add that 'Manchester historically was the great city and Wilmslow was the place where people lived in the large old houses that there are here'. However, it is clear that despite the decentralisation of employment to suburban and rural areas, commuting to the city centre remains important for Wilmslow residents, especially for those working in the public sector and professional jobs. For some, this commuting relationship continues to underscore the centrality of the city centre as their key focus. W14, for instance, saw Manchester as his central urban reference point. When asked if he was proud of living in the city he replied:

I suppose I am really yes, I do identify very closely, I grew up on the coast of Lancashire in Lytham St Annes and this is really my capital city if you like, so I identify with it and I am quite proud of it, particularly its football team and that sort of thing. (W14)

W14 worked as a lawyer in the city centre, and he and his wife continued to use professional services (such as its dentists) provided in the city. Unusually, his reflections were not premised on the city's visual appeal but suggested a different kind of interest and awareness of the city:

I am very fond of the City, I mean I have been here for 15 years and I think that it is – I mean it is not the most attractive city in the world but then that is because of its industrial heritage and you can't expect it to be the most aesthetically pleasing city in the world, it is a very straight forward city, it does not pretend to be anything else. I think it has a good range of shops and a good business centre, the perception of crime is a problem.

However, commuting has diversified for many households, so it is no longer the 'main' earner who commutes. Sometimes women commute to Manchester while their better-paid husbands work in Cheshire. In addition two men owned textile businesses based in the centre of Manchester but actually spent much time in international business trips. In only six households (one of which is W14's) does the male 'breadwinner' commute to Manchester on a daily basis. Even in Wilmslow, therefore, commuting to the centre is no longer central.

Narratives in Ramsbottom tell of the rise of commuting with the recent loss of the town's independent economic base and the rise of suburban housing. Although Manchester is seen as one area to which people commute, it lacks the centrality that it has for Wilmslow respondents. Actual commuting into the city was rather limited. Eight households saw some commuting, but in three cases this was similar to Wilmslow, with female 'secondary' workers going into the city while the main male earner did not. Chorlton was distinctive in seeing the highest rate of male commuting, with a large number of public sector professionals working in universities and colleges, local authorities and hospitals, as well as journalists working at the central BBC and Granada studios. However, these journeys to work were not interpreted as commuting by most Chorlton residents who actually saw themselves as working close to their area of residence. Chorlton was a kind of honourary central urban space, rather than a suburb. Finally, Cheadle was marked by virtually no commuting to the centre, with the exception of a few public sector professionals. Most Cheadle residents saw the city centre as a world apart from their own and would not think of working there. Urban centrality defined by a clearly structured commuting relationship is therefore of muted importance.

Contemporary research and writing on consumption (Corrigan 1997; Lury 1997; Miller 1995) and specifically on shops and shopping (Shields 1992; Falk and Campbell 1997; Miller 1998; Miller et al. 1998) has highlighted the role that such activity plays in identity construction, lifestyles, and as a means of understanding the significance of place. Table 5.1 also indicates the importance of shopping as a magnet for urban attraction. However, it is salutary to note that over half the respondents never visited the centre to shop at all, and only a quarter visited it on any kind of a regular basis, though this would often not amount to more than three visits a year. Nearly all those who visited the centre for shopping purposes did so for clothes shopping, with a smaller number reporting that they used its bookshops and music shops. Only for Chorlton residents do the numbers of regular users rise towards half the sample, while for Wilmslow and Ramsbottom residents it was much more common to visit Manchester shops on special occasions, usually defined as Christmas shopping or for a very particular purchase.

This mode of using Manchester defines the centre as a place that one visits for 'special' reasons and which is thereby set apart from the routines of daily life. Rather than urban centrality, with the urban core being the essential hub of life, this denotes a rather different meaning of the city centre in which it is available for special purposes, but the day-to-day business of life goes on elsewhere. This narrative is enhanced by the sense of several respondents that there are special shops, notably Kendal's on Deansgate, that one might wish to visit for special reasons but which one would not go to regularly. The significance of department stores as symbolic sites for special shopping or as 'Palaces of Consumption' (Bowlby 1985) has long been acknowledged (see also Corrigan 1997; Davies and Ward 2002).

Well Neil and I often go shopping, Neil likes to go to bookshops because there aren't really any good bookshops around here, even in Bury there aren't many, whereas I probably, it would be the bigger stores like Kendal's that there isn't in Preston, but on the whole because I know Preston and because it's a lot more compact, I would tend to go there. ... We don't go often. I go into Manchester for the bookshops, which I've got to make a special effort and go into Manchester. (R114)

We go in for special events. So if it's somebody's birthday we might go to a show. We might go specifically to a restaurant. My 15 years old loves Kendals. So if it's her birthday we might go for the day round the shops and perhaps have dinner and then out in the evening, so we would use the shopping. (W50)

I went to Kendal's for the first time for years and absolutely couldn't believe how good it was, but I wouldn't go just for the sake of going, we'd probably go on a Saturday with my daughter if she says do you fancy coming into Manchester and I'd say yes, I'll come to Manchester with you, but I wouldn't. (W69)

There is here a kind of paradox that by constructing Manchester as a centre of 'special' shops, the city centre becomes identified in the minds of its residents as appropriate for only occasional use, and is thereby removed from any kind of routine activity. The only real exception to this dominant pattern is for a minority of modern flaneurs who relate to the city in a more diffuse way. Benjamin (1999) sees the flaneur as an emblematic modern type, who moves between urban spaces in an unco-ordinated, fleeting way and thus both exemplifies the fragmentation of modern life but also can redeem it through his[3] ability to aesthetically link otherwise disparate phenomena (see Frisby 1985; Tester 1994; Gilloch 1996).

At the most generous definition, only 17 respondents (9%) can be taken to exemplify this kind of orientation to urban space, in that they articulate some, though often very limited, interest in walking round the city in anything other than a purely functional way. For a few residents, especially those from Chorlton, a pleasure in urban wandering is clearly articulated, as is especially manifest in Joe's case.

Joe: a contemporary flaneur?

Brought up in the Midlands, Joe (D34) had studied music, where he had formed a band which had made some impact in the city. Realising, reluctantly, that he was not going to make his living out of his music, he had decided to train as a music teacher. The rhythms of the city continued to intrigue him.

There is something about the place (i.e. Manchester), a bit love/hate.

What do you love or hate?

I think its this excitement of quite a lot going on in quite a condensed area but I don't know. What I don't like about it is more difficult to pinpoint. It's like a bubble around it, it's a point

---

of attraction but if like me you were attracted to Manchester from quite a few years back but when you get there, well it's like, well you haven't come from here. It's that sensation but it's all open arms but at the end of the day you feel you don't quite understand it, you are not quite with it…

What about walking?

Yes, I have to walk and I value the time.

Do you walk around Manchester or the countryside?

I enjoy a walk. If I decide I am going to walk to the shops at a distance or around town I make a point of covering quite a large area because I do enjoy the journeys in between and the sights you see. I like watching people in town. It interests me.

Would you go to the middle of Manchester, the centre, once a week or less?

No, it's less than that now. I miss my walks … the centre, the Library is the most important, although I just don't particularly find it attractive. I think it is a great building, a bit dirty, just inside it is a different place. That whole area of Manchester, Deansgate, John Rylands Library, Castlefield always amazes me. You cannot go there for a year and when you go again something major has popped up or you hear that Pete Waterman has had his studio there for all this time or that Ocean Software, a worldwide company, is just there. GMex is another place that amazes me.

For Joe, Manchester retains a 'porosity' a sense of mystery in which he is implicated, a mixture of open and closed. Like most respondents he relies upon, indeed relishes, his visual impressions of the city, but he juxtaposes the interiors and exteriors of buildings as a means of flipping between its unknowable and knowable elements.

Leaving Joe aside as a special case, most other respondents articulate a weaker sense of interest in 'mooching':

I enjoy going to town and that's certainly where we would go, you know, just to go shopping which we don't do very often at all. But increasingly I think not just for convenience, it's pleasanter to go up-to town and have a look around. (D13)

Mooch, sometimes go to Manchester for a mooch. Go to art galleries, just whatever I feel like, just look round the shops, go to Wilmslow. I have a friend and we get together. (D55)

Flanerie can be seen as an aspect of the aestheticisation of modern life (Featherstone 1992) as the wanderer assembles urban fragments into original artistic creations through their walks, in the same way that an artist can assemble raw materials into a work of art. A few respondents did talk about 'their' Manchester in terms of particular walks and sights that they used to take in, their own aesthetic take on the city. Joanne said:

Well, St. Anne's Square used to be ... well, used to be very nice and ... and you can ... at the back of St. Anne's is Parsonage Gardens and then onto the canal which has been tarted up a little bit now but they have a very nice bridge down there that I find attractive which looks like a sailing ... the riggings of a sailing ship. I like that, you know. And I used to like the old Corn Exchange and some of the buildings down there are very beautiful. Peter Street – some of the buildings along there are just quite breath-taking. And I don't like the Arndale – another letter I'm going to write! (R21)

It is easy to romanticise accounts such as these, in that they seem to evoke a more personal vision of the city. It needs to be emphasised that we have extracted the four quotations from the 182 interviews that represent the only clear statements of this kind in the transcripts. Most of the 13 others who can at best be seen to exemplify flanerie simply stated that they liked to walk between shops, or such like.

5.3 Manchester as site of high culture

Manchester's main function for most respondents is as a cultural centre, and in particular as a centre of 'high culture' (see Table 5.2). For many respondents, the city centre was a series of venues for classical music, plays, art galleries and museums.

And are you proud of living in the area?

I'm afraid so and travelling, oh and the theatre and the Bridgewater Hall, I love the Bridgewater Hall, I go to lots of concerts there. (W73)

Table 5.2 examines the use of the centre's leisure facilities, and shows that for residents of all four areas, the theatre and classical music are the main reasons for visiting the centre. The most frequently mentioned venues in the city are (in order of popularity) the Bridgewater Hall (home of the Halle orchestra), and the Royal Exchange (home to Manchester's leading theatre company). Perhaps surprisingly these eclipse Old Trafford (home of Manchester United) and the Nynex Centre (now the Manchester Evening News Arena and venue for popular music concerts and the then Manchester Storm, now Manchester Phoenix ice hockey team) in popularity for residents of all areas except Cheadle. The third most popular venue is the 'arts' cinema, theatre and art gallery that is sometimes seen as being at the vanguard of Manchester's cultural transformation from the 1980s, the Cornerhouse. Table 5.2 shows that its popularity is based entirely among Chorlton residents, and that residents from the other areas do not visit it.

In Chapter 1 we argued, following Benjamin, Bourdieu, and Appadurai that cultural taste needed to be understood in terms of the spatial range and reproducibility of its cultural form. The reproducibility of cultural forms allows them to be spatially dispersed and reduces the significance of

Table 5.2   *Use of cultural facilities in Manchester centre (percentages)*

	Cheadle	Chorlton	Ramsbottom	Wilmslow	All
Live sport	7	15	2	20	11
(Bridgewater Hall)	2	13	13	20	12
All classical music	2	17	17	40	19
Pop music	7	2	9	2	5
(Cornerhouse)	0	32	0	0	8
All urban cinema	0	38	2	0	10
(Royal exchange)	2	23	9	9	11
All theatre	14	55	32	49	38
Eating out	11	13	19	9	11
Pubs/clubs	11	11	6	0	6
Museums	2	4	8	4	5
Art galleries	2	19	4	9	9

Note:
Cultural activities in brackets are also included in the following generic category

particular places as venues. Table 5.2 suggests a neat relationship between central urban space and cultural participation. Central urban sites are not especially important for those activities which can be conducted in a variety of places, such as eating out and pub-going. However, for those activities which depend on 'live' performance, central urban location remains important. The role of the Cornerhouse can thus be explained by the fact that it shows films otherwise largely unobtainable in other formats. In this respect, our findings are consistent with those regarding shopping, that the city is a site for 'special' visits, and not one for routine activities. A few respondents clearly identified the city in this way, as the centre of 'cultural capital':

> I like Manchester. I'd rather live in Manchester than Birmingham. I love it because I love the theatres, I love the fact that it has universities around about, I love the fact that there are theatres that you can go to, shows that you can go to, shops, I just love it. (W35)

However, this articulation of Manchester as a desirable place because of its cultural facilities was in fact rather unusual. Precisely because the cultural events that it hosted were defined as 'special', hence unusual and not integrally related to other aspects of social life, it was quite possible for respondents to hate the city even while attending its cultural events with great relish, as in Betty's case.

Betty: High culture and urban loathing

Betty (W58) was an elderly woman who had originally come from Dublin but had lived in the Wilmslow area most of her life. Initially she had not liked the area, but having decided to 'make a go of it' she now felt at home. However, her attitude to Manchester itself had not changed.

I loathe Manchester.

Why is that?

It is a despicable place, I hate it. The only reason I go there is to go the theatre and concerts but I have never liked Manchester. It is not my scene.

Do you go to Manchester?

Yes

How often would that be?

Well as often as there is anything to see. The Royal Exchange you get something every 5 or 6 weeks, so we go every 5 or 6 weeks. If something comes to one of the other theatres we may go to that, the ballet. We go to, not now but have been … the Contact. … We have seen some very good plays there, we go the Library Theatre. Plays are usually on for a few weeks…

What about music?

I used to have a season ticket for the Halle but then I stopped buying a season ticket because I found that with going away more I was not using it and there is no point spending a lot of money so now I go when we are here, my husband is not very keen but he does come along because I don't like driving in town at night. So we go to the concerts as and when we want to.

To the Bridgewater Hall, have you been there?

Yes. I love going. It is really more involved in the music than the theatre but I enjoy both…

What about Manchester itself. Do you have a great commitment to Manchester?

No I don't like Manchester. I only like it for the theatre and music but as a place I don't like it.

Betty energetically partook of nearly every high cultural offering that Manchester could provide, but her enjoyment of these in no way detracted from her dislike of the city.

These points are quite consistent with our observation that Manchester is defined primarily in terms of its visual cues. Given that high cultural events take place in the interiors of buildings and hence face away from the public face of the city, there is no reason to suppose that however pleasant such events are deemed to be, they will have any impact on residents' views of the city.

In a sense people's use of Manchester for theatre and music exemplifies tensions between high and low culture. The majority of people only use the city – if at all – for exceptional purposes, to do 'special' shopping or to make an occasional trip to the theatre. The visit is both functional and ordinary, concerned to go to a particular venue in the city, but also charged with uncertainty (or extraordinariness) because of its relative infrequency.

The city is frightening but also still symbolically significant because of its importance for 'special' occasions. Around these complex relationships, we can understand the ambivalence of people's urban narratives.

5.4 Urban narratives

While few residents use the city centre on a regular basis, even fewer never use it. Only 13 respondents (8 from Cheadle, 4 from Ramsbottom and 1 from Chorlton) never go to the city centre at all. The vast majority of people use the city irregularly. The result is that the urban core of Manchester retains, indeed possibly enhances, its auratic quality. It is this enhanced aura for a special place removed from daily routines that makes sense of the kinds of urban narratives (see Finnegan 1998) that many respondents deploy. A number of common motifs surface. A particularly important genre is narratives of danger (see Taylor 1995). Concerns about danger are not so much about the city centre itself, but about the journey to the centre, through the city's poor areas. These narratives are to be understood in the context of unfamiliar journeys to 'sacred' places, but also because such journeys are unusual it is easy for these narratives to become mobilised around conventional urban 'myths'. A particularly common theme is the danger of driving casually through the inner city. R63, indicates clearly this juxtaposition between high cultural consumption of the city and the surrounding urban dangers:

> I think it's like any city, isn't it? I can't just pick Manchester out because I don't know enough about it. I do think that the outer areas a lot of them are getting very depressed. I mean Cheetham Hill has always been a bit like that, I don't know Mosside or around there although my son took me round in the car once after a concert of the Northern College … and when we were coming home he said I'll give you a run round Mum just to show you, you don't know what life is in Ramsbottom – he said that to me – he said you live cocooned and he took me and I was horrified at some of the things I saw. He said we don't stop and we don't get out, he said I'll just take you through.

> *What did you see?*

> Oh, dilapidation and people on street corners looking absolutely lost. It wasn't nice and when, I think it's been cleaned up a bit recently although I don't go by bus anymore, I always go by metrolink now – but when we used to go in on the bus, I have never seen such a dirty area as Cheetham Hill was. I have never seen paper and rubbish and it was horrible. I can't say anything about any other areas, I don't know them. I'm not a Manchester person that way, so as I say I can't really say.

The gap between lived routines and the city allows the city to be defined as a dangerous area full of unknown cues, which can nonetheless be visually detected. The car journey into Manchester takes on almost a mythical quality.

Well when I go to Manchester, I say I don't go to Manchester, occasionally we will go to Salford with my daughter, or I will and when you go through Moss Side you suddenly hear the doors lock and I think, we're round the rough area. You hear about people being robbed at traffic lights and things and a neice was queuing to get on the bus and she got her purse pinched, so I'm always very wary. It wouldn't have bothered me at one time, but I think now you have to have your wits about you. (C143)

Racialised perceptions of danger surface, either implicitly, or explicitly in the stories of respondents (see also Taylor et al. 1996: Chapter 8):

Manchester. I don't go in very often. I'm sure it's quite a nice city, but I don't know it and if I do go in I can never find my way out. I come out a different way each time if I'm driving. It's obviously a Victorian city. It's much bigger than Newcastle. We do have to go through Moss Side to get to it from here. [*laughs*] And I must admit I never ... I remember taking ... well my girls were both swimmers and they had a swimming gala and they were asked by their coach (to go) swimming at Moss Side and that's the only time I've ever felt a little bit nervous. I had to park my car with these two kids down in an underpass and I didn't see one white face and that may be wrong too, but I was unnerved by being in the minority ... I mean I've got nothing against black people at all, but when you're the only white one and you're down in the depths I was unnerved. (W3)

It sounds rather callous to feel that you want to distance yourself from it but I think most people given the opportunity would want to distance themselves from it, because I used to work in Manchester and drive through Longsight and Moss Side area and social deprivation and problems that are there don't exist here ... I've never heard of, perhaps, a drive by shooting, but when I drive through Longsight or Moss Side, I put the buttons down on the car. (W7, Deirdre)

We can understand this racialisation in part through the significance of visual cues to respondents perception of the city. Some Wilmslow residents specifically conflated blackness with the city itself.

I went to school in Manchester. Moss Side has never held any fears for me. I had coloured friends at school. We often went through the city centre to school. (W50)

By contrast, those large parts of the city that are largely absent from our respondents' accounts, tended to be areas of white residence, where whiteness was deemed invisible. Most areas of Salford and north Manchester, and Wythenshawe, at one time the largest council estate in Europe, were hardly ever mentioned. Wythenshawe is predominantly inhabited by white working-class residents, and although it was only a few miles from both Cheadle and Wilmslow, and although some Cheadle respondents had lived there, and some Wilmslow respondents had worked there, the place itself was rarely discussed. Sites such as these are largely invisible to respondents, even when they actually live near them. They are not the sites of negative identification, which people try to avoid (in the way that inner city ghettos such as Moss Side and Hulme are) but are invisible places.

Table 5.3 *Urban and regional identification of respondents (numerical counts)*

	Cheadle	Chorlton	Ramsbottom	Wilmslow
County	4	0	10	13 (1)
Manchester	15 (4)	31	10 (11)	14 (8)
Region	6	2	4 (1)	6
Local area	7	0	9 (1)	3
Other	3			
None	8	7	15	12

Notes:

County identifications: Cheshire for Wilmslow and Cheadle; Lancashire or Yorkshire for Ramsbottom.

Negative identifications in brackets.

Respondents could give more than one identification, and hence numerical counts, rather than percentages, are used.

Table 5.3 indicates how respondents from the four areas identified with Manchester, comparing it with other sources of spatial attachment. In two places, Cheadle and Chorlton, there is a strong positive identification with the city, and indeed Chorlton respondents are distinctive in their almost unanimous embrace of the city. By contrast, respondents in Ramsbottom and Wilmslow are more divided in their views of the city, with more respondents negatively identifying with the city. Even so, Manchester remained more important than county or region in providing positive or negative identities. To this extent, the imaginations of respondents in all four areas were fixed on Manchester. It remained an imaginary centre.

In talking about their views on Manchester, very few respondents articulated a sense that it was 'their' place which they identified with because they had been raised there. One exception was Ernest an upwardly mobile working-class man from Wilmslow who had become managing director of a medium-sized firm having started in manual employment. For him, invoking Manchester was a way of claiming roots:

Oh yes, certainly, yeah. I am proud of Manchester. I, I'm born in Manchester aren't I ... of course, I like Manchester, yeah ... but, but I think, yeah. I, you know I like living here and that's where as I say I was born, so yeah. (W1)

This invocation of local belongingness was most commonly found among Cheadle respondents who saw Manchester as a hook on which they could hang a sense of local pride. Liking the city and being proud of it tended to be related together:

Oh I love Manchester. I think it's a great place and I'm really proud of the fact that I come from Manchester, so we live slightly out of it, but I'm very proud of being a Mancunian and I've always felt like that. (C4)

So are you proud of coming from Manchester?

Yes, course I am, I'm proud of what Manchester's achieved...

Engineering was the first I think, now we're taking over with Manchester University, look at that for a place, it's a city within a city, it's one of the hardest universities to get into, it's easier to get into Oxford and Cambridge than it is into Manchester, it's got one of the finest medical schools going, it speaks for itself. ... (C52)

For some of these respondents, Manchester was a means of placing a regional identity:

Are you proud of living in Manchester?

Yes.

Why?

I like northern people, I've worked down south and they're just not the same, they're not on the same wavelength anyway, or they're slightly a bit too highly strung. They're not bad, but they're not as laid back or as nice or helpful as what northern people are. (C78)

In some cases, Manchester was also enclosed into an argument about nostalgia which was especially powerful in Cheadle:

I think my mother used to take us to Manchester, if my memory serves me well there was a coffee place on Market Street or somewhere, I can remember it all being white pinnies and little white hats, but I can't remember the name of it, I should be able to. They had lovely old machines full of coffee beans and the smell was all up the street, it was lovely, and my mother used to take us to those places. I think the reason we went, she had a friend who'd been in service, as she was as a girl, called Emmy and we used to go and visit Emmy, she sticks in my mind. (C26)

Mancunian identification was hence a means of positioning a sense of local pride in the institutions, values and lifestyles of their local area. It is hence an evocation of an autonomous, northern city. Table 5.3 shows remarkably unanimity in the identification of Chorlton residents with the city of Manchester, but they expressed their identification with the city in a rather different, more reflexive way. They were less likely to evoke local patriotism, and more likely to express ambivalent identification in which their identification with Manchester was an act of conscious decision. A number expressed concern about seeing this as pride, which they regarded as a problematic term:

Are you proud of living in the area?

I don't think it's something I actually take pride in, it's an area I've come to live in through my choice because of the job, I think Manchester's got a lot for it, I don't think I could take pride in anywhere I lived because a place is just a place. Would I be proud of living in say, Salisbury, with such a lovely cathedral, yes it's a lovely place and I might feel more attached to it, but it's still got it's good points and it's faults like Manchester. I think I tend to go to Manchester because of its background, the mix of people who've had to find work and sort themselves out, so I couldn't myself be proud of it but I'm interested in the history that's made it where it is and I wish it well in the future. (D70)

This account is related to an awareness of how Manchester might be seen by other outsiders, with a recognition that one is placed by others on the basis of where one comes from. The concern becomes that of justifying your identification to others, as well as stating one's own preference.

> I like Manchester and it feels like home. What I feel that other people would feel about Manchester if they were an outsider and they came and had a look, they'd probably think it was an ugly city and wouldn't like it very much and I think it probably takes a while to get to like it. (D14)

> I don't know, I keep trying to make my mind up about that. I'm very loyal to it when people slag it off. I feel very comfortable, as I say, even though I'm an outsider. A lot of the theatre staff ... a lot of the people I work with are, you know, proper Mancunian people: they read *The Sun* and they all smoke like chimneys and they're great fun to work with, so I like that. But the north is such a friendlier place to go to than the south. (D13)

A significant number of those who identify with the city do not come from it but instead 'achieve' Mancunian status by studying at a local university and choosing to stay. A good example here is John, who came to study in the city and became a teacher.

> *You say you love the city, that's quite a strong thing to say?*

> Yes I do. I mean I don't know many cities, I know London, but you don't know London, you know your part of London. With London I don't feel comfortable until I've crossed that river, the Waterloo sunset and all of that. I know Newcastle and I know Liverpool to a certain extent, maybe it's just that I've lived here so long, but I feel a sense of identity, a familiarity with the city.

> *Would you go so far as to say pride?*

> I think it would now, I mean I'm not a Mancunian in the sense I wasn't born here and having a pride and a loyalty is a bit iffy in some respects, but the city's done alright by me, basically and I feel comfortable in it and I think it's got a lot of potential, both in leisure and workwise and so on. (D98)

John's account shows how a sense of belonging and pride is related to his ability to settle ('the city's done alright by me, basically') and this sense is repeated by a number of other respondents who moved to the city from elsewhere.

Wilmslow narratives of the city tend to emphasise the distance between the town and the city. They are especially likely to invoke the idea of danger in travelling to the city centre, and also invoke a sense of leaving the city behind as they age. This can be seen as concomitant with their distaste for transience, and the idea that Wilmslow is now a place for those who have made a decision to put down roots:

> I used to work in Manchester and I used to go in every weekend; go shopping. But I suppose as my lifestyle has changed I would never consider going into Manchester now. You can't park; if

you do park it costs you a fortune. I like to get as much shopping and get somebody else to put it in the boot of my car. I can't really see the pleasures in struggling around Manchester with millions of shoppers; marching back and forward to my car, paying a fortune for car parking when I can get it free. (W7)

It's awful really … I mean I used to and it was really nothing to do with the bomb it's just that that was sort of … I mean, I think that is basically … I stopped literally going in there when I had my first child and it just … it's just too much hassle to even think about going in there and … I mean … because obviously from the shopping aspect, I mean, I used to quite like going to Kendal's and places like that but … I mean, now we've got John Lewis and all the rest of it it just … there's just no reason to go in there at all. (W23)

I might go to Knutsford, I don't go to Manchester very often now, I used to go there quite fre-quently when I was younger, but since the bomb – not because I am worried about the bomb I don't know what it is but I just don't go into Manchester, perhaps my shopping habits have changed, I don't go shopping quite as much now. (W40)

This articulation is also related to a concern to establish the status of Wilmslow vis-à-vis Manchester. As we discussed in Chapter 4, and as Table 4.3 indicates, a significant number of Wilmslow respondents identify with Cheshire rather than Manchester, and for many of these respondents this is related to a concern to establish their social position:

If you meet people out of the area and you are asked where you live you can answer Cheshire or Manchester to give an idea of where you live and I quite like to say Cheshire! Because when I said Manchester it is like 'Oh' people have a different view about Manchester, although in myself I feel thank God I am living near it … I feel that I can get to it if I want to but I am far enough away, I don't feel I could live in Manchester at all, but I feel that I can get to it very easily if I want to. (W10)

When I go on holiday and people say where do you come from I don't say Manchester, I say Wilmslow, Cheshire because we don't actually live in Manchester, isn't that awful, but people don't know where Wilmslow, Cheshire is so you end up saying Manchester. Yes I feel proud, I think there's a lot going for us, I read the comment that people make and send in and we get a lot of complaints but we get a lot of complimentary letters about how people found the city and most people find it very exciting and a nice place to visit. (W27)

I suppose to be snotty I would say I prefer to be regarded as Cheshire because Manchester, I can tell the way people say it, it has a bad image as a grey, industrial place, a rough image, rough people and they believe the Manchester accent is quite rough and there are some really rough people, but yes I suppose I would not really say I was from Manchester, well I do say I live in Cheshire not Manchester. I admit that. (W59)

Ramsbottom respondents were in many ways rather similar, except that they articulated a sense of greater distance from the city. There was a sense among Wilmslow respondents that they were still emotionally involved with a city with which they had historically close links and with which they were trying to distance themselves. Ramsbottom was historically more autonomous as an independent mill town. Even so, it is striking how little identification there was with its nearby urban centres of Bolton, Bury and Rochdale. Manchester remained a symbolically important place for respondents to position themselves against. As with respondents in all areas this sometimes was invoked as a story of personal development.

Stella: getting older and urban distance

Before moving to Manchester, Stella (R135) had lived in lots of places around Manchester, ranging from the student area of Fallowfield to Glossop in the Peak District. Having just had her first child she spoke about the safety that Ramsbottom now gave her, contrasting this with the city centre.

Manchester I find quite frightening now and I don't know if that's to do with age, but there seems to be a lot more people begging than there ever were, near where I work, and women with small children which I find extremely upsetting. On a couple of occasions last year I've just been extremely sad with it. It seems dirtier than it ever was but again when you're young and at poly and enjoying yourself you don't actually notice that. It is very clean round here so maybe in terms of what you're used to and what you then go and see it might just look worse. I don't know if it's got worse, I mean there are so many parts that have improved, like Hulme, when I was a student, I had friends who lived there and I remember going and seeing them there and it was just rat infested, disgusting, damp, a horrible place that should have been knocked down many years ago, and it seems lovely now, when I've seen stuff on Granada News they had a thing about how the residents had actually helped make their own places and put the gardens where they wanted and that seems a huge step forward from just shoving them all in. They've recently done one thing which goes completely against me, but probably if I was looking on the green side of things I would go what a good idea because it would stop so many cars going in, they've put ticket machines everywhere. It seems poorer in a lot of ways in terms of people begging, it seems better in a lot of ways because they have tarted it up and the bomb has actually improved certain things within Manchester centre which will be nicer.

For some respondents, their age allowed them to talk about Manchester in a more detached way, as a site that they might visit but without symbolic significance, in the way that Wilmslow respondents recognised it had. As Ronnie put it:

I think my only connection with a place like Manchester … I love the culture, I love especially the restoration. My only connection with a place like Manchester really and the bigger cities is the fact that they're … they seem more aware of the buildings that are around them as opposed to pulling them down and putting up these concrete jungles. I like architecture; I love to see an old building restored. You take G-Mex, the old railway stations, ok they're no longer functioning as what they were but they're no longer pulling these buildings down, they're looking at restoration now an awful lot. And I love the old Science Museums, love museums and things like that, you know, where they've got cars, planes. So my connection with a place like Manchester would be purely architectural, scientific, museum wise and just to see rather than pull them down, restore them. But apart from that shopping – no. No, don't go much. Very little contact with it, you know. (R28)

Conclusion

In this chapter we have explored the ambivalence of urban identity. Respondents do not see Manchester as the centre of their lives, or feel they belong – even in a relatively detached way – to the city. In this respect we do not subscribe to Le Gales's (2002) argument that cities exist, even in qualified form, as 'local societies'. There is little similarity in the way that the residents of our four areas talk about the city, and little sense that the city acts as an overarching unifying force in the lives and identities of our respondents. In contrast to Taylor et al. (1996) we do not think that there is a 'local structure of feeling', and certainly no evidence for any kind of cohesive or communal local 'culture'. Instead we see evidence that respondents view the city as a space largely hollowed out from social relationships, as a physical shell whose visual surfaces they scan for meanings. There is here a very different view of urban life to that which is standard in urban sociology which defines the city in terms of its routine everyday practices (for instance Simmel 1990). A model of urban analysis derived from models such as central place theory or Chicago school urban ecology which links places to their roles in a bounded urban system with a clear centre of gravity is of very limited contemporary value.

However, this does not mean that respondents were able to distance themselves from Manchester. Unlike images of the detached, fragmented suburb that are common in the writing of American cities, the city remained present and meaningful for the vast majority of respondents. In this sense, Le Gales (2002) is correct in saying that urban integration is more marked in Europe, even though we emphasise that this takes an individualised form. Manchester was seen in an individualised, reflexive way, as a means by which respondents symbolically position themselves. Respondents were rarely neutral about the city: they tended to love or hate it, with multiple narratives about Manchester, invoking elements of pride, nostalgia, despair, fear and hope. They generally talked about Manchester in a more emotionally charged way than other places that were salient to them, which they tended to portray in more fixed terms. Their stories were remarkably diverse and also rather difficult to predict on the basis of what they said in other parts of the interview. We can see how respondents' identity becomes implicated in stories about Manchester, and the city is drawn into individualised narratives of position and identity. This concern has usefully been identified by Castells (2002: 397) as the tension between 'individuation' ('the enclosure of meaning in the projects, interests and representations of the individual') and 'communalism' ('the enclosure of meaning in a shared identity'). However, whereas Castells sees tension between individuated individuals and communal cities, we see how individuals draw upon urban narratives to define their own individuality.

We therefore do not adopt the view of the 'LA school' that the city is a dystopic source of fragmented activities, networks and practices. There are some ways in which the city is unified through its continuing symbolic importance as a means by which respondents position themselves. We have seen the city centre function largely as a 'special' place. This is different from Los Angeles and other American cities where the city centre does not have this claim to be a 'special' site, and indicates that urban cores are likely to retain significance even while much routine practices are decentralised to suburban locations. This argument is germane to our emphasis throughout the book that people's sense of belonging is constituted relationally, through their attachments to other places, rather than to a sense of primordial belonging to a place in which they were 'born and bred'. Manchester mediates imagination and visual impressions with the complementary dynamic of the relationship between ordinary life and extraordinary uses of the city. Manchester thereby remains a crucial identifier to most respondents, and acts to provide some kind of framework through which the four areas are differentiated. Thus, the sense of belonging that Chorlton residents have to their area needs to be seen in relation to their positive, though also agonistic, attitude towards the city, while Wilmslow residents are torn between the recognition of the historic link between the city and the suburb, and their sense that the city carries negative status connotations. In Cheadle, senses of local identification and pride are hooked onto Manchester, rather than to other possible referents. Only in Ramsbottom is there a more detached orientation to the city, though even here it serves as an important reference point.

We see the symbolic importance of the city not as resting in its importance in everyday life, where it is unimportant. Instead we see the potential for the city to serve as a key symbolic marker through the increasingly visual and 'auratic' relationship that many local residents have with it. Respondents from all four areas use the city centre predominantly for cultural purposes, and the city thereby retains its centrality in part because of its continued monopoly of many 'high cultural' pursuits. Even though there is a sense among some respondents, especially those in Wilmslow, that they would rather not have to endure going into Manchester in order to see the opera or theatre, there is also a halting sense that it remains appropriate for such venues to be located there. Even with the decline of the urban public realm, the cultural infrastructure of the city centre remains crucial therefore in centring the city and providing a common reference point for respondents in diverse places.

Notes

1 Theoretically, these arguments have been developed with reference to claims about the possibility of agglomeration effects in global city places (Krugman 1991, 1995), and the possibility of knowledge transfers in dynamic urban places (Audretsch 1998). For a powerful critique in keeping with the arguments developed here, see Amin and Thrift 2002, Chapter 3.

2 Sites within Manchester referred to here and in subsequent quotes are indicated on Map 5.1.

3 On the masculinity of the flaneur, see Wolff 1987.

6

Work Cultures and Social Ties

It is all too evident that people's life chances depend critically on their social class, certainly in more stark ways than three decades ago (Savage 2000). Increased polarisation in the economic rewards associated with professional and managerial occupations on the one hand, and routine non-manual and manual occupations on the other, is related to a wide range of other inequalities, such as those in health and longevity (Bartley 2004). Sociologists have often emphasised that people's experience of different kinds of work extend into their domestic and leisure lives, with the result that experiences of class at work were linked to broader processes of class formation (see generally Savage et al. 1992; Giddens 1973). Parker's (1976, 1983) account is especially well known. He noted that in demanding and absorbing professional occupations there was a process of *extension* whereby work spilled over into leisure, for instance, socialising with work colleagues. By contrast, among manual workers in extreme and dangerous occupations, such as mining and fishing, there was *opposition* when people compensated in their leisure time for difficulties of their work. Here one might also socialise with one's work mates, but in hedonistic ways or through leisure defined in reaction to their paid work. Finally Parker detected *neutrality* among clerical or white-collar workers, where the domains of work and leisure run in parallel and do not intersect.

Parker's approach has been much criticised in recent decades. His 'neutral' category is largely residual compared to those of 'extension' and 'opposition', even though there are far more people likely to be employed in such occupations. He relies on gendered assumptions that men's social lives tend to be defined by work (Deem 1986; Green et al. 1990, Roberts 1995, 1999) but not women's who are more likely to be working in clerical and white-collar jobs. It has also been emphasised that the changing gendered division of labour and the growing numbers of women in the labour market has changed the relationship between home and work. Hochschild (1990), for instance shows how some people find employment less stressful and demanding than childcare and housework (see also Halford et al. 1997; Scraton and Watson 1998). The dominant approach today, following Rojek (1995), argues that the boundaries between work and leisure have become increasingly blurred, with the result that in post-modern social relations it is not possible to distinguish the social spheres of work and leisure with any degree of clarity. Thus Wittel (2001) claims that IT professionals engage in 'network sociation' where their work involves extending one's social networks, with the result that social life segues into work with little differentiation.

Lury (2003) shows how idioms of game-playing also structure working relations in the IT sector; du Gay (1996) argues that workplace relations in retail organisations address their workers as consumers using motifs generated from outside the workplace and McRobbie (1998) emphasises the fluidity of boundaries in the cultural economy.

These studies, important though they are, focus on particular employment sectors and on the experience of work, rather than leisure. With some exceptions (notably Hochschild 1997), they do not look at whether leisure activities and neighbourhood relationships are structured by work. In this chapter we consider how people's work experience informed their perception of place and affected their social lives. This involves returning to familiar issues in the study of community, where the extent of overlap between these two spheres was a major source of interest, especially for occupational communities where ties of work and neighbourhood reinforced each other (e.g. Dennis et al. 1956). In addition, by assessing how people's patterns of sociability are related to those of their work, and how far people's friends and social ties are socially exclusive, we are able to assess the nature of contemporary 'class formation'. In addressing these issues, the first part of the chapter examines the way that respondents talked about the way that work affected their social lives and their leisure, while the second part examines how people talked about their best friends. By connecting up these two issues we draw some broad conclusions at the end of this chapter regarding the nature of contemporary class formation.

6.1 Workplace sociability

Hours spent at work sapped the time and energy of many of our respondents, and there was ample evidence in our interviews regarding the sheer demands of the working day in driving people's lives. For this reason, when we asked respondents whether they thought their job affected their social life, few replied in positive terms, as if it provided positive potential for their social lives to be enriched. In most cases, this question was seen as an opportunity to talk about the constraints which work placed on their social life, mainly through the impact of their working hours, or the general demands of the job. As one educational administrator put it, 'I suppose that one of the key things is that perhaps I'm a bit too tired to do as many things as I might want to' (C110). This response was widely reported across the four areas, especially in public sector employment:

And would you say the job affects your social life at all?

Oh yes definitely.

In what ways?

One thing the hours that I've got to put into the job … I get up early in a morning, 5.45, 5.30 and I'm tired when I get home, mentally tired which I sometimes think is worse than physical stress. It also puts some stress into your lifestyle, there'll be times when you'll be thinking of jobs still at work when really you should be switched off and enjoying. (R13)

Few employees reported significant spillover of their work lives into their social lives. In part this was due to the fact that few employees worked for large organisations concerned to provide opportunities for their social life. Public sector professionals in all four areas, and especially in Chorlton, often worked for large organisations (such as local authorities, schools, hospitals and universities) but had usually moved between organisations and showed little loyalty to any specific one. In Cheadle, although many men had worked in large factories in the past, they now tended to be self-employed or working for small firms (especially in the building and engineering industries), and women worked part time in white collar jobs. In both Ramsbottom and Wilmslow there were large numbers of men, and a few women, in technical and managerial jobs, but in most cases they had moved between firms, and tended to work for companies which were spatially dispersed and did not have large offices on any one site, and needed to travel extensively in the course of their work which reduced their ability to develop social relationships. Deidre, who we saw in Chapter 4, emphasised her detachment from her surrounds and also insisted on her emotional distance from work colleagues.

Deidre: distance from work

Deidre (W7), who we met in Chapter 4, worked as a trainer for a large financial organisation and succinctly revealed many of the main motifs about how people talked about their work.

Do you think your job affects your social life?

Yes. Well, it means there isn't any. Don't get me wrong, that's not a hardship.

So you don't mind that; it's not something that bothers you?

No.

To what extent does your social life overlap with work?

It doesn't. ... When I'm working there's a different me. As I often say to people, my job involves training inter-personal skills. Teaching people how to deal with other human beings; how to get the best out of them. How to sell something to somebody ... and they say to me: 'It must be marvellous when you get home', and I say to them: 'No, it isn't'. I don't use it because it's manipulative ...

And would you say you have much social interaction with your colleagues, you know, when you're chatting with them is it mainly about work?

Totally about work.

You wouldn't chat to them about your hobbies or something, or would you?

Well, they say to me: 'What have you won most recently?', only because they know I do comp(etitions) … I don't know how it's come up. I suppose what it is is that I've obviously gone into work at some stage and said: 'Oh, you know what I've won!', and they've said: 'What do you mean, what you've won?', and I've told them and they'll say to me when I see them: 'Have you won anything decent recently?'. But really that would be the limit of it.

You wouldn't say you've developed any friendships at work?

I suppose as friendly as you get is with my co-trainer, John, who I do the outdoors with. Friendly is probably the wrong word. It's friendly business rather than friendly personal. If you can imagine going up a mountain, which is quite steep, and you're stuck on some gorse, right, and you go: 'John, I'm stuck!'. It's not personal, that's business, but if you're so reliant on somebody, you work so closely with them, it's unreal to say that you can't be friendly, of course you're friends, but it's not kind of a social friendly.

You wouldn't go out for dinner with him would you, or anything like that? It would just be a work situation.

Oh no. When we're staying in a hotel I'll say to him: Do you want to go for something to eat?', or we'll see what's on the menu have something to eat and then I'll say: 'I'm shattered, I'll see you in the morning'. We wouldn't necessarily even sit there and have a drink together. I mean, because while you're walking along you sort of talk about, you know, social, political interactions. So that, if you like, is the social bit but it's still in work and it's not personal.

On the whole, employees reported limited forms of involvement with their colleagues. Most employees prized being able to get on with colleagues at the workplace, and many partook of the culture of the Christmas office meal, the birthday drinks session in the pub, and the occasional party. Many respondents reported that they had no time to take lunch or find a break so that they could socialise with colleagues. One nurse reported:

Well I would say probably 70% of the time you don't get a break, and when you do get a break you have to stay on the ward because there's only two qualified nurses, so if I disappeared there would only be one nurse around. Up until very recently we didn't even have a room to go to, you just had to sit at the desk, but now we've converted a room so we can go and sit and get a bit of time out. (C114)

Many respondents grabbed breaks or chose to get some relief from the pressure of their work by deliberately seeing their breaks as a chance to be by themselves. One optician from Chorlton described how she spent her lunches in the office kitchen with the other workers:

But to be perfectly honest even though I'll spend time in their company while I'm in the kitchen and I'm not antisocial, but I'll tend to go off and read, which they quite understand because I like to switch off completely at lunchtime. It depends really, sometimes I talk to them, sometimes I don't, more often than not I tend to sit and read whatever's hanging around in the kitchen. (D12)

This emotional distance from work was the dominant motif across all four areas. There were only a few older respondents who revealed in their accounts a kind of fascination or compulsion about their work which preoccupied them to the extent that they talked about their work before we specifically asked them about it towards the end of our interview schedule. A retired policeman from Cheadle talked about the collegiality of the police force, the way that he had made his best friends in the force, and the extensive social life it generated, in his case through his involvement in its brass band, its football club, and its tennis and table tennis teams. But this was exceptional.

One important reason for the relative weakness of informal work-based socialising was that members of dual earner households with children had little opportunity for informal socialising because of their need to co-ordinate being at home to cover for each other's shift and working arrangements. This was especially marked in Cheadle, where nearly every household had to juggle hours so that one partner or the other could work at weekends, in the evening, or shifts. There were only two households in Cheadle (out of 30 households with both partners working), where neither partner worked outside regular 9–5 working hours. In several interviews the issue of balancing hours surfaced as a source of tension between partners, with women reporting how their husbands assumed that their working demands had priority:

At one point the job that he used to have, he worked nationally and he'd have to go away and it wasn't so much the work. I think it was the way he organised it. He'd sort of come home like at the last minute. Again I was working and um he'd come home and say, Oh I'm going to be away next week three nights, and it did then 'cos I felt all the responsibility for like E. arranging child minders and … even now if he doesn't, I suppose it's something we'd had to cope with but I said to him, If you're going to be away and I've arranged to go out and you know, it's up to you to sort out a child minder. And even though we say that it's me that always does it. (R4)

Pressure of working hours was not the sole reason for these patterns. Many employed respondents without dependent children also reported that they did not socialise actively. They explained this in terms of stress, burn-out and disillusionment. This feeling was especially evident amongst public sector workers, many of whom sought emotional distance from their work. Stress was reported especially in Chorlton and Ramsbottom, though it was largely absent in Wilmslow where the men, predominantly private sector executives, backed up by their wives' domestic labour, had more relaxed working routines and pressures on their time. For one teacher:

You just walk in in the morning and the phone starts ringing and it never stops so you just keep going. So it's hard to have a break and sit and chat to somebody, there's too much to do, students queuing outside the door, the phone ringing, mail to open. (D71)

Several respondents spoke about declining sociability in their workplace, often seen as a generational shift. John (D98), who claimed he had been highly sociable in his early teaching days reported that:

I don't know what your experience are of schools, but it's an aging profession and that may be one of the reasons why we don't seem to have as much oomph as we used to, but because of that you tend to find that increasingly there are very few young teachers in the schools, particularly in Poundswick* anyway, those that are there have got commitments outside school with families and so that tremendous exciting social life that was based on being 24, single, in a school where there were lots of other single people, has gone. I think the average age must be late thirties, and that's only because of the infusion of two or three very young teachers.

So that's something that just doesn't happen any more?

No I'm not really interested in a social life based around work. (D98)

These feelings crossed class divisions. Most employees, whether they be professionals, manual workers, or white collar workers sought ways to avoid extending their already intense work demands even further into their 'personal' lives. Parker's class distinctions between professionals and manual workers is not borne out. Thus, a skilled manual worker reported feeling demoralised by the intensification of work in a way not dissimilar to the professionals (though using somewhat different language):

Yeah, yeah … ah, it's not as good as it used to be … I mean you … used to be able to have a really, really, good crack but things with the improved customer relations that we don't know if the customer's walking around the place like when we're playing football. All that's taken over now, it's become very serious. Work has become very serious.

You can't have a laugh in the same ways?

No, you can't. Everyone takes everything so seriously you're that scared … frightened of losing your jobs … I wouldn't go out on a works do with people that I work with all day long 'cos I work with them all day long … I wouldn't choose them as my mates like – I happen to work with them. … We get supervisors telling us what to do – go faster, this isn't good enough, that's not good enough, mop the floor up, stick a brush up your arse and you can sweep up at the same time. (R30)

Our findings above should not lead us to the conclusion that respondents were always emotionally detached from their work. Some respondents were heavily involved in their work, but these nearly always reported their involvement in individualised terms, as something that took up their time and energies and which took them away from collective leisure pursuits, or social ties, of any kind. Stuart, a manager in an engineering firm, reported that he did not go out during the week:

certainly in the last year, because I've just joined a company belonging to a friend of mine, it's a fairly young company and I'm working all the hours God sends at the moment. I was back home tonight at six, that's the first time I've been home before quarter past seven since I remember. I've had four days holiday this year up to now. It's a bit of all hands to the pump.

So what would a typical weekend be then?

Well I do go into the office for a couple of hours, which annoys my wife, I say that I'm only going for half an hour but I end up staying for two hours. My son has a job in the car park for United, so I take him in and I nip into the office and work for a few hours and then when he's finished he comes up to the office and I bring him home.

Can I ask you more about how your work life affects your social life?

At this moment in time, in the last year, it has taken my life over, in fact we were just talking about it half an hour before you arrived, it has taken my life over. (C13)

When a university lecturer was asked how his job affected his social life he replied 'silly question', before going on:

Being a lecturer at a university is not a 9–5 job. The preparation, the research which you're expected to do, the number of publications you're expected to publish each year are such that 9–5 does not cover it. You usually find yourself working weekends, evenings and once you have done x number of lectures in one week, you tend to need the weekend as a flop. It's the same with any teaching, Jackie's the same, after doing a week of teaching you need a weekend to flop, and then to suitably motivate yourself to lecture again. It's not that the job itself isn't enjoyable, it's just that it does take something out of you. (C38)

Some of the more ambitious, younger respondents, talked about how their career interests were best served by distancing themselves from an active work-based social life. One junior doctor talked reported that:

I don't actually socialise with the people that I work with. I work in quite a small team and I actually fastidiously avoid major heavy nursing nights out. You've got to be made of strong stuff to cope with those, and they're all a bit false so I try to avoid … I'm not very close … I don't really socialise with the people I'm working with immediately. The people that I am friendly with are people that we have [got to know] over quite a long period, and because of the nature of my job I'm working at different hospitals every 6 months, and so it takes quite a lot to sustain a friendship beyond what is often quite an intensive period. So there will be a few people who you do maintain contact with over the years but not very many, but they're quite robust friendships. … Probably sort of once every 6 months there will be a 'do' of some sort, a meal or something, and depending on how things are going with that job and especially in intensive care: intensive care is a very strange place to work, it's very intense and it's made up of a core of permanent nursing staff who are extremely specialist, high-skilled, advanced, blah, blah, blah … , and if you don't get on with them you might as well shoot yourself. … And we are notionally senior to them on paper … and so I feel the key to actually delivering a decent service is cohesive relationships between the people at work, and I will actually make quite a calculated decision as to whether I feel I need to go on one or two of those outings in order to make my life easier. (D13)

The individualisation of the career as a project of the self (Grey 1994; Savage 2000, Chapter 6) entailed a delicate balancing act involving the cultivation of appropriate contacts but refusing to get too 'thick' with colleagues from whom it might then be difficult to extricate oneself from.

Having identified the power of the boundaries that were drawn between work and 'private' lives, it is important to recognise exceptions. Those who had large amounts of economic or (some kinds of) cultural capital were able to extend their work sociability into their leisure. Especially in Wilmslow, employers, senior managers and self-employed men, like Ernest, used their leisure contacts to develop business ties, with the result that there was a very fluid relationship between social and working lives.

Ernest: the sociability of the chief executive

Ernest (W1) was the managing director of a local engineering firm, which he had built up from scratch, from a working-class backgound in Manchester. He began playing golf shortly after he got married. He had become a keen player and every Saturday morning was spent on the golf course. His wife was also involved in the club, and attended dances and social events with him, and his son had become an excellent player. Like most golf club members, he was exercised by the status and standing of different clubs, which led to different queuing times since the most exclusive clubs took longer to get into. This had led to him joining a less exclusive club but hoping he could get into a better one 'by the back door'. His involvement in the club overlapped with his business. Because he was in engineering construction:

> I used to help out insofar as if they were doing any (I used to help with) sheds for all the equipment and so on and so on. You'd get a price you know, people and contracts and [buyers] and you want to [sort out the] contract.

However, when the club did not take his advice 'I backed off then, and I've not done anything with them at all other than I play golf, that's all'. However he did still feel very attached to other club members, going for weekend retreats with them. In addition, his social life in the club 'greased the wheels' of his business activities. One golf club had 'a fabulous golf course. I do know people in there. Not many but I do know quite a few and so it would be handy for me you know business-wise it would be handy.

Yeah. It would be a good place to take people?

Yeah that's right.

Yeah. Is that what you'd use it for rather than ...? Meeting people as well or?

Yeah meeting people as well and taking yeah ... and ... I was considering joining the golf complex at Low Barn* ... but I was thinking of actually joining there and ... 'cos I like the

---

> [Lake*] ... .a very good club. It's great for taking clients, but [pause] it's very difficult to get on the course ... it's a much better place to take people really.
>
> For Ernest, golf club membership was a means of maintaining business contacts, similar to the way that his firm had season tickets for Manchester United where he regularly took clients to home games.

Ernest's case is by no means unusual. W93, also a managing director of a small firm, spent every Saturday afternoon at a local golf club, and would normally stay there in the evening when his wife would often join him to have dinner and possibly attend a social event. He was explicit about the business advantages of club membership:

It's convenient. Because it's a private club and I can typically have people show up off a train or a plane, it's the kind of place that happens to have dining facilities from eight in the morning 'til eleven at night, and 16 years ago when I joined you still had restrictions on licensing laws so you would go along somewhere, nothing to do with that, but a pub or a hotel would close and somebody would turn up in the middle of the afternoon and you couldn't get a drink or a snack. Things have changed drastically and a private club like that had all of those facilities, I believe that's why they've been very successful, so that was the reason I joined it, plus I was getting very interested in golf and it's a good course ... I would say that there are many entrepreneurs and private business owners, I think there are many other people that join there because it's good for their business they believe, people like bankers, accountants, lawyers, who believe they can network and meet people.

In fact, it transpired that W93 also belonged to a golf club in Florida which he used on his American business trips.

A second kind of extension, which overlapped with the first, was evident among those who made a living out of their social and cultural skills, especially in Chorlton, where 16 respondents (34%) – double those from the other areas – reported that there was a strong overlap of their work lives on their social lives. Many of these were employed in the cultural sector, and give some support to the claims of McRobbie (1998) regarding the distinctive nature of work in this sector. A self-employed development consultant reported a lot of overlap between her work and her social life 'because there's loads of people who I'm friends with who end up doing some work or who I've ended up working with because we're both interested in the same sort of things. So there's a lot of interface and movement' (D11). This is the world of de-differentiated spheres, whereby work, leisure and socialising become fused. A few employees employed in the cultural sector also fell into this category. An orchestra musician reported that his work and social life 'were one and the same' (D52). Another musician reported that 'well my hobbies are my livelihood, I teach here, I've got a recording studio upstairs, I've got two or three bands I play in' (D42). A buyer for a designer clothes outlet talked about how he depended on his leisure contacts:

> I run the northern area for a fashion company, so it affects it quite a lot, really, because you tend to mix with the same people you're involved with, don't you. So again, it involves going to the clubs now and again and also the people that you meet tend to be of the same ilk. Obviously if you're a bricklayer you would probably go the Bricklayer's Arms a lot more often, so I think where you go to eat and things it does revolve around the people you've probably met through work, etc., and also I work quite unsociable hours sometimes and as I say, work the odd weekend. (D23)

Similarly, the two journalists we interviewed reported a fresh and lively social scene around their work, reporting that it was common for colleagues to decide to eat out or go for a drink after work. For D115, her job:

> affects my social life in that most of the people who are involved in my social life are people I work with, but other than that, not massively, although it also has some sort of implication for my social life because we finish work late and can't get to the supermarket, maybe that's why we eat out more ... nearly everybody who's my friend up here is from work or connected to the business somehow, 95% of them.

For a TV producer:

> Mainly I work very, very, long hours and all my social life is related to work, and mainly it's going out for meals, cooking at home, going out for drinks, occasionally the cinema, occasionally clubs, occasionally a walk in the countryside with somebody at the weekend but it's pretty much, almost all that I know, people that I've met through work ... (D56)

When asked if she had become friendly with anyone because of leisure interests, she replied that:

> No, because of work really. I mean I've become friendly with people that like going to ... at work. I have to be brutally honest because we've moved up here with my job because it takes so much time my only friends are friends that I have made through work.

A few similar cases were evident in the other areas. A self-employed craft-worker (R59) in Ramsbottom, for instance, talked about how she made friends among her clients. But only in Chorlton was this kind of overlap common, and even here it did not predominate.

In general, most employees demarcated their work firmly from their other social ties, and it was only among the self-employed, and to a lesser degree male senior executives, that much overlap was reported. In general, our findings do not support the 'post-leisure' argument that employment and leisure are becoming de-differentiated, at least at the level of people's accounts of the relationship between these realms. Indeed, our evidence points clearly towards the increased differentiation of these spheres. This is due to the intensification of employment relationships, the way that career advancement was often defined as involving distance from work peers, and the fact that men could less easily rely on their wives to provide domestic support systems. Within this framework, work contacts were valued for providing collegial support. You do not want fellow workers to be too distant, since this might make one's work more difficult, but you did not want them too close either. This is the kind of relationship between work and social life which does not appear to be conducive to marked processes of class formation, in which people's experiences of work and employment become to define their identities and social ties more broadly.

6.2 The practice of 'best friendship'

Given the relatively limited overlap between people's work and their social relationships, as well as the relatively distant forms of neighbouring we examined in Chapter 4, we now turn to consider how our respondents do talk about their 'intense' friendships. How far are these really detached from their everyday routines of work and residence? Many recent commentators have emphasised that the practice of friendship and intimacy has indeed become disembedded from wider social relations. Silver (1989, 1990) and Pahl (2000) argue that the decline of communal social relations brought about by capitalism and modernity more generally led to a radical restructuring of sociability. Commodification and commercialisation entails the crystallisation of intimacy in particular, significant 'others', with emotional withdrawl from people routinely encountered in daily life. Those who were socially and spatially mobile, and who worked in modern bureaucratic settings, were seen as most likely to differentiate friendship from other social ties. Bott (1957), Bell (1968) and Allan (1979) argue that the middle classes were more likely to identify friends who they are specially intimate with, whereas more stable and locally rooted working-class people were less likely to differentiate friends from acquaintances. In their recent work, Beck and Beck-Gersheim (1995) and Giddens (1991) focus on the dynamics of the 'pure relationship' in which the relationship itself becomes the object of participants' concern, with the result that it becomes an object in itself, stripped out of context. Modern relationships, it is hence argued, are different from earlier understandings where friendship is embedded in, and grows out of, social relationships, and potentially intimate relationships can exist at considerable social and spatial remove. This argument dovetails with Granovetter's (1973) analysis of the 'strength of weak ties', where acquaintanceship and casual contacts are often more useful for instrumental purposes, than are the deep ties of friendship. It is thus possible to differentiate non-instrumental, de-contextualised intimacy, from casual, instrumental social relationships.

There are, however, numerous critics of this view of the 'pure relationship' (e.g. Jamieson 1998). Social categories, especially that of gender and to some extent of class, still appear to structure practices of friendship in a way which indicates the enduring power of social relations to configure forms of intimacy (Adams and Allan 1998). Furthermore, following Bourdieu (1997), intimate relationships can be seen as a means by which forms of exclusive (or in Putnam's 2000 terminology, 'bonding') social capital are generated. We are interested here in whether the practice of best friendship actually disembeds people from their social relationships.

It is well known that more and more people claim they have 'best friends'. Pahl (2000), citing Lynd's Middletown studies that up to 40% of Americans in the 1930s did not feel they had a close friend in whom they could confide. In our study only 10% stated that they did not have a best friend 'who they confided in' (see Table 6.1). In line with other studies (Allan 1979; Willmott 1987), those without such friends tended to be elderly working-class men, with a concentration in Cheadle, the least affluent of our four areas. Many of those not reporting best friends were locally raised, whereas nearly all the in-migrants in all four areas reported having best friends. Those without best friends appear little different in terms of their sociability from those with them: if anything they seem more gregarious. This is in keeping with the well-known finding that the sociability of working-class men relies on extensive 'weak-tie' acquaintanceship. Indeed, one respondent saw their sociability precisely as the reason why he did not have best friends:

> Not really, friend-wise no. I don't get that involved with people. I do have friends, good friends but I don't get that heavily involved with them purely because I have had my own things to worry about. So you don't really want people coming to you with their problems and complaints, you know what I mean? They tell you anyway but you know it's just a passing comment here and there, nothing that deep. I don't think it's a good thing to get in too deep with people, no. Because they tend to get to rely on you and invariably people will always let you down, its human nature. So I tend to be, I wouldn't say I was a particularly good judge of people, because I am generally too outgoing, I will always help regardless of who or what, if somebody asked me for help I will help them no matter what it is. It doesn't matter what it is, I don't do it because I know they are going to help me, you know what I mean, I am just that way inclined, I will always help people even if they do me a wrong after – which has been known on several occasions! (C70)

It is interesting that there is an awareness of what a confiding 'best friendship' might entail, which indicates the normative power of this conception. Here, not having best friends invokes a different conception of the self from that discussed by Giddens (1991) and Pahl (2000). Rather than seeing the self as being positively developed through intimate interaction with significant others, the self is defined as a fixed, private entity whose health depends on protection from external threats. Given the predominance of elderly male skilled manual workers who expressed this view, this concept of the self may be linked to the culture of male craft autonomy in which it was deemed vital to allow workers to retain inviolate control of their own work-space and routines (on this conception of the self, see Savage 1998, 1999, 2000). Having best friends does not involve a more developed self-awareness, rather it indicates a different kind of self-awareness:

Table 6.1   *The organisation of friendship (percentages)*

Location of best friends	Cheadle	Chorlton	Ramsbottom	Wilmslow
Manchester area	64	48	36	40
North of England	11	8	38	11
Rest of England	5	28	12	32
Other nation	8	9	12	14
No friends	14	8	3	4
No. of best friends with named location	64	65	69	85
Met through:				
School/as kids	41	48	30	63
Work	23	22	27	6
Family	18	15	12	16
Leisure	18	0	18	13
Neighbours	0	15	12	2
No. of best friends where known how met	22	27	33	32

Note:
Numbers add up to more than number of respondents since some respondents named more than one best friend.

I think if we were having difficulties in anything we wouldn't confide in them [friends]. If we were going through a very bad financial crisis or something like that, no we wouldn't confide in them. I mean general problems, yes we probably would, but nothing too specific. (C34)

I would not think I have them [best friends] that close who I would confide in because I have on one or two occasions thought I had friends like that but they have let me down. You only find out when things get back to you. You think from now on keep it to yourself, that is the only thing. I have found now, keep it to yourself. (D9)

Having best friends demands a certain confidence, and implicitly requires the persistence of relationships, and hence their ability to be abstracted from time and space so that it can endure over these dimensions:

I have had (best friends) over the years. There was one lad who was my best man, I used to go out with him every single night of the week and we did that for about three years, very close, but then because we moved away down south, you lose that tie. Then we got ties with people in the Air Force and we moved back up here again and it's like we've got these half ties everywhere. I still know him and we get on really well but it's not what it used to be. (C65)

Not really, no. I have had in the past. I tend to let go of people. I don't like to cling on to the past. (D92)

No I don't actually see them much now, but I have seen them in the past they have come up to see me and I have been down to them but it might only be twice a year but I think as the years go on you get more involved with the family life and maybe that turns off your friendships. Moving away from the area doesn't help as well, that's too far to travel to go and see them you just tend to drift and get involved in day-to-day activity. (W42)

No, they've all gone their separate ways now. The best friend that I grew up with, occasionally I'll see him, perhaps once in the last 20 or 30 years, something like that, but when you meet them again they're nothing like you remember them, so they're not really your friend any more. There's nobody now that I could turn to in times of trouble or anything like that, I'm very much alone now. (D42)

In these various quotes, all from men, rather than best friendship being seen as entailing distinctive inter-personal qualities it is the possibility of sustaining such ties in the lack of routine day-to-day interaction – their abstraction – which explains their failure. This sense is related to the idea that intensity cannot be sustained when out of physical contact, as Harry's case indicates.

Harry: the difficulty of best friends

Harry (C55), was a very friendly and sociable security worker. Having been brought up on the Wythenshawe council estate, he had moved to Cheadle 20 years ago, and was pleased he had done so. Although he had an active social life, he denied that he had friends he could confide in:

I've never had friends like I had in the army. I know it was a different kettle of fish because we were living together, but that's what I would call friends, I've never had any really close friends, because basically most of our time is spent with the family anyway.

You didn't keep in contact with anybody in the army?

No … I actually did meet one once in Hyde, and I went looking for one two years ago and found him in Newbury in Berkshire. We were very close in the army, really close, and when we came out we actually wrote to each other and sent Christmas cards for a number of years and he used to write to my wife and everything, then it died off and I kept writing to his address and I never got a reply and I often wondered what had happened to him. We went for a week to Oxfordshire in Spring last year and I said let's go see if I can find him and we went, well what a shock, I wish I'd never been, because as I knew him he was a very big lad, very strong, and when I got there this little old man come out and no exaggeration, he had grey hair in a bloody pigtail, same age as me, but he was small and weedy whereas I'd known him as big. I said I'm looking for Andy Twistle, do you know him? And he said, it's me. I nearly fell off my trolley. None of us realised that we all look different, but this bloke had completely changed.

This revealing account indicates how the changed appearance of a former friend exposes the lack of endurance of the friendship itself, which here cannot be abstracted from his physical appearance.

What we see here is related to the limits of local belonging we have identified in Chapter 2. It is not necessarily that the locally raised are less likely to have developed 'best friendships'. Several of them report that they have had best friends in the past. Rather, such friendships are not seen as enduring. They are also aware that they are different from the norm. All respondents without best friends understood what the idea of having a confiding friend might entail, and recognised that they deviated from this norm. Some respondents labelled themselves as 'loners', 'non-mixers' or 'lazy'. Those who had best friends, by contrast, did not explain this in terms of their personal characteristics, because it was deemed to be the social norm Thus R78 who reported that:

I'm a loner, I don't confide totally in anyone.

This 'defensiveness' around not having best friends could also lead to respondents seeking to account for this abberation:

I haven't, I don't have, but then I have a sister who's only 18 months older than me and we were best friends really, so I think I never had to make best friends. (D43)

We can see these responses as running parallel to the limits of local belonging that we identified in Chapter 2. Just as those locally raised no longer felt at home, so those who could not sustain 'best friendships' felt they were somehow lacking. Can it be argued also that best friendship is the concomitant of elective belonging?

Table 6.1 indicates the spatial range of best friends and the venue in which friendships were forged among the sample as a whole. The most common way that best friendships were formed, in all areas but especially Wilmslow, was through childhood relationships, especially those from school or university. In some cases such friendships were traced to a very young age. Respondents rarely met their best friends through their current work places. In some cases best friends are defined as family members, normally partners, occasionally siblings or children (but never parents). Those met through leisure include a significant number met through holiday encounters, and rarely include people met through clubs or associations. Some neighbours are defined as best friends, though in many cases these are former neighbours, whose contact has been sustained.

Spatially, in every area except Cheadle, the majority of best friends live outside Manchester, the result being that contact has to be on a planned basis. One implication is that best friends were largely personal, characterised by dyadic ties, with third parties rarely knowing both the respondent and his or her best friends, with a small exception of some cases where couples defined other couples as best friends. Very few people would ever be likely to hear anything about their best friends from anyone other than the best friend themselves – they were thus clearly removed from any kind of extended social networks.

Very few respondents saw their best friends as people they had much to do with, or indeed needed to have much to do with. Rather, once formed, the relationship persisted. In this respect they are rather different to the idea of the 'pure relationship' which in Giddens's formulation involves ongoing work and reflection. As W99 reports, migration need not affect one's friendships:

> I have still got the same best friends I suppose that I always had. Two of them are in Canada and I met them at school. I emigrated to Canada when I was, or my parents did, when I was eight. So I grew up in Canada, went to primary and secondary school and didn't really come back to England until I got married really. The two girls I am still in touch with and phone them and my daughter has just been out to stay with them. Obviously I don't get to see them much, only every couple of years but I still feel the same about them as I did then and I would say I have maybe about six in England. All of them I would consider very close. A few of them were neighbours when the children were very small in London and I still keep in touch with three or four of those girls. We see each other once a year and maybe two or three in and around the Wilmslow area that we met when we moved up here and they have stayed.

For many respondents, best friends were rarely seen face to face:

> I've got some friends that I've had since I was 12.
>
> *School friends?*
>
> Yes, one lives in Preston and I see her every year, I have kept one or two close friends.
>
> *And you meet up with her?*
>
> Yes, just once a year, either here or at her place. The friend that we made in South America I see her quite regularly and she comes over here or I go over there.
>
> *Once a year would that be?*
>
> No, not as often as that, but every few years. (W73)

Striking here that seeing a friend regularly involved less than annual contact. This kind of friendship was revealingly discussed by W42 in terms of the fact of the very nature of good friendship entailing the need for less frequent contact:

> I don't really have contacts with old school friends although there are a couple of people I occasionally see but being good friends, I wouldn't actually see them on a regular basis now. The people I have met in various places around haven't really continued a friendship although at the time you could say that there was a strong friendship, but it's something that when you move on you tend to make new acquaintances. (W42)

The key phrase here is 'being good friends, I wouldn't actually see them on a regular basis now'. It is almost as if best friendship is defined in terms other than participation in shared social activities, with it being given a different kind of status as an enduring relationship which persists even with little support from routine social practice and activities. This was not always the case. Some respondents saw more of their best friends, and a few identified their partners as best friends. Revealingly, this was often then qualified by an unease as to whether partners could 'really' be best friends. In response to being asked whether she had best friends, C120 replied:

No, not really. As I say, I've been very family orientated. Friends, yeah, but not best friends, and I think, alright, when I've got a husband that's your best friend isn't it? And then when they go you can't sort of pick up a best friend out of the air.

For another Cheadle man, his wife was his best friend which he saw as 'a bit sad' (C101). Cheadle was generally distinctive since a significant number of respondents identified best friends with whom they did regularly socialise and who were embedded in their leisure and kinship. However, many with best friends living close by subsequently made special efforts to distinguish these friends from other acquaintances, as if to guard against the implication that all people living close to them were their best friends. They also often emphasised that the friendships were not derived simply from local interaction.

No. Lots of friends, lots of acquaintances, but there's only a few who I would say are extremely close friends.

When did you make those friends?

A couple of them from school, some of them made a bit later in life, one of them I met when I was in the police, we still see, and a couple from the army. (C79)

Well outside my family, you inevitably have those relationships, a lot of people say I've got lots of friends, I think most people say that when they don't mean it. I think that a lot of us have got what I call associates or acquaintances, probably most people don't have more than six or eight true friends throughout their life. People in my position you tend to find that more people want to be friends with you and therefore you have to be more aware. It's a sad part of life, if you've done well people want to know you and you get invited. If you perhaps haven't done so well but you might be just as friendly a person, people don't migrate towards you. So that's why people that are wealthier who have attained a lifestyle, you live in your own home and you've got your surroundings and you tend to be very contented there because you actually want to be quieter because you've got a very hectic life. And I think it's not because they're snobs, and people say they might be, they just relish the short amount of time they have on their own to recharge their batteries. So I probably have six to eight people and they've come both from business and socially. Outside that I probably have another 30 or 40 people that I would say that we'd be quite happy to go and spend one or two nights away with, many of them are business associates, but they're different than friends. (W93)

Hence this is a somewhat different point to the familiar argument that working-class respondents are less likely to have intimate friends. Such people in fact seem concerned to create some kinds of boundaries between acquaintances and friends, though this can be difficult when the latter are seen as closely embedded in his social life.

Fundamental to best friendship is the idea that the friend endures, not only in terms of being long-lasting but also that the relationship is no longer dependent on any specific practical context to maintain it. For many respondents this meant friends made while they were children, with whom a relationship has been maintained. This trait characterises many of those with local friends:

Yes, friends that I've grown up with really and kept in contact with. For instance there's one I met yesterday I haven't seen for about three months and I'm going to stay with him and his family on Saturday night, the two of us will just go out, his wife will stay in with the two children, and we'll talk about a range of things during the evening, and we'll both confide in each other, both in personal things in our lives, even tax matters, the whole range of things.

Where did you meet these friends, at school?

Yes, some were at school and some were out of school, some we all trained together in the mid-seventies, so our career paths were similar as well. (C136)

In some cases it was clear that endurance is related to a common theme of being able to connect if necessary, which exists even when contact with one's best friend is rare. It is clear that in some of these instances, especially among men, actual intimacy is rare but the idea of its possibility persists:

It's one of those funny situations, yes we do talk, but no we don't, I know it sounds daft. We don't have the contact like we used to do, nothing about because I won't do it or he won't do it, it's just we know that if anything would happen, he'd be here straightaway, and he knows that if anything happened with him, I would certainly be there straightaway.

So you don't actually need that week-to-week contact?

No, not at all. It's one of them things where, I can't put it, there's no way with Terry, he's there if you need him. (C71)

It is no exaggeration to say that this is the dominant narrative of best friendship, which is found in all four areas and for both men and women. It is a narrative which explains how someone can be insignificant in ones actual social life yet still be symbolically and emotionally important:

We write to each other, we make the odd phone call. We don't keep in contact as much as we used to, we had things to talk about really when you're writing, but whenever he comes back it's like he's not been away really, I just know that we'll be friends. (C17)

They are friends who you could pick a phone up and they'd be here tomorrow or tonight if necessary, but that wouldn't mean that we'd see them on a very regular basis, so sometimes once a month, some weeks you might see them every week, it does vary, at the moment I haven't seen them for about three months.(C21)

I'd probably say I've got about three or four best friends, ones that I would confide in. I don't know it's just happened really over the years, I have ones that I don't see for a year, but when I see them it's still very close. (W88)

We don't see a lot of each other. We don't even phone each other much. Our friendship is just one of those very strong friendships that will just keep going .... I have this friend in America who is a very good friend and I have another one in Germany. I just feel that they are good friends, you don't need to see them very often and catch up with them. Whenever you see them it may be two years have gone, you just pick up where you have left off. (D50)

Its one of those things, we can go a year without speaking, but I still know she is a close friend. I do write, occasionally I phone but not often. (D51)

Pahl (2000: 72) talks of the idea of 'fossil friends' as a means of characterising these kinds of relationships, 'who were particularly important at one stage of life ... but who move away and are not part of an individual's active personal community. However, if circumstances happen to change, the "fossil friend" may be reactivated and the friendship would carry on "just where it left off"'. This definition however implies that the real friendship depends on being reactivated, and that fossil friendship is not the 'real thing'. In fact, our respondents accounts suggests that respondents are quite happy to have best friends at a distance and that the rhetoric about reactivating the relationship is a narrative device to explain why such friends can still be held to be intimate when in reality they may be relatively unimportant.

A number of narrative genres go alongside the view of best friendship. One of them is the idea of contingency, the idea that because close friendships do not come out of routine encounters, there is a remarkable chance element in their development. This is especially commented on by those who met friends on holiday, such as Sallie:

Sallie: contingent best friendship

Sallie (D51), was a graphic designer, enthusiastic about living in Chorlton, though she noted that she was not a 'Manchester native'. Living with a partner, but with no children, she relished her exciting holidays, where she had met her best friends.

I actually met them sailing funnily enough. We were there a fortnight, we were together, we just fell in with them, there's one, Lesley, on the first day was walking around with a mask, vertical, and was falling about all over, and she just creased me up laughing. She was with these other two people and we just got to know each other and we had such a laugh, the same sense of humour. The night before we left we stayed in the local bar and drank it dry and then actually as we were sitting round feeling terribly ill the following day, we started talking about what we were coming back to and it turned out two of them were in PR and the other worked for Blenheim Online, she's an accountant but in publishing, and we all worked in the same sector, and we'd never mentioned it for the fortnight.

Forming a real friendship is seen by her as invoking qualities and relationships abstracted from the practical world of work and employment. In this respect this is congruent with the 'pure relationship' idea, since it is not any kind of social similarity or link that is seen as key to the friendship. It seems that friendship here is positively created, invented, by stepping out of the routines of daily life. Sallie went on to note:

> They hadn't done sailing before, we'd done sailing before, and we'd done windsurfing before, and one of them was about 17½ stone, and she'd gone on this holiday not realising that sailing was going to be quite so much a part of it and the boats were tiny. She wasn't very agile, quite overweight, and trying to dip under the mast she just kept scraping her knees and she didn't do a lot of sailing but we kept inventing these diseases and that was what made us friends.

> *So it was less the sailing, but it was being in this situation?*

> Had we not been on that holiday at that time we would never have met. Had we not been who we were we would not have remained friends. That was 1985 I think. In the interim one of them, Poppy's been to work in New York for three years and then went to South America, she's travelled a lot, she's been to Australia, Val went and lived in Australia for a bit, Lesley's changed his job about three times, got made redundant, come up here in a desperate state just to get away from everything down there. We share a lot in each other's lives and so we just happened to meet on holiday but it was the humour. We've been to Menorca now four times and we've never made other friends like that. You get on well with everybody while you're there, but they're the only ones we've actually remained friends with.

Sallie emphasises the contingency of the friendship and the 'spatial stretching' of their friends:

> it's funny really, because even though when I'm with the younger one, Liz, the one who's been working at the airport, she worked on cosmetics with me at Stockport, she is really my daughter's age but when I'm with her and when I'm with the other one who's got the two small children, we felt like we're all the same age because we all talk on the same level and we all discuss everything from things that frighten us to death, spirits, crazy things, to gossip at work, so we've got a lot in common. (C108)

Contingency allows people to have friends who can know one outside one's current practical daily life. D27 for instance, was a very sociable and friendly woman, who had developed friendships in a number of contexts. However, although clearly gregarious she only had 'one friend who I would confide in – but only one'. She had known her for over a decade and she did have a reasonable degree of social contact with her because although she lived in a nearby city, they would often meet at the weekend. She completed her remarks with the interesting observation that:

> I feel that I relate to her not just because of children or work and I think it's actually significant that we knew each other before we had children, so I feel like she knows me as a person and not just a mother and that is significant. I mean, I do feel with my friends I've met via the children, I don't feel they know me as well as someone would if they'd known me before children.

Best friends are distinctive in knowing people in a different way, in reinforcing a sense of the self that is different to that evident in daily life. Best friendship can be seen as a form of 'abstract' friendship. To be sure, respondents value the 'personal' qualities of their friends, but the fact that the relationship is disembedded from pragmatic daily routines gives it this abstract quality. Abstract friendship might thus be seen as a kind of objectified social capital in a rather similar way that Bourdieu talked about the way that cultural capital is objectified in particular cultural artefacts such as works of art, literature, music and so forth. Abstract friendship is seen as a socially approved and sanctioned mode of friendship which becomes the norm against which friendship more generally is evaluated. Like objectified cultural capital, abstract social capital is sedimented and relatively enduring. Part of the process of abstraction involves a claim on time and space, that is to say the friendship endures over spatial distances and over time. Seen in this context, abstract friendship can be seen as a mechanism for providing guaranteed support in the future or in situations 'at a distance'. By claiming your friend as 'best friend' you are leaving open the potential of calling on them in ways which need not be directly reciprocated. Abstract friendship allows you to store social capital outside pragmatic daily routines.

Seen in this light, abstract friendship can be seen to be a correlate of elective belonging. It involves disembedding people from their current place of residence by allying them with people living elsewhere and which identifies people as belonging to social groups scattered in space. Yet in another way, it also facilitates the effectivity of informal social relationships based on situational networks. By stripping intimacy out of interactions based on neighbouring and work it becomes possible for such interactions to be organised on a pragmatic basis, less likely to be troubled by a clash of deep personal feelings.

Conclusion

Elective belonging involves clear differentiation between personal and situational networks. This is in keeping with the twin localising and abstracting processes of elective belonging. Sociability is structured along an axis which distinguishes abstract from daily, situational, contact. 'Best friendship' can be seen as an abstract social relationship that takes people out of the lived routines of daily life, and which links them to spatially dispersed others. They have huge symbolic significance. Just as places are connected to other places through the organisation of a network of the imaginary, so one's network of best friends connects you to other places. Best friendship, to a large extent, is an imaginary relationship. By contrast we can see that situational, daily sociability around work (as well as around neighbouring which we discussed in Chapter 4) is largely detached from friendship practices. Employment does not generate solidaristic feelings or intense social ties that might permit class relationships to spill out from the workplace. On the whole, relations with work colleagues do not lead to extensive informal socialising, especially in bureaucratised forms of employment.

We can thereby see how elective belonging largely entails the eradication of class formation, if this is to be understood as a process where social ties and identities are to be organised on the basis of class position. In recent years sociologists of stratification have become increasingly aware that class formation is a fragile creation, and that there are numerous reasons why it might not take place. Even so, there remains a temptation to suggest that class formation may take place under certain conditions (Erikson and Goldthorpe 1992; Savage et al. 1992). However, this argument no longer seems a useful one to draw. There may be some conditions under which class formation could occur, but these are so far removed from the nature of daily life and the organisation of work and residence for most people, that these are largely of hypothetical value (see Savage 2000).

Our scepticism towards the class formation paradigm does not, however mean that issues of class and inequality become unimportant. Rather, drawing on Bourdieu's work, we can see an implicit social coding of friendship which allows those in more advantaged social positions to best evoke it. We have also seen some striking exceptions to the limited overlap between work and leisure amongst privileged groups. Those with the highest amounts of economic and cultural capital were the most likely to report an active social life and overlap between their work and leisure, whether this be Wilmslow's affluent business class or Chorlton's cultural workers. It is these elites who are able to bridge these otherwise differentiated fields with relative ease. The apparent weakness of class in the accounts of most of our respondents is actually testimony to its profound, yet largely invisible, power (see Savage 2000).

7

Mediascapes in the Mediation of the Local and the Global

The significance of the media for undermining place-bound social relationships has been emphasised by numerous theorists who make much of the capacities of the media to transmit information rapidly over vast distances as a key globalising force (Meyrowitz 1985; Giddens 1990; Castells 1996a, 1997; Lash 2002). Some accounts go so far as to suggest that contemporary social life is media life (see Baudrillard 1988). Held et al. (1999: 363), in their careful survey, argue that there has been marked 'cultural globalisation', as a result of 'a series of decisive shifts in the geographical scale, immediacy and speed of cultural interaction and communications'. Yet, despite these claims, we still know relatively little about the reception and use of the media in everyday life in ways which allow the thesis of cultural globalisation to be tested (as Held et al. 1999: 373 readily admit).

In fact, it is clear that many media ethnographers are somewhat sceptical of the claims made regarding the significance of the media. Morley's (2000) impressive synthesis of research relating to 'media, mobility and identity' is instructive here. He insists on the continued relevance of local belonging, and draws on Tomlinson's (1997) work to note that 'it is ... in the transformation of localities, rather than in the increase of physical mobility (significant though that may be for some groups) that the process of globalisation perhaps has its most important expression' (1997: 14). Furthermore, Tomlinson's suggestion (as quoted by Morley (2000: 15)) that 'the paradigmatic experience of global modernity for most people ... is that of staying in one place but experiencing the "displacement" that global modernity brings to them', is highly germane to the account of elective belonging we have developed in earlier chapters.

There is thus something of a stand off between social theorists who proclaim epochal importance to the media, and media researchers themselves. We ally ourselves with the media researchers in studying the media sociologically as part of the patterning of the everyday (see also Spigel 2001). Our approach here involves showing how Bourdieu's conception of cultural capital and the cultural field can be developed through a fuller analysis of the role of the mass media in everyday life. Despite its sophistication, Bourdieu's work is insensitive to the proliferation of the imaginary made possible by the new media. Drawing on the work of Silverstone, Morley and Appadurai, we show how we can retain a modified conception of cultural capital only by recognising the complex spatial reaches of varying technological media and their power to form specific kinds of cultural connections.

In the first part of this chapter we discuss theoretical issues before turning in the second part to consider our respondents' narratives of ordinariness and defensiveness around television viewing. Thirdly we consider how respondents underscore distinctions in the areas of musical taste and fourthly, reading practices. The final part of the chapter explores the global reach of our respondents' cultural referents to show how respondents made reference to cultural sources from different parts of the world to position their cultural tastes.

7.1 Cultural capital, media and everyday life

In this book, we have interrogated how Bourdieu's analysis of stratification can be modified to take account of global flows. Leaving aside his early Algerian research, Bourdieu's empirical research was conducted in France, and many of his most famous studies are accounts of French society (and in some cases, as in *Distinction* 1984, they might better be read as accounts of Parisian metropolitan culture). Comparative applications of Bourdieu's work have tended to encourage the view that it is possible to measure national variations in forms of cultural, economic and social capital (Lamont 1992; Savage et al. 1992; Bennett et al. 2000; Vester 2000; Lamont and Askartova 2002). These projects, interesting though they are, are subject the powerful criticisms of Urry (2000) that 'national society' is not the best frame for understanding contemporary social and cultural relationships.

We have suggested in earlier parts of this book that Bourdieu's approach can be made more sensitive to issues of fluidity and mobility. After all, he makes no great theoretical claims for the national level of analysis: he pays little overt attention to the role of the nation state (see for instance Wacquant's Foreword to Bourdieu's *The State Nobility* 1996). His theorisation of capital can be made more spatially sensitive. Bourdieu (1997: 47f) claims that cultural capital comes in three forms: embodied, objectified, and institutionalised. In the first dimension cultural capital is embodied in people's dispositions and demeanour, and is thus not spatially fixed. People carry their embodied cultural capital around with them: it can hence cross national boundaries, leading to transnational cultural capital where people from different nations congregate. In its institutionalised forms, cultural capital is certainly mainly dependent on national agencies, most importantly educational systems. Here however, it is possible to argue for the increased significance of transnational institutions such as multi-national media corporations. This is indeed the claim that Appadurai makes in highlighting the significance of contemporary mediascapes which refer 'both to the distribution of the electronic capabilities to produce and disseminate information (newspapers, magazines, television stations and film production studios), which are now available to a growing number of private and public interests throughout the world, and to the images of the world created by these media' (1993: 278). Objectified cultural capital is found in 'material objects and media, such as writings, paintings, monuments, instruments etc.' (Bourdieu 1997: 50). It is an empirical matter whether such objectified forms are defined in terms of a national canon, and it can indeed be argued that the kind of classical high cultural capital emphasised by Bourdieu is a form of European transnational culture, represented by an appreciation for German, Italian, French and its Graeco-Roman lineage.

We argued in Chapter 1 that cultural practices which do not depend on display or performance in fixed sites are less likely to be bound up with struggles for distinction than those that are. Bourdieu's arguments regarding cultural capital rest primarily on the power of 'auratic' cultural capital, consecrated in art galleries, museums, theatres, and such like. However, the media may disrupt the significance of these kinds of cultural practices through allowing the mobility of cultural artefacts. Thus, for Scott Lash (2002), the media reduces culture to depthless information. It is within this media saturated society that the cultural omnivore (Peterson and Kern 1996) emerges. The omnivore is able to roam widely across cultural genres and references because of the capacities of the media to readily provide diverse cultural cues in an easy and accessible form. This mobility also involves spatial mobility, the capacity to appreciate cultural forms from different parts of the globe.

We are therefore interested in assessing whether people's use of the media invokes cultural distinctions or whether it is consistent with the arguments of the omnivore thesis. As we have explained, we see it as essential to explore this issue in relationship to the media's ability to either break down or construct senses of place. Insofar as the media does indeed generate 'no sense of place', this is good reason to suppose it generates a more omnivorous culture. Our approach builds on the work of Roger Silverstone (1994) who argues that television is central for understanding how individuals live their lives in contemporary society. Building on Winnicott's discussion of the role of the transitional object in human development and Giddens's consideration of the centrality of trust relationships in late modernity, Silverstone argues that television is crucially important to the maintenance of contemporary ontological security. Our senses of belonging, self and identity in a changing world are crucially structured by our immersion in television.

In contrast to those mainly Marxist influenced accounts that offer extended critiques of 'everyday life' as marking popular incorporation (for a summary see Gardiner 2000), and those more populist approaches – influential within cultural studies – which see everyday television consumption as part of a resistance to hegemonic power (for example, Fiske 1989), Silverstone argues that the role of media in everyday life should be conceptualised as entailing searches for security. He thereby offers a 'neutral' account of how the media is related to everyday life (see also Drotner 1994). For Silverstone, 'Our everyday lives are the expression, in their taken-for grantedness, as well as (in popular culture) their self-consciousness, of our capacity to hold the line against the generalised anxiety and the threat of chaos that is a *sine qua non* of social life' (1994: 165). Consumption and in particular the consumption of television, is 'both the oil and glue of structure and agency within everyday life' (1994: 131). Silverstone indicates here how media consumption may be relevant to the themes of belonging, self and imagination that we have explored in this book.

On the basis of this general theory Silverstone also argues that television can be located in place, through its implication in the development of suburbia (see also Silverstone 1997). It offers programming about suburbia that deal with suburban anxieties, and is part of the suburban transformation of public life, entailing commuting, privatism, nuclear families, set gender roles, consumption and so on. While some (for example, Medhurst 1997) argue that his claims about programming misunderstand the most popular form of television in Britain (soap opera, or the British continuous serial), Silverstone's argument is generally valuable. However, in keeping with the concerns of this book, it is important to probe behind Silverstone's generic emphasis on suburbia, to consider more complex ways that the media may generate networked senses of place.

In his summary of arguments concerning the domestic nature of television and its role in households, Silverstone draws a useful distinction between home, family and household (see also Morley 1986, 2000). Crudely, home is that produced, often in idealised ways, on the basis of household relations:

> Home is what is produced or not (we feel or do not feel at home in the spaces we occupy and create); it is produced as the result of productive and reproductive work by its members, and also by a whole range of other activities, principally consumption activities, that have as their end product a more or less powerful statement of identity, ownership and belonging. Households are the social, economic and political systems in which that work takes place. (Silverstone 1994: 45)

Families are also variably constituted and cannot be assumed to have a particular form. In Silverstone's analysis, 'Families create homes and live in households' (1994: 33). This means that studying media in everyday life requires attention to what Silverstone terms the 'moral economy' of the household. However, it also entails, we suggest, looking at family relations, in a way that goes beyond the interactional dynamics of households, despite their importance, to the wider identities that are bound up with everyday life.

Silverstone offers a powerful framework for the study of media in everyday life in which the construction of everyday, ordinary identities are given greater emphasis than the kinds of struggles around distinction that Bourdieu highlights. However, we still lack a developed understanding of what this construction of the 'ordinary' involves. A number of commentators on the cultural omnivore thesis have argued that we need to explore the subtle claims to distinction which may be entailed when people have the capacity to move across cultural genres. This may involve the elaboration of a kind of 'ordinary distinction', where cultural expertise does not appear to be based on overt snobbishness or elitism (Bryson 1996; Warde et al. 1999). We explore these issues by comparing the similarities and differences in patterns of media consumption in our four areas. We are interested in showing how media are important in the narration and reconstitution of senses of the self – concerned with belonging in places, being a part of particular types of social groups, distinguishing oneself from other groups and in the location with kinship groups. This involves us in unravelling the paradox that while media might not appear important as generators of identity they are crucial in the mediation of identity and the performance of identity in everyday life in societies that involve large media consumption (see Abercrombie and Longhurst 1998).

7.2 Television: routines, defense, pleasure and identity

We begin with television, probably the most universal form of global communication, which has been the focus of many of the strongest claims regarding the media's role in changing people's attachment to place (e.g. Meyrowitz 1985). And indeed, only one person in our sample claimed not to watch television. Table 7.1 offers a characterisation of the broad patterns of television viewing in our four study areas. We should note that the data in this area poses particular issues of interpretation. The ubiquity of TV in everyday life and its role in everyday interaction makes some people more prone and comfortable to talk about TV than others. It was not always easy to gauge the importance of viewing particular programmes. A person may mention that they watch *Star Trek* or *The X Files*, but this does not itself indicate whether this is a programme that is crucial to them or just part of the background to their lives. In addition, our data is accounts of people's viewing practices, rather than more objective data on what they actually watched. Given that this taps people's senses as to what kind of programmes they can 'own up' to watching, this is actually rather valuable for our purposes.

Table 7.1 shows that in all four areas there were rather similar patterns of viewing, with little marked difference according to the economic and cultural capital of respondents. Three common reference points were evident. Firstly, respondents often reported watching documentaries and news in their television viewing, with a very common first response to our question of whether people watched TV being to mention these genres. Some of these responses can be attributed to defensiveness, with respondents wishing to appear that they watched 'respectable' programmes. W31's response that '(I) Never watch TV, well I watch the *Nine o'clock News*' is typical. Certainly, the popularity of news programmes among our sample is greater than might be supposed from reported audience figures.

Table 7.1 *Non-prompted mentions of television programmes*
(percentages of sample in each place who mention programmes[1])

	News[2]	Soaps	Sport	Comedy	Police	Films	Others	Total
Ramsbottom	27	16	15	8	9	5	21	131
Wilmslow	26	15	15	5	9	5	26	88
Chorlton	10	22	8	13	7	0	(42)	93
Cheadle	22	13	13	6	6	5	36	104
Total	91	67	52	33	32	15	126	416
	(21.9%)	(16.1%)	(12.5%)	(7.9%)	(7.7%)	(3.6%)	(30.3%)	(100)

Notes:
1. All specific programmes mentioned coded as one mention of genre. For example, a list of comedy programmes coded as one comedy mention.
2. Includes all news, documentaries and current affairs programmes. A respondent mentioning news, current affairs and documentary coded as three mentions.

Soap opera was also popular in all four areas, with little direct link between people's stock of cultural capital and the extent to which they watched soaps. Soap operas provide a common vocabulary which people can draw upon in casual conversations in a similar way to sports talk (Erickson 1996). People discussed their relationship to soap opera in both positive and negative ways and it drew the longest and most complex spontaneous narratives regarding television. Respondents often placed their preferences as a simple statement of their taste: 'I like *Coronation Street* – I follow that' (C29); '*Coronation Street*, I always watch that' (C91); 'I do like the soaps, but I'm not avid, but I could pick up just about any of the soaps' (D56); '*Coronation Street*, which I think everybody watches' (D84); 'I am addicted to *Coronation Street* and *Emmerdale*' (W10); 'I am addicted to *Coronation Street*. I hate *EastEnders*. I like *Brookside*. I like those two' (W59); '*EastEnders* and *Coronation Street* – those are the two I would video' (W82); 'Oh yes, I watch *Coronation Street* of course' (R32); 'I like the soaps of course' (R47).

Unlike the news and documentaries, which few people had controversial views about, soap operas divided respondents into fans and critics. Many people were negative: 'I don't like the soaps' (C99); with respect to *Coronation Street*, 'I've never liked it' (C52); 'I refuse to watch *EastEnders*, *Emmerdale Farm* or anything like that, because they're too gloomy. *Coronation Street* I admit I do watch' (C13); 'I don't watch soap operas, I find them trivial and boring' (D74); 'I can't stand *EastEnders* and *Coronation Street*' (W93); 'I can't tolerate serials like *Coronation Street*' (W7); 'like watching paint dry' and 'as soon as I hear that music it's totally repellent to me' (R127). What is interesting here is that respondents do not feel defensive about either liking or disliking soaps: reference to this genre allows people to establish their ordinariness (see Longhurst et al. 2001; Savage et al. 2001). Indeed, only a small group were relatively indifferent: 'it's just habit isn't it' (R114); 'I do watch the soaps but it wouldn't worry me if I didn't, I'm not addicted to them, if I miss then it doesn't bother me' (R12); 'Not regularly no. Occasionally when *Coronation Street*'s on, but not *EastEnders*' (D106); 'I find if I am in here cooking and someone is watching, I will say what is happening' (D66); '*Coronation Street* when I see it, but I'm not addicted to it' (C97); 'I watch *Coronation Street* if it is on' (C55).

Part of this relationship to soaps lay in the way that it was acceptable to watch alongside other members of the household who might be deemed to be more interested in the programmes. While both men and women watched soaps, men often stated that they watched them because their female partner did. For example, 'Most of the soaps, I've got no choice really' (C78); 'Tina likes the soaps' (D25); 'with the wife' (R156). In addition, people talked about their changing viewing as a means of talking about their own tastes: 'I used to watch *Coronation Street*' (C 48); 'Well I'm going off *Coronation Street* a bit but I watch it and *EastEnders* and *Emmerdale*' (D101); 'I used to watch *Coronation Street* avidly, but it's just immoral now, it was the only one I felt was of any interest but it has gone off a lot now' (D70); 'I used to watch *EastEnders* and never miss but I have gone off that now. I click in and out now and then just to see what is happening but I am not addicted to any of them' (W99); 'well most people watch it [*Coronation Street*] well they did, I don't think it's as good as it used to be' (R32). One person watched more: 'I've recently got interested in *Coronation Street*, since it's changed the people it's become more entertaining, plus they're doing a lot more real location shooting, my next door neighbour's house was in it' (D71).

We can see then, that narratives of soap operas at one level confirm the omnivore thesis (since most people talked about them), yet they also allowed people to position themselves by being fans and critics of different soaps. Before we consider this point further, let us note that the third main programme mentioned was sport. It was very common for men spontaneously to volunteer the importance of television sport for them. This was often in the course of a longer list of programmes that respondents preferred, rather than being pulled out for emphasis at greater length, as was the case for soap opera.

Table 7.1 also illustrates some similarities and differences between the areas. While people in Ramsbottom seem more likely to talk about TV than people in the other places, Cheadle, Ramsbottom and Wilmslow are broadly comparable in generic TV tastes; the exception is Chorlton – the area with the most cultural capital. Here there is television taste that can be characterised as 'omnivoric' (Peterson and Kern 1996). Chorltonians are less likely to mention news, documentaries and sport than others and are much more interested in soaps and comedies. Chorltonians are less defensive about their TV viewing. They exhibit less need to emphasise their news and documentary viewing when in conversation with a university professional than others – which might account for the high news and documentary figures elsewhere.

There were very few people who straightforwardly talked about television as an enthusiasm (Abercrombie and Longhurst 1998), or displayed the taste

Table 7.2 *Possession of cable and satellite television*

	Have	Used to have	Do not have	Do not have but would like to	Missing	No.
Ramsbottom	15	4	59	0	22	46
Wilmslow	32	0	34	0	34	44
Chorlton	13	0	49	0	38	47
Cheadle	28	2	28	5	37	43
Total	39	3	77	2	59	180
	(21.7%)	(1.7%)	(42.8%)	(1.1%)	(32.8%)	

of a univore interested in only one type of programme (Peterson and Kern 1996). There were some examples of this, for instance fishing programmes for a keen angler, dog programmes for the pet lover, blues on German satellite channels for the music fan. Edward was an unusual case. He talked at length about the pleasures of TV, noting that 'I enjoy my television such a lot' (C34). Most of those who were more enthusiastic about TV were cable and satellite enthusiasts who, for example, thought that 'normal telly today is absolute crap' (R147). It is well documented that satellite and cable TV have taken on particular niche meanings in the UK (see Brunsdon 1991 and especially Moores 1996, 2000). In contrast to parts of mainland Europe (particularly the low countries) and parts of the USA, Britain was and is, a country where TV is accessed primarily through terrestrial means, with a choice of five channels. At the time of this research the figure for satellite TV take-up was 18%. The position for our sample is given in Table 7.2. One motivation that has been reported for watching satellite TV is that it enables the viewer to move out of a national restricted diet of TV (Moores 2000). However, the dominant pattern revealed by our data was rather different.

Table 7.2 shows that overall 22% of the sample had satellite or cable and 43% did not. 2% had ended a subscription and only 1% made it clear that they would like to have it but were prevented due to the cost. Wilmslow (our most affluent area) with nearly 32% and Cheadle (our least affluent area) with nearly 28% have above average figures for possession of these technologies. Table 7.2 collates the preferences and patterns of viewing for those who had these technologies. The patterns are not surprising, with sport figuring highly as what is watched by those who have cable and satellite. The patterns also give an aspect of a potential explanation for the relatively high take up of these technologies in Wilmslow, with people here being the only ones mentioning golf as the sport watched. Golf continues to have high cultural capital associations in England (though much less so in Scotland) and is infrequently shown on terrestrial TV (with the exception of 'The Open'). Similar narratives would also be relevant for other more 'minority' sports such as tennis. As with terrestrial TV some people emphasise news and documentary (especially the *Discovery* channel) or the appeal of cable/satellite for children. Others display particular enthusiasms such as fishing, and blues music.

One keen Sky viewer (R147) emphasised the importance of sport and football:

Is sport the main thing you watch?

Yes, all the time. I've got Sky, last night I watched football, tonight I'll be watching the football, Friday night City's on, I'll be watching that, and Sunday like I say. So yes, sport's a big thing with me, watching it. I stay up half the night watching cricket.

Was that the motivation for getting Sky?

Yes sport definitely.

Any other things that you watch on Sky or on terrestrial TV?

She watches a lot of the documentary channels, the history channel, the discovery channel and she likes sci-fi, she's a big *Star Trek* fan. So she does get to watch what she wants and I get to watch my sport, it doesn't cause any problems really. I mean I think normal telly today is absolute crap, it really is, yes *EastEnders* and *Coronation Street* she watches, but there's very little else on the normal terrestrial telly, I mean sport is non-existent now on normal telly.

Finally in this vein here is D68:

What about the television do you watch that?

I watch too much especially at night, I do like *Star Trek.*

Are you a bit of a Trekkie then?

I don't like to think so.

So what do you like to watch then, you mentioned Star Trek?

I like medical things; I watch a lot of Discovery Channel.

I was going to say do you have Satellite?

We have cable.

And would you say you watch more cable than ordinary TV?

Yes, we very rarely watch the normal channels.

Those who don't have cable/satellite are often opposed to it. For example, when asked about this topic D106 replied 'oh, no, no', other responses include 'I would not want a dish' (R37), 'I do get fed up with that because

I haven't got Sky TV and I'm not going to pay it just to watch golf, but it does annoy me. It's the same with rugby on Saturday but what can you do?' (W60).

It has become increasingly common to suggest that television can only be adequately understood as a domestic medium (for example, Morley 1986, 2000; Lull 1988, 1990; Silverstone 1994), where it is an essential aspect of domestic interaction (Silva 2000). Television is an integral part of the way that households organise time and space. The overwhelmingly domestic nature of television came through when people discussed television with respect to their partners or children. People would often talk about watching together or how they separate to watch different things. In the latter case it was often the case that women would leave the main TV for their male partners, for example, 'if he's watching sport I go upstairs' (W109) and 'we usually watch *EastEnders*, my husband watches it as well, or if he's away I record it for him, but I'm not really desperate if I miss an episode' (W109), 'she won't generally watch sport, she would rather go out' (D74), 'she buggers off upstairs' (R147). In this respect it is clear that TV is as an aspect of the gendered spatial organisation of the household.

Television is also clearly used in talk about how the day and the week is structured into a pattern (Gauntlett and Hill 1999: 21–51). Thus on the former: C17 talked of 'flopping in front of the telly' at the end of work, TV was 'a part of winding down' (C2), for R145 TV 'is a relaxation from work', W96 would 'crash out and watch the television', R82 will 'slouch on the couch and watch TV'. We found much less talk of how TV structured the week, though several respondents drew attention to the symbolic and organisational role of Friday night television. Thus, for example, 'on a Friday night we invariably do watch TV, have a take-away curry or Chinese and sit and watch, Friday night's good on Channel 4' (R59). In some sections of our sample, especially younger people with younger children this was very common:

Friday nights … sometimes we go swimming on a Friday evening with my sister and her two children, and then we'll come back here and we'll have chips for a treat. They stay around for a bit and eventually they go home and we'll go to bed. Friday night tends to be, if we're not going out, we'll sit in and have a bottle of wine, watch TV or a video, something like that. Friday night is like a big relaxing time (D12):

Yes, it's a sporadic thing. I probably watch a fair amount, very unselective, there's a couple of things that I bother to watch.

Which would be?

It's really light entertainment now, things I can name, I used to watch *Friends* religiously, Friday night Channel 4 stuff, *King of the Hill*, *Father Ted*, things of that sort. They are the sort of things that I would bother to video if I wasn't going to see them. (D103)

Other younger people had a different sort of Friday night routine: 'we watch when we get in from the pub' (D64).

For smaller numbers of our sample other parts of the week had a similar significance. For mainly older viewers Sunday night was mentioned particularly as a key time for relaxation. Some of those with younger families also talked of Saturday evening TV in such a fashion. It was less common for weekdays to be marked out in this way, the main exception being the way that *ER* fans might see their viewing as central to their Wednesday evenings. These patterns obviously connect to the scheduling of TV, but it is important that viewers did not time shift to take account of when they liked to watch. There was a clear interaction between what is available on a particular night and the meaning of that night.

Nearly all respondents talk of TV defensively. Given that they spend a significant part of their lives watching television, the scale of this defensiveness is extraordinary. No other activity that we examined, with the partial exception of shopping at large supermarkets rather than local shops, was discussed with this degree of defensiveness. The following give examples of a denial of TV watching: 'I'm not a great fan of watching telly' (D109), 'we watch a bit, not a lot' and 'just odd things, not very much really' (R138), 'we don't really watch a lot of TV, do you?' (C4), 'I don't say I watch an awful lot but it's generally on' (W3).

Such denial is often contextualised by the perceived seductive or addictive nature of television or by the emphasis that their viewing is planned or selective. Thus, for example, 'That's the trouble really, I switch the television on and I should be going and doing things' (D101), 'I don't like it when I start sitting there and just can't be bothered to move and I start thinking I can't be bothered to switch it off so I just watch all night, that annoys me' (D9), 'we never have it on during the day, but in the evening we watch it, we pick out what we want to watch' (R139), 'We watch TV, but I try not to have it on unless there's something I want to watch because ideally most of the time don't really want it on while the kids are around, sometimes I watch *Coronation Street* while J. is just calming down for bed, but I try not to' (R59), 'we're not addicts' (C17), 'we are quite selective' (C13), 'it doesn't go on automatically' (C38), 'we do watch TV, I have to confess it' (W33), 'unfortunately I do sort of fall in front of the box in the evening but I'm not really interested in television, it's just sort of a way to a means really' (W25), 'we're fairly particular ... And we look at the *Radio Times* and see if you know if there's a *Horizon* programme or a *South Bank Show* [science documentary and arts documentary programmes respectively] or something and it obviously looks good we'll watch it, but it's not a question of it being there' (W2), 'I watch but I am selective, I don't just watch like a zombie' (W58).

Respondents are keen to emphasise their agency in selecting which TV to watch, through careful selection and planning of viewing and through placing boundaries around acceptable viewing (see also Gauntlett and Hill 1999). One case exhibits such strategies in quite an extreme way: 'Well

I can't say yes or no, you see it's not in our sitting room, so that if you want to look at it you've got to be slightly uncomfortable … and it's absolutely deliberate' (W67). In some cases children figure in the narratives of protection from TV, or defensiveness around it. Comments such as the following are illustrative: 'it takes too much time up, especially for my teenage daughter' (W98), 'I end up watching a lot of children's videos which is nice, although again I don't let her watch a lot of TV' (R135).

TV is therefore an ordinary culture (see also Morley 2000: 109 in discussion of Scannell 1996), which leads to defensiveness as people protect their ordinariness. Those people (a significant number, if still a minority) who were not defensive also tended to emphasise their agency through their deliberate TV choices. With respect to particular forms of TV: 'I like watching the TV. I like watching films a lot. I like watching videos' (D59), 'I do like *Star Trek*' (D68), 'I love that animal programme, *Animal Rescue*' (W59), 'Well I'm mad on watching sport on television I'm afraid. I love sport of all kinds except snooker and I watch everything really' (W73), 'I love the things about real people' (C97), 'I like a good film' (R12). As mentioned above some people often talked about cultist or fan type programmes as clear favourites. For the relatively few people who did this, *Star Trek* featured quite heavily (on *Star Trek* fandom see, for example: Bacon-Smith 1992; Jenkins 1992; Penley 1992; Tulloch and Jenkins 1995): 'we're big *Star Trek* fans, we tape all the *Star Trek* stuff and watch that in the evening, we have the video set up' (R138) and 'I like a lot of the technology. I like watching old episodes because you see a lot of stuff in old episodes, which is actually now in place. There was lasers and stuff and the idea of travelling faster than light and the escapism' (D20). In addition, there were some people (most often in Chorlton) who exhibited a degree of reflexivity in their defensive narratives of TV watching. Here, the culturally confident are able to own up to watching 'rubbish' or 'crap' without seeing it as staining their character. For example, 'All the crappy things really … all the chat show things that are so bad they're good, all those kind of things, that's it and just the news, I like to watch the news' (R114), 'any old rubbish when I need a break' (D52), 'but I do tend to watch quite a bit of crap TV' (D87).

In general, in line with other studies, people do not invest greatly of themselves in television as a medium, with the exception of a few enthusiasts who tend to subscribe to cable and satellite. We have the paradox that television, which promotes omnivorous tastes, is regarded with suspicion by respondents who are reluctant to identify closely with it. Whereas people generally talk keenly about how they moved to their place of residence, this kind of talk is largely absent from TV narratives where respondents fear that they will be positioned as lacking agency. The TV is hence part of the everyday, but it is also something to be resisted. This is a somewhat different pattern to that detected by Silverstone (1994) who sees much more popular immersion and involvement in television. Watching is both normal yet something not quite acceptable for most people. The role of TV in people's sense of who they are is often negative in general terms. However, as we have seen TV is significant in the playing out of home, family and relationship identities, in the sense that it works in relation to gender and households and is overwhelmingly talked of in such terms. Thus, very few people talked of TV in public places such as pubs or clubs. TV is a part of everyday family and household life.

One way that individuals emphasise their agency in watching television relies on narratives which allow them to draw together individual, family, place and class belonging through invoking particular programmes. Soap opera figures especially strongly here. W10 stated that 'I am addicted to *Coronation Street* and *Emmerdale* because we were married in that church. *Coronation Street* started the evening before we were married, but I like *Morse* and that kind of thing'. These narratives are often articulated through a concern with 'northernness', in which the north is a means of linking biography with the media. Here *Coronation Street* played a very important role. It evoked more comments than any other programme, and a contrast was often drawn between *Coronation Street* (which is set in Wetherfield, a fictionalised Salford in Greater Manchester and *EastEnders*, a fictional community in London's east end): so D63 while liking the former, was explicit in saying 'I don't like *EastEnders*'. Or W69 compared many soaps:

You like television, is it a whole variety of things you like?

A huge variety, sport, we've got Sky Sport, we don't have Sky Films or anything like that, much to the children's upset, we've got Sky Sport, we watch sport, we watch the soaps.

Do you have a favourite soap?

Well I quite like *Coronation Street*, I mean I watch it and talk about it and have a laugh about it to other people, I think *Brookside* is much more realistic, but I have got quite annoyed with *Brookside* and phoned and written when they do these things in the public interest and I watch *EastEnders* even though I think it is really quite miserable, I won't watch the others, I mean if *Neighbours* is on after we watch the 1.00 news, or watched Emma's show and we were sitting there I'd probably keep it on, and I would never really stay in and my husband doesn't really know how to work the video so if we miss *Coronation Street*, we miss it.

R54 linked together a number of different themes:

I watch a bit of telly. I like Corry. A lot of people who say they never watch Corry watch it. I like documentaries.

So you watch Coronation Street *most nights?*

That's the only soap I'd watch, I can't stand any of the others. When I want to put myself in a bad mood I'll watch *EastEnders*! I used to watch *Brookside* when the guy from Flying Pickets were on it, it were quite funny in them days, but now that's gone all morose.

So what is it about Coronation *Street that appeals?*

Well I think it's on the turn as well. It was quite amusing and there was some very good acting in it, some of it was quite true to life, but now it's getting over the top and it's not true to life, they haven't researched it like they should. Like the other week when Ken Barlow fell through that ceiling of the bedroom, and this guy's supposed to have lost his betting slip next door, he didn't need to go through all that performance to retrieve his old betting slip, because what you do if you lose your betting slip you just write another one out, because you know how you write, your writing style is your particular thing, you write it out, you put the stake on, the date and the time and you give it in and they'll pay you. Anybody who knew would know that was a load of rubbish. And this guy going and spoiling his wedding, a middle-aged bloke wouldn't resort to that sort of thing, he might have give her one or something like that, but he wouldn't have done that. I find it's going a lot worse.

Other comments on this issue were brief and straightforward. For example: R18 liked *Emmerdale* 'because it's north Yorkshire'. R33 liked *Coronation Street* 'because it's northern and it's down to earth, I like the characterisations, I think they're quite funny'. Other examples include:

I usually watch the soaps. *Coronation Street*, because when we lived in the south we didn't have a television at first we rented this cottage when we moved house and it had a television and for the first time I saw *Coronation Street* and that for some reason that reminded me of the north so I have watched it ever since. It isn't really anything like the north.

What about EastEnders?

I started watching that because these southern friends watched it and out of curiosity and I watched. (W21)

For W59:

Do you watch much TV?

I watch too much. I am annoyed with myself. It is only because I am tired and I am slumping. I try very hard to really choose carefully. I hate watching rubbish just for the sake of it.

So you look in the paper and see what is on. What kind of things do you watch?

I am addicted to *Coronation Street.* I hate *EastEnders.* I like *Brookside*, I like those two. I love that animal programme, *Animal Rescue.*

Why do you like Coronation Street? *What is the appeal?*

Well it has always been very amusing; there are some very funny people in it. Also one or two of the people in it live round here so you see them. I suppose also because it is northern.

Therefore, while at one level people talked of soap operas in terms of entertainment, escapism and with respect to reality, it was also used to mobilise narratives of belonging. By locating soap operas through specific reference to their own biography, it becomes more acceptable to own up to liking it, since its generally addictive character is downplayed in favour of a more individualised one. This therefore means that people do not simply evoke straightforward nostalgia for the north or its supposed working-class community in their accounts. Rather, it enables the construction of aspects of the self that locate the individual biographically, culturally, spatially and socially. Perhaps the most telling comment in this respect is that it 'reminded me of the north ... It isn't really anything like the north'. (R33) This qualification is similar to the way people could claim that they belonged to places without being part of the 'community'.

These matters come further into focus when soaps are used in wider discussions of culture and social change. Thus for example R82 uses the example of a 'problem' family, which had just, at this point moved into the fictional soap, *Coronation Street* to talk of change in the local area (see also Gillespie 1995 for a discussion of the role of *Neighbours* in this respect):

And do you think it's the sort of place that's going up, going down, staying about the same?

We have quite strong views on this, because our neighbours next door, he's actually a policeman and his wife is a nurse, we get on quite well, the whole area's actually quite nice, lots of nice people, but we've just had some new people move in who we've nicknamed the Battersbys, which probably indicates our feelings. But other than that isolated example I think it's about the same. It's a reasonable area.

Further, here is R127, who fed TV into a discussion of the class-based nature of consumption:

A perfect for instance to me is, it's like a reflex thing, you can have somebody winning a million pounds in Liverpool who's always lived in one of these terraced houses, and they might be very nice people, don't get me wrong, but it's conditioned, and that million pounds, in five years time, the odds of them having any of that million pounds left is very little. They will have blown it; they might have one or two things they've purchased with it, the fantastic telly that's worth seventeen grand. Whereas if someone wins a million pounds from a slightly more middle-class family, they're more likely to say, well alright then we'll have a few good holidays and we'll invest it, and I don't have to work again.

How, then, do we understand the role of the TV in these narratives of belonging? We have seen that while it does generate omnivorous references, these lead to anxiety and defensiveness on the part of viewers who are concerned to present themselves as individuals able to pick and choose what they watch. Part of this emphasis on agency involves the generation of media narratives which allow people to show how particular programmes can be mobilised into their own personal account. People thus deploy media narratives to buttress their own elective belonging. As Morley has pointed out: 'home may not be such a singular physical entity fixed in a particular place, but rather a mobile, symbolic habitat, a performative way of life and of doing things in which one makes one's home while in movement' (2000: 47).

7.3 Music: ordinary and omnivoric

Diversified musical tastes have been seen as a key aspect of claims that an omnivoric culture is developing among the middle classes (see, for example, Peterson and Kern 1996). It has been argued that taste in music among the middle classes is widening and this increased pluralism is representative of a general widening of taste, which itself may be leading to new modes of distinction. In addition, music is considered in the context of Goffman's attention to the performance of everyday life (see DeNora 2000, see also, Bull, 2000)

As is shown by Table 7.3, listening to music is a popular activity for our sample. It is less popular than television or radio but over 80% of people listen to music overall. There is some variation in this figure, with Chorltonions being the most engaged and the Cheadle residents least. Unlike television viewing it was possible to identify four distinctive taste groupings: the 'traditional classicists', the 'fans', the 'consumerists' and the 'omnivores'. The former is most common in Wilmslow and consists of those people who express a clear preference for classical music, which they often characterise as 'light classical'. These are often those who listen to Classic FM on the radio. They may attend live classical concerts, but are just as likely to attend musicals. 'Fans' express a clear preference for one genre or performer of music. This is a comparatively small group, who, for example, like the blues, 1970s progressive rock, or who follow a particular group such as The Fall. However, most people fall into neither of these categories, but rather express an 'omnivoric' refrain, within which there are two broad groupings: the consumerists and the omnivores.

It is common for people to begin a discussion of their musical taste with a statement along the lines of 'I like all sorts of things' or 'I have a wide taste in music'. When this statement is qualified, it sometimes reveals a relatively narrow set of tastes, sometimes characterised by respondents themselves as 'easy listening', covering a broad range of popular performers. These people are best classed as consumers (see Abercrombie and Longhurst 1998), where music is a backdrop to everyday life. The other group are more clearly omnivorous, and often discuss their wide musical tastes at some length and most commonly in generic (rather than performers) terms. The consumers omnivoric refrain is most common in Chorlton (66% of those who listen to music), weaker but still significant in Cheadle and Ramsbottom

Table 7.3 *Type of reference to music by respondents (percentages)*

	Omnivoric Refrain	Social context	Car	Family children	Live	Life cycle	Professional interest	Listen	Sample
Cheadle	43[1]	33	33	33	24	12	3	81[2]	41
Chorlton	65	14	2	23	52	5	14	94	47
Ramsbottom	41	15	18	26	33	10	0	89	44
Wilmslow	24	12	0	21	56	12	0	83	41
Total	67	27	19	38	63	14	7	150	173
	(44.7%)	(18%)	(12.7%)	(25.3%)	(42%)	(9.3%)	(4.6%)	(86.7%)	

Notes:
1. Percentage of those who listen.
2. Percentage of sample.
3. Columns add to more than 100% since respondents can identify more than one type.

and weakest in Wilmslow. Moreover, the 'true' omnivores are most common in Chorlton.

This discussion of taste relates to patterns of attendance at live musical events. As we would expect, live attendance is most frequent among the 'light classicists' and 'fans', and therefore less popular among Cheadle and Ramsbottom residents, but a majority pastime for those in Wilmslow and Chorlton. Again, there is great variation here from those who attend a country and western club on holiday to those with tickets for a classical season. However, what is perhaps most significant is that live performance is commonly discussed in connection to space and place, especially, as we saw in Chapter 5, with respect to use of Manchester city centre. Live music was nearly always linked in respondents' narratives to a particular venue, such as The Apollo or the Band on the Wall. As we have argued, live cultural performances continue to be importantly anchored in place.

As Table 7.3 shows, there is some variation in the extent to which respondents in different areas discussed these issues. There is a similar pattern to radio listening, where music is described in relation to the home, doing tasks, at times of the day, with respect to children and partners sharing the same living space and within the car (where it is often difficult to disentangle music listening from radio consumption). Respondents also considered music in relation to their stage of life, or place in the life cycle, saying things that suggested that their taste had been formed at a particular time and so on.

Music can also be significant in different ways: domestically and in its centrality as an activity for many people (there is a significant number of respondents who play instruments and a number of professional musicians live in Chorlton). While as we have seen, many people articulate a clear set of musical tastes, this is more often contextualised by what we have called an omnivoric refrain. Thus, it seems, especially in Chorlton respondents reinforce their imagined cosmopolitanism by drawing attention to their wide and differentiated tastes in music. They both consume lots of it (by contrast with the widespread denial of TV watching) but also listen widely.

There is significant confirmation here of aspects of the omnivore thesis, which seems particularly suited to discussion of musical taste (see, for example, Bryson 1996). Credibility is gained, especially for the younger groupings in Chorlton, by the display of their particular mode of cosmopolitan taste. The badge of omnivorous musical taste reinforces cosmopolitan distinction (see also Carrabine and Longhurst 1999). While this exists everywhere, it is weakest in Wilmslow, where only a quarter of those who state that they listen to music contextualise this with an omnivoric type of statement. The majorities in the other areas are less concerned with this sort of strategy. In particular the taste of that significant group in Wilmslow who enjoy the light classical seems to suggest a rather unreflective consideration of this mode of taste, it is something assumed and commonplace. The consumerist taste is similar, it seems to assume a set of tastes as part of the everyday, rather than produce a set of juxtapositions as a mode of distinction. Despite the prevalence of the omnivoric refrain in these places, there is an everyday ordinariness to musical taste; it is lived in the habitus in relatively unreflexive and unreflective way. The discussions of the topic tend to be brief and relatively 'commonsensical' here. Chorlton is different. Music, it can be suggested, is very important here as part of the performance of an omnivoric, cosmopolitan self.

7.4 Respectable reading

Reading is almost as ubiquitous as television and radio. Unlike TV, respondents are virtually never defensive about reading, especially books, since they are seen as a culturally respectable form of cultural pursuit. Even magazine reading is not discussed in any defensive sense. The broad differences between the areas are set out in Table 7.4

Apart from Cheadle residents, the majority in each area read some kind of newspaper, if not every day. A significant part of the pleasure of the newspaper is doing the crossword. Magazine and book readership is also common. There is clearly a difference in the amount of reading done for work purposes with Chorltonians doing far more of this. Despite these differences between the areas, some broad general themes emerge. As with radio, reading is, for some people, part of the fabric of everyday life. People sometimes include reading when asked to describe what happens at the weekend or during a day. People go to bed with a book or other reading material, even if they are often too tired to read very much. Reading may be done while watching the TV, or while the TV is on. This is especially the case with newspapers and magazines.

Reading of books (and to a lesser extent magazines and newspapers) is significantly affected by the other demands of everyday life. This is often considered in relation to the tiredness produced by work on the pressures of having young children. This lack of time would nearly always be expressed in terms of regret. The overwhelming sense was that those people affected

Table 7.4 Reading practices

	Local paper[1]	Rout	Area/shop	Holiday	Paper	Magazine	Book	Pass on/family	Enthus	Cross	Work	Sample	Total
Cheadle	15	24	22	10	42	34	42	10	37	5	2	41[2]	43
Chorlton	15	21	28	13	60	55	60	2	36	17	23	47	47
Ramsbottom	21	19	9	19	57	43	55	0	32	9	6	47	47
												100%	
Wilmslow	16	24	9	11	56	51	44	2	40	7	11	45	46
Total	30	40	30	24	97	83	97	6	65	17	20	180	183
	16.7%	22.2%	16.7%	13.3%	53.9%	46.1%	53.9%	3.3%	36.1%	9.4%	11.1%	98.4%	

Notes:
1. Percentage of sample
2. Percentage of total

in this way would like to read more. This is backed up by another theme, where people discussed reading on holiday. An important part of the pleasure of the annual holiday is that allows the space and time to read that is not available at other times of the year. This is a significant sidelight on the debate about the pleasure of holiday and travel. While seeing and experiencing new things may be an important aspect of this, another aspect is the desire to engage in the ordinary pleasures of reading, so that the holiday allows the experience of what might be termed the 'ideal ordinary'.

Reading is connected to other aspects of the fabric of local and everyday living. Newsagents are emblematic of an area and represent aspects of what may be good about an area – the papershop is handy – or used to point out the disadvantages of another area – you have to drive to the papershop. Local bookshops are often welcomed as part of the description of the significance of particular local amenities. As we saw in Chapter 5, a trip to the bigger bookshops in Manchester is part of the exceptional pleasures of the city. As with cinema, the absence of these sorts of place could figure as part of a narrative of local decline. Likewise, as with Wilson and Kelling's (1982) 'broken windows' thesis, old newspapers lying around can be seen as a symbol of a declining area, or an area to be differentiated from the current place of residence. This can even extend to the way in which the reduction in the title available in the local library is discussed as part of a local decline, or the vagaries of differential local government funding of libraries (C136). Newspapers sticking out of doors are sometimes connected to crime (C102). Local newspapers continue to have resonance in a number of ways, as both a site of local information and as a way of narrating how, for example, a particularly good or new job was found.

On a different tack, in Cheadle reading is part of the ebb and flow of family and friendship. Magazine subscriptions are sometimes bought as presents by family members and can thus be seen as part of the reciprocation and reinforcement of family bonds. Further, magazines are passed on, or passed from others. Networks of this kind are seriously under considered in much media sociology (on the family reciprocation and objects in the home, see Money 2003). More often commented on is the male readership of women's magazines (Hermes 1995). Several men offered comment on how they read the women's magazines that are part of the household. Significantly, this never works the opposite way round. Women do not read men's magazines, or at least they did not talk in this way.

Magazines and books connect to enthusiasms in fairly obvious ways. It is common to reinforce an enthusiasm or hobby by reading material – most commonly magazines, though this is the case with books as well. There are clear patterns in this respect where the gardener will read books and magazines as well as watching TV programmes on this topic. In this respect, enthusiasm needs to be considered across a variety of media, which interconnect in ways that are relatively neglected. Even less commented on is the way in which reading substitutes for the actual day-to-day engagement in an enthusiasm. Magazines and books can be considered therefore to fuel the imagination for particular activities (Abercrombie and Longhurst 1998). They can also be a way of preparing for engagement in something, such as a 'craft' enthusiasm, or listening to a new or unfamiliar type of music. Reading can in itself be described as an enthusiasm, for a significant group of people it is something that they are very keen on and as we have pointed out, they would like to spend more time on it.

7.5 Globalisation and cultural capital

We have shown how people's complex use of the media offers cautious support for the omnivore thesis. Whatever their cultural capital, people are wide ranging in both television and musical taste. Despite this, their degree of defensiveness, especially regarding television watching, indicates a fear that their ordinariness may be revealed as being 'common', leading to strategies to re-embed media use through local and biographical references. We have also shown that there are complex ways in which our respondents draw subtle distinctions in the way they use cultural genres and seek to emphasise their agency in developing narratives of media use. We conclude this chapter by considering in more detail how these patterns of use are related to global references and the organisation of cultural capital.

We examined how people mentioned English and non-English referents in the visual arts, music, cinema, and television, field (see Table 7.5). Any named programme, book, and film is coded in terms of its nation of origin[1]. Table 7.5 shows that fully 70% of all cultural references are to English sources. Of the remainder, the vast majority, 75%, are to references from the United States. To put these stark figures another way, a mere 7.5% of references are to cultural products which come from outside England or the USA. Of this very small number, about half (3% of the total) are to European sources, and another half (3%) to Australian or Canadian ones. Only 1% of references are to other parts of the world, including all of Asia, Latin America, and Africa.

In general, these cultural tastes mark out our sample as part of a white, English speaking diaspora with a geographically limited range of points of cultural exposure. If this is evidence of a global culture, it is one highly skewed to the Anglophone nations of the former British empire. There was very little engagement with non-English language cultural forms, with only one reference to a writer who was read in translation (Kafka). Only 12 respondents (7%) mentioned any interest or proficiency in non-English language reading, and of these, two did not speak English as a first language. Outside Chorlton where there was a significant minority of non-English speakers (15% of respondents), very few used other languages. It is therefore not coincidental that the main European referents were in the area of music, or less commonly the visual arts. It was also in the area of music that black cultural forms had some popularity, with there being considerable enthusiasm for jazz and soul. Nat King Cole was easily the most popular

173

Table 7.5 *Geography of cultural referents (numerical counts and specified percentages)*

	Cheadle	Chorlton	Ramsbottom	Wilmslow	All
American cinema	15	16	14	5	50
American TV	4	27	9	3	43
American music	25	33	13	6	77
American literature	1	11	6	1	18
American other	3	2	3		8
Australian	6	5	5	1	17
Canadian	2	3			5
European	10	13	4	4	31
Other	2	4	1	5	12
All English	144	173	136	151	604
% English	69	60	71	86	70
% US of all global references	71	78	82	60	75
All	210	287	191	176	864

black artist for our respondents. With the exception of a handful of references to reggae and world music there were no references to cultural forms deriving, however indirectly, from Africa, Asia, or South America.

Music and cinema are the most 'mobile' of cultural genres, with the fewest proportion of national references, and not coincidentally both play important roles in the definition of popular culture itself. In both cases, American influences were very strong, They were much weaker for television viewing, where Scannell's (1996) argument that television performs national community is amply born out by the dominance of national reference. Silverstone's (1997) emphasis that television allows the performance of 'domestic suburbia' would appear to have considerable resonance. American programmes only had appeal in a few niche areas, where they seemed to have established themselves as 'quirky'. The most important here was *Star Trek*, which had an aura of its own, and which had cult status among a handful of respondents. The same was true to a lesser extent of other American programmes, such as the *X Files, ER* and *Friends*.

Let us consider more specifically how the spatial reach of cultural references is related to economic, social and cultural capital. Firstly, if we compare the references of respondents in four different areas it is clear that Wilmslow respondents are systematically less likely to mention any non-English sources. Only 14% of its cultural references were to outside England (compared to 29% in Chorlton, which reported the highest). Even for the cinema, nearly three quarters of references were to English cinema (mainly through references to *The Full Monty* or *The English Patient*), whereas in every other area, Hollywood held sway (with *Titanic* being the referred to most frequently), see Table 7.3A on p. 180. This finding is interesting in view of the common assumption, evident in the work of Bauman (2000) and

Castells (1996a) that it is the corporate elite who are most global in orientation. Although Wilmslow respondents often worked in the global corporate sector and reported considerable overseas contact on a personal level, at the level of their cultural taste they were the most nationally focused. Economic capital appears related to a strongly nationalist frame of cultural reference.

Secondly, references to English cultural sources were not usually used as means of establishing distinction. Rather, in line with Rose's (2001) account, they were used to establish common cultural referents which were known to be widely shared, a means of emphasising belonging to an 'imagined national community' (Anderson 1983). Thus the two most widely cited cultural references, *Coronation Street* and *EastEnders*, were popular in all four areas, even though there were some differences in how they were discussed. References to popular sources such as these were often linked by the same respondents to references to more 'high brow' national references such as the literature of Jane Austen (interestingly, the most popular novelist among our sample, in part due to the recent serialisation of *Pride and Prejudice* on TV), or Charles Dickens. This kind of national cultural taste which appear to bridge high and low was especially evident in Wilmslow. W68, an elderly woman married to a former scientist, first appeared to exemplify a veneration for high culture. She spoke of her fondness for the Royal Shakespeare Company at Stratford, and she had also been to Manchester's main venues for high culture: the Royal Exchange Theatre and the Bridgewater Hall (home of the Halle orchestra). But then she went on to note that:

> Most days we have a cup of tea at half past four and watch *Countdown*, so we watch *Countdown* and there's a children's news programme that we watch afterwards, it seems a bit silly but it's quite interesting and one or two programmes: *Question of Sport* we watch; *University Challenge*. Actually, my daughter was on *University Challenge* a long, long time ago when she was at Cambridge, but something like that, and I quite like an opera.

She had also been to see the *Full Monty* and *Mrs Brown* at the cinema. Unusually, her entire cultural repertoire was restricted to English references, but these spanned the range from high to low. A similar pattern is evident for W33, a 51-year-old pharmacist. She was a devotee of opera and classical music, regularly attending the Bridgewater Hall and she had recently read *Pride and Prejudice*. However, she also reported watching *Brookside* and *Heartbeat* and spoke especially fondly of the cookery programme, *Two Fat Ladies*. Again, like Susan, she made no references to any non-English cultural referent, except disparagingly to Spielberg's film *Schindler's List* which her husband had videoed but she thought was 'too long'.

It should not be thought that it was only the affluent Wilmslow group who were able to extend their taste downwards by reference to a national canon. The same kinds of references can also be found in Cheadle, the least affluent of our four areas, showing how many of those, without significant amounts of economic and cultural capital, were nonetheless able to refer to English classics.

Cheryl (C51) was an enthusiast for the popular TV programmes *Coronation Street*, *Emmerdale Farm*, and *Soldier Soldier*, she also said:

I like *Morse*, that's a good series. I like *Soldier Soldier*, *Sharpe*, period dramas I like, I liked some of Jane Austen, things like that. I've read quite a lot of the classics, Charles Dickens I've read, I've read *Pride and Prejudice*.

Of course, we do not mean to argue that there is a homogeneous national culture and that Cheadle and Wilmslow respondents were similar in their cultural taste. Differences in the ways that people used and talked about various national references could easily be found. Rather, our point is that people did not use references to national cultural sources to make any obvious claims to class distinction, but used them to lay claim on membership of a shared (white English) national community.

Thirdly, white popular (or 'low') culture in England has been strongly inflected with American references. Cheadle, the area where respondents had least economic or cultural capital, showed the greatest prediliction for American cinema and music (though not television or literature), and Ramsbottom was not far behind. Generally, across all four areas, American cultural referents were utterly distinctive compared to those from any other nation. Respondents referred to a particular cultural genre or artist from most countries as a sign that the respondent wanted to announce (in a coded way) their ability to appreciate a 'difficult' cultural form. Certainly, liking a cultural object from a non-English speaking nation was usually as a clear indication that respondents wanted to emphasise their 'taste'. However, this was not true for American referents. Respondents felt at home in American culture (though of course what they are appropriating is a particularly (northern) English reading of aspects of American culture (see, for example, Ang 1995 on the appropriation of *Dallas*)). Respondents often had a sense of a wider cultural field within American culture in which different genres jostle for position and popularity. Thus Jane's (W91) current social life saw her live out American idioms. She endorsed an 'Easy Rider' lifestyle, had just celebrated her 50th birthday with a motorbiking holiday in the American west (unfortunately she was too small to be able to ride a Harley Davidson), liked the Eagles and Eric Clapton, and watched Hollywood films. Her husband was also an Americo-phile and had just returned from line dancing at a special 4 July event. She liked rock and not Country and Western music (although her husband did, a fact which had led to evident dissent within the household). Although extreme, this was not unusual: respondents could position themselves with respect to various genres of American cultural forms, so allowing them to sustain localised claims to status and position through their references to American icons and images.

This leads to the fourth point: this sense of the imbrication of Americanism in English mass culture meant that one of the ways that people sought to establish cultural distinctions in their taste was by contrasting American culture with European culture, a point strikingly indicated by Dave.

Dave: Europhilia and antipathy to American culture

Dave (R127), an export manager from Ramsbottom made a clear link between his opposition to Americanism, his antipathy to consumerism, and his own cultivated taste.

> I would not walk round an Arndale whether it be the new one being built in Trafford Park, that will never see my car in the car park, I'd much prefer to go to somewhere like Chester and look at the shops in the high street.

Why is that, because you like the high street?

> I prefer the high street definitely. I'm not into anything that the Yanks do we should follow kind of thing. It's the same thing in business, all the courses and things, they all start in America, 90% do anyway. Why can't we align courses to our business? We're British, a bit different, I'm not saying we're better, but we're different.

Dave's antipathy to Americanism was intrinsically related to his pro-Europeanism and his interest in high culture.

> I travel extensively through Europe so I'm looking a bit further afield. I paid for my wife and daughter to go to a family wedding in the States but I wouldn't go, the States doesn't interest me, I can't be doing with it, so I stayed here, I had the week off as well, I got my own things out, read my books, opened my wine, a game of golf.

When asked how he became interested in art he replied:

> I think just the love of art. I could spend hours walking round an art gallery. If I'm in Paris and I've got half a day to kill, I'll invariably go to an art gallery. I've seen a lot of the paintings, especially Renoir, but I could go and sit at one of these paintings for an hour. I'm not one of these people that looks at an object and says, what do you see, I can't be doing with that. I like art.

Interestingly, Dave was not a university graduate and his hankering for Europe might be seen as a strategy to try to announce a cultural capital which he actually felt he might not otherwise have.

A few other respondents articulated a sense of hostility to American culture as commercial and championed the values of other national cultures. Susan (D11) took this antipathy to mass American culture to justify her championing of Manchester's art cinema, the Cornerhouse, where she liked the 'variety of films and foreign films, otherwise you just get the American epics, you don't get anything else'. Another respondent positioned British alongside European cinema:

> I suppose together we're quite interested in the recent resurgence of British cinema, although it's a bit patchy. I'm not saying we don't particularly like Hollywood films, there's the odd good one now and again, and there's a few reasonably entertaining ones. I'm quite interested in some of the foreign films, particularly Spanish ones. (D71)

Similarly a retired hospital consultant in Wilmslow who was actively learning German at the Goethe Institute and had been an active member of the Anglo-German medical society also articulated a clear endorsement of high culture (W67). This having been said, Table 7.5 shows that the appeal of European cultural references was relatively weak, and indeed, few of our sample seemed concerned to 'claim' high culture in this Europhilic way.

This leads on to a fifth point which is that there is evidence of a reflexive redefinition of high culture away from European culture towards 'offbeat' American forms. This is especially true in Chorlton which has a wider range of US references for TV watching and literature than any other area. Chorltonians, those with the highest stocks of cultural capital, are the most American centred, with respondents reporting 82% of their non-English references to US sources, compared to 75% overall. The kinds of cultural capital displayed by Chorlton respondents is rather different from what might be seen as 'standard high culture'. The culturally privileged in Chorlton showed a predeliction for American sources, but these tended to be relatively off beat – the feminist crime writing of Sarah Paretsky, the black feminist fiction of Toni Morrison and the writing of J.D. Salinger and Richard Ford. They liked the distinctive kind of Channel 4 American programmes such as ER, *Friends* or *Cheers*. Indeed, it is especially American television that appears attractive.

Our point is that the embrace of American culture allows respondents to seem to have the best of all worlds. They can keep a certain distance from stuffy, middle-brow English culture, they can appear to be open to popular culture through their embrace of American culture, but at the same time by championing only certain elements of it, show a kind of reflexive taste. In short it allows a kind of positioning in which you can appear to be culturally distinctive without being snobbish. D64 tells an instructive tale here:

> Yes, I've got a real passion for cheesy American films like *My Best Friend's Wedding* with Julia Roberts I saw that last week and I really go in (video shop) and think it's really great because Chorlton's so cosmopolitan they do actually have quite a good selection of older movies in Blockbuster they have all the old black and white originals and I go and think I should have an attempt to broaden my horizons but then I end up going for the latest release. (D64)

Although Jenny was attracted to the cosmopolitan range of videos being available, she ultimately ended up with American films.

Conclusion

There is no doubt that the media allows extensive communication at a distance, and that our respondents draw on a remarkable range of references in their narratives of media use. Compared to people's concerns with their choice of residence, their schooling, and the kinds of places which they aspired to, there is no doubt that media use allows significantly more spatial and social diversity for our audiences. In some respects, we have shown that the media do allow the weakening of cultural boundaries away from any kind of rigid distinction between high and low culture. We have emphasised the way that it permits the elaboration of an ordinary culture which has widely shared cultural referents in all four places. We have especially emphasised the significance of music as permitting a kind of omnivoric cultural repetoire. Appadurai's concept of the mediascape allows a powerful way of indicating how media use allows the cultural imaginary to have extensive spatial reach. Yet, despite this, there are clearly specific patterns of use which indicate that media use is incorporated into narratives of elective belonging.

We have shown how the media need to be understood in relation to the other dimensions of daily life, and connect to the meaning of place and imagination in crucial ways. The imagined cosmopolitanism of Chorltonians is displayed as much in their media consumption as it is in the way that they narrate their liking for Chorlton and its comparison to other places. Family life is played out in relation to television and cinema as much as it is with connection to schooling and membership of the PTA. We have particularly argued that more subtle ways of establishing distinction are also in evidence, in large part as people draw imaginary links between cultural referents, so that their idea of the ordinary has a latent geography. Four points stand out by way of conclusion to this chapter.

Firstly, although television use is generally identified as a backdrop to everyday lives, and respondents rarely see it as allowing them to pursue particular enthusiasms or interests, people are defensive in talking about their TV use, emphasising the gap between themselves as individual agents and their viewing. Those who were enthusiasts, especially for sport, could often present this as the result of their individual choice to subscribe to satellite or cable TV. In short, respondents did not conflate their everyday lives with their television viewing. TV was appropriated back to local narratives of identity and belonging, with many people's most extensive comments being about how media use was related to their relational sense of place.

Secondly, the more that a particular practice is spatially fixed, the more likely it is to be concerned with elaborating social distinction. Music is distinctive because people listened to it at live events as well as through transmissions and recordings. It is instructive that here it was possible to differentiate four types of musical taste (classical, enthusiastic, consumerist and omnivoric) in ways that were not possible for television taste which had no developed 'live' aspect. Similarly reading (as well as radio, on which see Longhurst et al. 2001), the most spatially mobile of cultural forms since books can be read in any number of spatial settings, are subject to even less concerns over distinction than television. Rather, reading is surrounded by fantasies of desire in ways not found for the other media.

Thirdly, we can see how media use is structured by a powerful spatial axis that can be associated with the power of cultural capital. We can see our respondents being pulled between European high culture – difficult and esoteric – and American popular culture – accessible and fun. Cultural referents from these two continents define the meaning of high and low culture, entailing that national culture is positioned – often uncomfortably – between them, with the result that it does not sustain strong divisions between high and low. Few proclaimed the values of high culture, since to do this would imply you were a snob who revelled in difficult art forms. Placing cultural references in a global frame does not eradicate the power of cultural capital but places its effects on a wider spatial stage.

This leads on to our final point, which is that there is evidence that new kinds of cultural distinction are emerging, formed through a concern to re-appropriate American culture. By championing more unorthodox or cultish aspects of American culture, one can claim expertise and personal taste without appearing to be a snob. We see the appeal of 'serious' American culture as marking out the cosmopolitanism of Chorlton's young professional middle class. Despite the potential of the media to make global connections, they have actually led to the hegemony of Anglo-American cultural references. We turn to consider this point more fully in the next chapter in examining respondents's global awareness.

Note

1 For the purposes of this exercise, Scotland, Wales and Northern Ireland were regarded as other European nations. We coded according to the nationality of the author, musician, or producer/production company.

Table 7.3A: *Number of English references for particular cultural forms, and their % of the Anglo-American total*

	Cheadle	Chorlton	Ramsbottom	Wilmslow	All English
Cinema	4 21%	9 36%	5 26%	13 72%	15
TV	88 96	82 69%	87 91%	80 96%	22
Music	20 44%	37 53%	25 66%	36 86%	39
Lierature	26 96%	30 73%	7 53%	14 93%	13

8

Cosmopolitanism, Diaspora and Global Reflexivity

Over the past decade interest in cosmopolitanism has mushroomed across the social sciences and humanities (see for example Cheah and Robbins 1998; Vertovec and Cohen 2003; *Theory, Culture and Society* 2000; *Public Culture* 2000). In the hands of writers such as David Held (1995), Ulf Hannerz (1996), Ulrich Beck (2002), Bryan Turner (2002), Turner and Rojek (2001) and John Urry (2000), cosmopolitanism is seen as intrinsically related to globalisation and holds out the promise of 'an orientation, a willingness to engage with the other' (Hannerz 1996: 103). It has been seen as an emergent cultural form offering the potential for a new kind of tolerance based upon pluralism, dialogue and a recognition of difference. We currently, however, lack an elaborated sociology of cosmopolitanism. As Tomlinson (2003: 240) remarks, '(c)osmopolitanism is still largely a speculative discourse'. Despite the subtlety of many of its leading theorists, unexplored hyperbole abounds. For Beck (2002: 17), 'the study of globalisation and globality, cosmopolitanisation and cosmopolitanism constitutes a revolution in the social sciences'. In this chapter, we examine our respondents 'awareness of the world' (Robertson 1992), to explore the nature of contemporary cosmopolitanism and its relationship to daily life.

Many commentators see a key feature of cosmopolitanism as its global awareness (see Beck 2002). In many respects, this idea follows in an Enlightenment tradition (Fine and Cohen 2003) which saw it as 'an attitude of mind that attempted to transcend chauvinistic national loyalties' (Schlereth 1977: xi), with cosmopolites being interested in many parts of the world, borrowing ideas from different cultures and using reason and intellect to come to informed decisions. Critics, however, point to the socially exclusive nature of cosmopolitanism and the way that it reinstates a white, liberal worldview rather than any genuine engagement with 'others'. Thus the American poet Pinsky criticised Nussbaum's influential view of cosmopolitanism as one that recognises the rights of non-citizens as an ethos of 'people like ourselves', living in a global 'village of the liberal managerial class' (see Lasch 1995; Robbins 2001: 15f). Calhoun (2003: 106) sees cosmopolitanism as 'now largely the product of capitalism, (which) flourishes in the top management of multinational corporations and even more in the consulting firms that serve them'.

Given these criticisms, we are interested in exploring whether the global references of our respondents indicate that they may better be understood as a form of diaspora identity of the white English, rather than as a more developed form of cosmopolitanism. Diaspora involves the spatial dispersion of ethnic groups away from an original homeland so that their location and identities are stretched between points. It has special relevance for those ethnic minority groups, notably Jews or African blacks, who have experienced a forcible removal from their homeland (Gilroy 1993). Some writers argue that diasporic identities need not be confined to these particular cases, though Cohen (1997) traces the existence of a British imperial diaspora which spread from Britain throughout the territories of the empire. We saw in Chapter 7 that the cultural contacts of our respondents are focused nearly entirely on the anglophone nations of the former British empire, in a way which suggests that this imperial legacy still resonates several decades after decolonisation.

In this chapter we examine the relationship between specific Anglophone diasporic and more general cosmopolitan identities among our sample. In conducting this exercise we reiterate that our sample is definitely not a representative group of Mancunians, many of whom are members of ethnic minority groups, such as the large Jewish communities in both south and north Manchester, or Pakistani immigrants, whose global connections have been skilfully traced by Werbner (1990, 2002). However, we can turn the ethnic exclusiveness of our sample to our advantage by considering how the 'whiteness' of our sample is articulated in our respondents' own narratives. Our questioning threw up many opportunities for people to mention activities, influences and practices that connected respondents to non-English phenomena, and by revealing how the global is 'configured' in people's narratives we are able to show the ways in which global influences could be used to reinforce – possibly challenge – everyday routines and practices.

The first part of this chapter considers our respondents' ethnic identifications, before exploring the extent to which people had experience of living outside England, or had kin living in different nations. The second part briefly considers how people talked about their experience of holiday-making, as the activity which nearly everyone engages in and which often is taken overseas. The final part of this chapter examines how respondents talked about their global connectivity.

8.1 A white northern English diaspora

It has been argued that 'whiteness' depends on a dissimulation from ethnicity, so that as a category it holds itself above and apart from ethnic attachments (Roediger 1991; Frankenberg 1993). Whiteness is thus an unacknowledged reference point from which other forms of ethnicity become visible by deviation. It thereby helps underwrite the kind of 'normal' identity that we found in Chapter 7. It is indeed striking that our respondents proved remarkably reluctant to identify themselves in any kind of ethnic terms. They were much more reluctant to talk about their ethnic than their class identities (although, as we discuss in Savage et al. 2001,

Table 8.1   *Ethnic identification of respondents*

Ethnicity	Cheadle	Chorlton	Ramsbottom	Wilmslow	Total
None	15	17	21	10	63 (45%)
White	7	13	9	12	41 (29%)
Caucasian		3		3	6 (4%)
English		6	2	1	9 (6%)
British	1	1	1	3	6 (4%)
Jewish	1	1		2	4 (3%)
Irish	1	5			6 (4%)
Scots			1	1	2 (1%)
Other	2	2	1	2	7 (5%)
Missing data	16	1	12	12	41

Notes:

Percentages are of those for whom data is available.

White includes qualified responses (e.g. white British).

Other includes 1 Anglo-Singaporean; 1 Yorkshire; 1 Northern Irish; 1 Church of England; 1 Methodist; 1 Western European; 1 hybrid.

they were also ambivalent about their class identities). Table 8.1 tabulates their responses to our question: 'Do you regard yourself as a member of an ethnic group?'. Nearly half said no, usually tersely and with no elaboration. Those respondents who were prepared to talk about this issue sometimes indicated how they saw ethnicity in terms of 'other' ethnicities, so that the term has no purchase for them:

> I don't know, to be quite honest with you. This is really strange; I see ethnic groups as anything other than my own. Do you know what I'm saying? In terms of ethnic groups are anything that isn't British. And I suppose ethnic group then would be all coloured; all non-English speaking, but not my own. So I don't think of myself as ethnic. I suppose I am; middle-class white. (W7, Deirdre)

This reluctance to name whiteness as ethnicity was also manifested by the fact that those who did say they were 'white' frequently appended it to other qualifying terms. Twenty-three of the 41 who identified as white added qualifying terms such as 'White European', 'White British', 'White Caucasian', 'white middle class' or 'white anglo-saxon'. The term 'Caucasian' (sometimes by itself, as indicated in Table 8.1, or in the term 'white caucasian') seems to be indicative of a concern to hide whiteness behind what is seen as a 'scientific', rather than an emotive, label. It proved difficult, in short, to elicit from respondents a clear acknowledgement of their ethnicity. In this respect they differed from the few ethnic minorities in our sample who could always give a clear and articulate account of their ethnicity. This was often linked to their sense of diasporic attachment to a 'homeland', a sense especially strong for those from neighbouring nations:

> I am Irish. I feel very strongly about it.

> *Would you go back?*

> No.

You say you feel very strongly about it, can you say a bit more.

I don't know why but I do. I suppose because I was very happy there. It is a wonderful country to grow up in. Even then there was a quality of life that I can't describe that was completely different from here. Unless you have lived there and it is different now but when I grew up, first of all the church was very strong, and I am not saying that is a good thing, I am not a Catholic, but it created a certain atmosphere. In my day if you passed a church you crossed yourself but it did not matter what religion you were, not now though. I think of all the countries in the world Ireland has changed at least as much as anywhere. (W58)

I suppose I feel very Scottish and that probably increases as you move away from Scotland and it reaches it's peak during the rugby season of course so I guess in the work situation there is a lot of banter about that and this is a very difficult area because if one was sensitive one could say that this was discrimination … there is lots (of) things said about the Scots and about other groups … and in the wrong setting that can may be misconstrued and so on. (W38)

The only other significant ethnic minority in our sample were four Jewish respondents, none of whom were orthodox believers, who all talked crisply about their Jewish identities. This having been said, none had an unambiguous sense of Jewish identity, largely because of their uncertainty about the relationship between their national citizenship and their ethnicity:

Well it depends if you think of Judaism as a religion or a race and I'm never sure whether I'm British and Jewish, or I'm Jewish and maybe my loyalties lie with Israel, I don't think so, but we do tend to, not really a ghetto life existence, but because I think Jewish people have been persecuted, you tend to have Jewish friends because you know your not going to get criticised. (W68)

For the majority of white respondents our question about their ethnicity was often not welcome. Indeed, we sometimes did not feel able to ask this question because we expected a hostile response (one reason why there is significant amount of missing data). For instance, when asked, 'Do you see yourself as belonging to any particular ethnic group?', one respondent retorted, 'What a bizarre question'. Sometimes, when we tried to engage in dialogue, this led to further contestation, as in the following example:

Do you think you belong to any particular ethnic group?

A strange question that!

Well on equal opportunities monitoring forms they have a ticklist for that.

Well just through the sheer physical assets, white or black I'd put white, but I'm not sure about the reasoning around that question.

Well you wouldn't respond by saying you're English or British white or whatever in the first instance particularly for example?

Well I haven't got any particular racial overtones.

No it's not a question about belief in that respect it's in some ways a question about how people identify themselves.

I'll put it another way then. I always vote Liberal Democrat but in the European election I voted Conservative because I don't feel European, I do feel British, and especially being married to an Irishwoman, I don't feel English. But I don't particularly feel European, I must admit, so I suppose in that aspect I wouldn't normally vote Conservative but I did it because it was a specific purpose, I think probably a lot of people did the same thing. (R164)

In this case we can see how ethnicity is actually rather an important part of this man's identity, when placed in context, but when asked outright, he is hostile to us. This sense of uneasiness at ethnicity is in part linked to uncertainty about national identity, and its overlap with ethnicity. People were sometimes uncertain as to whether they were English or British. In view of recent arguments that devolution within the 'British Isles' may give rise to heightened forms of English nationalism (see Paxman 1999; Kumar 2003), it is interesting that very few respondents articulated a strong sense of English identity. One of the few examples was:

No I don't think I do (identify as an ethnic group), other than I'm very proud to be English and think Englishness is being swallowed up and lost, but I think it's a uniqueness around the world that wherever you go an English person is perceived today as really honest, probably slightly naive, living slightly in the past. But I think in business circles we're starting to gain tremendous respect because we are an educated country. (W93)

However, on the whole, respondents were not happy to give a clear English identity as their ethnic identity, and preferred the more generic and ambivalent identification as British, with some using even broader transnational categories such as 'white European' or 'white Caucasian'. Hesitant responses could be an indication that they did not conflate their whiteness with being English, leading them to distance themselves from what might be seen as racist responses in replying to this question.

I guess I'm a white caucasian, but again, colour and race to me doesn't really count for a great deal because I've got some close friends in this country who are black, I've got a lot of friends who are Thai, so for me race isn't really an issue at all. (R82)

It's difficult isn't it, certainly English, but again how do you define English. An Asian boy born in this country is English. English, British, certainly rather than European. (R156)

This tendency was especially marked in Chorlton, where respondents were distinctive in being considerably more reflexive and 'comfortable' in addressing their ethnicity (which explains the lesser amount of missing data in that area). In line with the cosmopolitan culture of Chorlton, a number of respondents rather sought to play up their ethnicity through talking about the (usually) fractional component of their descent which could be attributed to non-English, or non-white blood:

> It's funny, I don't really feel as though I do (have an ethnic identity), and I suppose I do, but I hate the question when people say what do you think you are, because I mean I'm British, I even feel funny about calling myself English, and I don't know why, I'm always really pleased that my parents have got bits of other countries in their blood, we've got Spanish and Irish, it's ridiculous but I think I like that feeling. So common sense tells me that I am but I don't really feel as though I am. (D53)

> I would call it a hybrid, because I'm a quarter Irish, a quarter English and half German, so when I want to characterise or make a caricature of who I am, I would say something like white middle class English, but I think there's more nuances in me with my whole upbringing and cultural background. (D11)

There is hence considerable fluidity in people's identifications, with a halting recognition that they are white, and a recognition that they are not in any simple terms English, but have wider ranging, transnational attachments. Stuart Hall's (1981) account of 'new ethnicities' may thus be applicable not only to ethnic minorities but to the dominant white population (see also Back 1996; Solomos 1989).

Numerous writers have emphasised the contemporary significance of transnational migration (Papastergiadis 2000), in the British context often related to the trading role of British empire (Cohen 1997). And, although most of our sample was rooted in the north of England through upbringing, work and long-term residence, this was compatible with considerable spatial dispersion of their contacts and previous history around selected areas of the world. Nearly one half of the sample mention some kind of salient transnational connection or experience during their interview. Twenty-two (12% of the total) had lived abroad for significant periods of time, the main location being the Middle and Far East. Very few had lived elsewhere in Europe or the US, though a handful had lived in Australia. Most of these had lived overseas when they were children, or had been at college or University overseas, and only a handful had ever worked abroad.

Kin contacts also indicate the power of the imperial connection. Of the 51 (27%) with kin overseas, most lived in the former British colonies, and especially Australia (9), Canada (8), New Zealand (6), South Africa (4), the United States (8), Singapore (4) and Thailand (2). These have all been sites for out-migration from England. The only other area where significant numbers of family members lived was in Europe (including Scotland, Wales and Ireland), where ten of our respondents had kin. There were no family members living in Asia (other than Singapore and Thailand), Africa (other than South Africa), or South America.

Table 8.2   *Overseas contacts of respondents (percentages)*

	Cheadle	Chorlton	Ramsbottom	Wilmslow	All
Lived overseas	12	11	6	20	22 (12%)
Family overseas	28	32	17	16	51 (28%)
Friends overseas	7	9	13	16	20 (11%)
Works or has worked abroad	19	13	8	42	37 (20%)
(Regular current work contacts)	(2)	(6)	(6)	(40)	(25)
Leisure contacts	0	4	4	0	4 (2%)
All personal contacts	42	38	38	76	88 (48%)

Notes:
All personal contacts is less than the sum of rows 2–5 because some respondents report ties
on more than one dimension.

A significant amount of work related international mobility was reported
by our respondents. Thirty-seven (20%) reported some kind of work contact
overseas. In some cases this was no more than irregular conference attendance, but 25 respondents (13%) reported that their work demanded
regular international visits. Table 8.2 shows that Wilmslow residents with
international business contacts either in United States or the Far East
formed the vast majority of these. Perhaps surprisingly, rather less contact
with Europe was reported. There was still slight evidence of Manchester's
19th Century legacy as the centre of the world textile industry, with two of
the wealthiest households we interviewed comprising of textile importers
and exporters (both with business interests in the Far East). Those working
in the public sector, even in senior positions, reported much less international contact than those in the private sector, which is one reason why
residents outside Wilmslow reported fewer international links.

In addition to kin, a significant number of respondents mentioned having
'best friends' overseas. In all, 20 (11%) reported that someone they could
trust was living abroad. In most cases these were English people who were
currently living overseas. Although several lived in Australia and Canada,
the highest number of such friends, nearly half, lived in Europe. As we have
seen in Chapter 6, having friends overseas allowed respondents to articulate the idea that friends do not need to be seen regularly but that when
they are contacted, they can immediately connect with them.

Finally, a small number of respondents enjoyed a particular hobby that
involved them in global contacts, often because it was highly specialised so
that there were not enough fellow enthusiasts within England. Donald
(R78) exemplified this most remarkably. He was a member of the English
team for a rare dangerous sport which meant regular overseas competition.
He went every year to the European championships, and as a result of his
activity 'I know Americans, New Zealanders, Australians, and although I've
talked about the European competition there's world competition as well so

I know people from across the world'. Donald was unusual, but there were four other respondents who belonged to voluntary associations with international spans. There were three others whose hobbies or interests led them to sustained international contact (a member of a rotary club, a member of the Swiss Alpine club, and a member of an international summer camp).

We asked a range of questions about respondents' use of the internet, email and telephones as a means of communicating with people at a distance. It is perhaps revealing that few respondents spoke with any feeling or substantial interest about these topics. At the time of our fieldwork, internet usage was rising rapidly, and many of our sample said they expected to become connected to the internet in the near future. Forty-one respondents (22% of the total) used the internet, and 53 (29%) used email in some form. Most of those using email did so only for work purposes. In Cheadle internet use was particularly limited, and it is interesting that those living in the more suburban locations in Ramsbottom were the most internet-active of any of the areas. Those respondents who reported using these technologies for global communication did so entirely to maintain contact with people they knew through face-to-face contact, normally friends and kin. There was here a sense that virtual communication could be useful for purely instrumental reasons (to make bookings or purchases), or to maintain relationships originally established by 'normal' face-to-face means, but little sense that it could actually generate meaningful relationships. There was little evidence from our research that virtual communication was of major significance, though we would note that at the time of our research these technologies were expanding rapidly and our findings may no longer be true at the time of writing this book (see generally Woolgar (ed.) 2002).

If we add together all these contacts, 48% of our sample had significant personal contacts or experiences outside England, having worked abroad, having some family members living outside England for an extended period, or having spent significant amounts of time overseas on business or leisure. Wilmslow was the most globalised of the four areas in these terms, with 58% of its respondents having international experience or contacts, while the proportions in the other three areas varied between 25% in Ramsbottom and 38% in Chorlton. What we see, therefore, is a population with contacts that do spread beyond national confines to embrace broader global contacts, which are strongly oriented to former British imperial colonies. We now turn to consider the extent to which these ties are related to other aspects of our respondent's identities.

8.2 Holiday-making and everyday life

In recent years, social theorists have drawn attention to the importance of tourism, seen less as a departure from normal routines and more as a means by which older boundaries between work and leisure have become more permeable (see Urry 1990). It is certainly true that holidays are the main way that our respondents visited other nations, and for most they were the only reason for spending time outside England. Only one person we spoke to claimed never to have a holiday, and 139 (79%) had been on at least one overseas holiday in the past three years. One interesting feature is that respondents do not mainly go to the English-speaking world that we have seen dominates its cultural and personal contacts. Most overseas holidays are taken in continental Europe, with only 35 people (20%) having been on long-haul flights to destinations such as the USA, Australia, the Caribbean or the Far East in the previous three years. Spain, France and Greece are by far the most common holiday destinations in Europe, among residents from all four areas. Four respondents had a second home abroad (all in Spain). It should be noted that British holidays are also common, Wales, Scotland and the South West of England being particularly popular destinations. In the most affluent area, Wilmslow, there was an unusually high frequency of British-based holidays, as a result of the fact that several respondents owned second homes (mostly in the Lake District), and also that this group were more likely to take additional holidays on top of the main overseas one.

There is a dominant narrative regarding holidays. Although holidays are seen as rare opportunities for freedom in contrast to the workaday world of everyday life, very few people presented them as a matter of individual free choice, but defined them in terms of family needs or expectations. More generally, they become ways of marking out and symbolising family relationships and stages on an annual or even less regular cycle (see Roberts 1999; Rappoport and Rappoport 1995 for discussion of impact of life course and lifecycle on patterns of leisure). A particularly common refrain was the contrast between holidays for single people or couples, which allowed independence and adventure, compared to the family holiday which was more constrained, as Fiona indicated.

Fiona: children and holiday-making

Fiona (D12) had moved to Chorlton after having lived in other parts of Manchester for many years, where she lived with her partner and had a small two year old daughter. She continued working part-time as a computer engineer, and emphasised how important holidays were to them because of the demands on her time.

Yeah, we used to love going abroad. We used to have several holidays a year, especially when we were in Stretford and had a lot of loose cash. Not exclusively on holidays but a large chunk of it went on holidays abroad.

Did you go all over the place?

Yeah, we've been to Egypt, Mexico, a lot of places in Europe. What we'd try and do is have a sort of city break at Easter and then a 2 week somewhere.

> *And now that's stopped has it?*
>
> Yeah. Yeah, the first year we had Rosie we went to Anglesey which – she was 4 months old so we didn't want to travel very far – we went en masse with all the family and with the other grandparents as well. Last year we went to Tenby and it rained, with the family, but we also went to Greece for 2 weeks.
>
> Fiona looked forward to the future when she would be able to holiday independently again.
>
> We'd like to get abroad and maybe even have a short break, just the two of us, when she's a bit older and she can stay with my parents for the weekend.

Children are defined as key agents in limiting holiday freedom and ensuring that holidays become consistent with local routines and practices. W12 reported that [we]:

used to go abroad before we had Matthew and then we decided after having him, when he was little we didn't want to go abroad and we didn't for a couple of years, we went down to Devon actually – for a couple of years we did that. We did go to Cyprus – that was in January – that was unusual for us we never – it was something different to do really – we tend to stick to England really.

Where did you go for your last holiday?

Turkey.

And is that a typical holiday for you or not?

Fairly typical, I suppose since we've had the children we've had our holiday restricted really, before we had children we went round the world and took 9 months off and went to America and worked in Australia and things like that and we travelled to the Far East one year, but since we've had the children it tends to be package holidays.

Beach type holiday?

Yes. Oh last year we went down to Cornwall to one of those really nice family hotels with everything inclusive, children's entertainment and that was good …

Holidays thus become means of accounting for freedoms and the limitation of freedom through the role of family narratives and structuring a sense of the changing position, of family members. They can thus be seen as the necessary mirror of 'elective belonging', in which holidays figure as potential freedom which is then reined in through the extension of family relationships. At times this could take a prospective form as respondents talked about their plans for future holidays:

Can you tell me where you went for your last holiday?

Last bank holiday weekend we went to Oasis in Penrith.

Do you go abroad much?

When we were expecting the baby we went on our last big holiday, we went to California, we've some family over there, we did a bit of touring around. This summer we're going to Northumberland, we've planned while he's small to have holidays in this country really, there's a lot of places we've not seen. When we first got married we were short of money and we went up to Scotland and it's quite a surprise what you can see in this country, it's probably not any cheaper by the time you've finished. (D107)

The power of this narrative of the family history was such that some single respondents articulated a sense that package holidays were not normally 'for' them. Interestingly, respondents rarely report that holidays have broad enduring significance for their social lives, and people rarely report following up their holidays with broader reading or cultural engagement, the exception being a few respondents who brushed up their language skills or were interested in aspects of European culture. As we identified in Chapter 6, a few respondents reported making enduring friends on holidays, though these were always to other holiday-makers, rather than 'locals'. Thus, as liminal experiences, holidays, even to non-English speaking nations, generally help to reinforce the 'normal' boundaries of everyday life based around a northern middle-class habitus. Only four respondents hankered to retire overseas, especially to somewhere like Spain, and these few do exemplify forms of what we will call 'global reflexivity' where they are able to see themselves in very different settings to those of their current residence. However this does not extend to those three respondents from Wilmslow who own holiday homes abroad (all in Spain), who see such homes as an extension of their current living practices.

8.3 Cosmopolitanism and global reflexivity

In this last section of the chapter we examine in more detail those respondents who exhibited more developed forms of global reflexivity. At the most general level we can define global reflexivity as an ability to look at their lives, thoughts and values from a perspective that did not take English referents as the implicit frame for judgement, but which was able to place them in some kind of a broader global comparative frame. This is in keeping with Robertson's (1992: 27) emphasis that globalisation involves the *'comparative interaction* of different forms of life'.

At the broadest level only 23 of our respondents (13%) exhibited some kind of comparative frame at some point in their narratives. The predominant form of reflexivity involved the ability to place local affairs into a broader frame of comparison extending outside England, thereby indicating that the respondent was aware that things 'here' might seem strange or peculiar to those from other nations. Most did not display the kind of reflexivity which indicated that their own identity was placed in a global context. Only seven respondents articulated a deeper kind of reflexivity in which their selves were positioned through global referents.

The first kind of limited reflexivity depended on making cultural comparisons between their lives and those in other nations through finding a comparative frame of reference. Invariably, this involved seizing aspects of the city of Manchester as their 'home' frame and comparing it with other non-English cities. D42, for instance, compared Manchester with Milan:

> I don't see an awful lot of Manchester itself, I don't really use it at all, mainly because parking wise it's such a hassle. … When we go to see my daughter in Milan, outside her front door you go down into the metro and you're in the centre of town in no time, she's always going into the centre because it's dead easy, but here there's no chance, I don't even know which bus I'd get to go into the city centre, never mind when it's coming, or how to get back. I suppose everything to do with travelling becomes a hassle one way or another. (D42)

W27 shows the same reflexive capacity to place Manchester in an international context, indicating how this ability was directly related to the expertise she had developed in her job as tourist development officer:

> I think the centre (of Manchester) is getting better and I think that when it's rebuilt after the bomb it will be an awful lot better than it was, but I think the short time I spent in education, going to different schools, for some people it's not changed at all. I think it is still quite a deprived area in some places of Manchester, particularly north Manchester, and the fact that in Europe we are classified as objective 2 area level of deprivation, so we obviously have got quite high levels of deprivation within Manchester. But I don't think you notice it so much in the city centre, it's like any other big town, as I said I was in Dublin the other week and it's lovely, but outside it's very deprived, it's objective 1. I think it is improving, I think it will get better and I think things like the Metrolink, I think it's being in Europe, I think that the money the city's getting from Europe, places like the Bridgwater Hall, the money that's gone into Moss Side. (W27)

Sandra (R81) thought Manchester was 'brilliant' and when asked what changes had taken place she said:

> Well obviously the physical changes, the buildings, the development that's gone on, I think it has actually come on a par with other European cities, where I think it could match facilities of other places in Europe. That was brought home to me last year particular, again through work that Pete did, because they have an international conference every year and it was in Basle the year before, and last year it was in Manchester, which was a bit disappointing from my point of view! It was suggested that it's viewed internationally on a par with those sort of places.

For Kerry (D27) this kind of global reflexivity permitted a more cynical sense of the limits of Manchester in true global context, in her doubts about the city's real credibility as an Olympic bidder:

Well, I think the city council is working incredibly hard to turn it around and I mean I think it was in decline before the IRA bombing and, you know, something really good can come out of it because it has been a way of getting money from central government invested in the city centre but then battling against competition which will inevitably come from Dumplington and Trafford. I think its aspirations are tremendous but sometimes a bit laughable. I mean, I think it was great bidding for the Olympics but you know when you walk round Manchester it just looks like a really tired, sad city centre and you sort of think about the other countries that bid for it, you think. … My sister in Australia thought it was really funny, sending all these city council postcards and the picture would be of Manchester and getting her to display them in the shop she had. I think it has been in decline, I think maybe that decline has been stopped and maybe it'll be turned around. I think the important thing with Manchester is to build on it's strengths and its strengths are that its the gay capital if you like and it's very vibrant and exciting in the gay village and I personally think that's very positive and also there's a lot of excellent bands that have come out of Manchester club culture. I mean, I'm not into that because I'm too old for it. I think that is a definite strength that Manchester has and I think, you know, it's important to maybe build on that. Not to try and make something it isn't. I mean, I just went into the centre yesterday, it is full of old warehouses and run-down places. I mean, it looks like it's in decline, it needs a heck of a lot of investment to turn it around.

Kerry draws on the visual cues of Manchester, in ways we have examined in Chapter 5, to evaluate the city with others. Her account, along with others, indicates how a limited kind of global reflexivity is garnered around the site of Manchester itself, so that rather than there being reference to generic global awareness, comparisons were made to particular sites. Global comparisons are specified in terms of a home point of comparison – in this case the city itself – against which evaluation can be made. Secondly, reference is mainly to European, rather than British imperial cities. Indeed, it was more common to compare Manchester with (often unnamed) European cities than it was with other English cities (such as Leeds or Birmingham) with which it might appear to be vying with for national status and position. In this respect, perhaps Manchester's concern to market itself as a 'European city' has indeed permeated through to the thinking of a significant minority of residents.

A particularly interesting way that global references of this kind were made was with respect to the 'local' football team Manchester United, the city's main claim to having a global 'brand' (see King 2000). Several respondents were aware that Manchester United gave them a means of positioning themselves to those outside the white diaspora in global terms.

Well I suppose it depends who I was talking to, if I was talking to somebody from another country I'd say I come from Manchester, because everybody's heard of Manchester United, but if I was talking to somebody in this country I would probably tell them I came from just north of Bury, because most people have heard of that, and if I was talking to somebody in the region then I'd say Ramsbottom. (R81)

Well yes, I'm not ashamed of (living in Manchester), I think it's a positive thing to live outside of (London) particularly in terms of the work I do, … and it's good, it's easy, when you say you live in Manchester people all go, oh Manchester United. … So anyway, that's a way of having an identity. (D11)

It's very easy actually I went on a wonderful trip to South America and we were sitting in a park place and a few little boys came up, they wanted to shine your shoes and they were lovely little boys and they spoke English and said where you come from, so we say Manchester because they all know Manchester United, it's incredible. I didn't used to say that in England because in the south if we used to go to parties and things round there and you used to say Manchester they used to start talking in this silly Lancashire accent which was very annoying so after that I always used to say Cheshire and they don't know where Cheshire is. But if you're abroad if you say Manchester, you're well away. I thought that was just incredible, this poor little beggar boy and he could speak English and he knew about Manchester United. (W73)

Perhaps appropriately given its global branding, actual attendance at Manchester United games varied little between areas. It was highest among the well-heeled executive men from Wilmslow, several of whom engaged in corporate hospitality from its boxes, and lowest among the less affluent men in Cheadle. Positioning Manchester United as a global brand has involved aligning it with corporate culture.

It needs to be emphasised that this kind of global reflexivity does not involve any deep awareness of oneself as globally positioned, but a much more limited sense that Manchester's specificity could be understood by reference to other parts of the world. It was thus quite consistent for this kind of global reflexivity to be anchored back to a form of local or nationalist identification, as Stuart indicates:

Stuart: the cosmopolitanism of a 'northern lad'

Stuart (W74) had a glittering career working for one of the area's best known transnational firms. He had worked overseas and was a major authority in his area, yet he was clear that his attachment was to the north, even though he had the contacts and experience to work further afield if he wished.

Oh yes from time to time I've looked at posts abroad and also elsewhere in the country and I guess my inclination is I'm a northern lad and I'll stay in the north west, I've lived in different parts of the country, I've worked and lived in the north east, I've worked in London, I've worked in East Anglia and I've also worked on the Wirral and I kind of like this north west area.

While aware that Manchester existed in a global context, this in no way detached Stuart from place. Indeed overseas allowed him the possibility of 'liminal' experiences in which he could step outside his normal routines, call his values into question, but then reaffirm them. He related how after he had completed his medical training his decision to work in the private sector was related to a business trip to Sweden.

... within 6 months of qualifying, I had a research paper published in the *British Medical Journal* with my consultant and I got into this thing about, this is an anecdote, but as a senior house officer in 1976 I took home £200 a month, but I told you that over and above a busy working routine I worked a one in two rota, one in two nights on duty, every other weekend on duty and it was a hard life and nevertheless I still found time to fit in research, writing papers and going to the odd meeting and if I did go, I was invited by ICI and one or two other pharmaceutical companies to speak at symposiums, they paid me £50 and I remember I was asked by ICI to go on a lecture tour to Sweden as a senior house officer and so they organised the tickets and I got to the airport at Gothenburg in Sweden and this was like big time, I mean you could come out of med school and you really don't know anything about the world or how to get a mortgage or how to organise anything and so I was very green, but I was not naive, so I got to the airport at Gothenburg and the rep met me and he said what's your honorarium, let's go to the bank, so he takes me to the bank and as I'm walking to the bank I thought what shall I tell him, if it's £50 in London, it must be £100 abroad, so I said my honorarium's a £100 and he looked at me and said, oh no, and I thought he's rumbled me, and he said £150, so I thought that's nice and I tried to not let it show and he said have you got any expenses, now my wife was expecting and I didn't have two halfpennies to rub together, by the time I'd paid the rent on the house and the loan on the car and living expenses, it was like breadline and so I'd managed to scrape together £18, to take on this trip and somebody told me they don't have pubs in Sweden, you have to buy them in the hotel and it's really expensive and I'd scraped together £18, so rather candidly I said to the guy, I'm awfully sorry I need to cash a cheque because I'm thinking to myself now I've got £150, I've been on duty on the hospital and I haven't had time. Oh not at all he said, let me give you some expenses, so he gave me another £50, so he gave me £200 as krona, I was there for 3 days and I didn't have to spend a penny, they would not let me buy anything. I remember getting home and having changed the money back to pounds and I got home and I went in and she said how have you got on and I put £200 pounds on the table, and I said life is hard, we have a one in two rota, we have a hell of a career in front of us, but there are other ways forward, I said because I've been prepared to go that extra mile to do clinical research and work extra hours, there's a months salary, what's that telling you? And that's why when I finished my GP training I wrote to ICI and said can I have a job and I thought they might put me in a laboratory with caged rats, but they said do you think occupational medicine is for you and I remember joining ICI some months later in occupational medicine and listening to all the changes that were coming through about training and specialisation and feeling a bit overawed and a bit daunting thinking what have I done here and now some 20 years later I actually chaired the UK committee that oversees all that sort of training and approval of specialist training for UK occupational medicine, so life goes full circle.

Stuart's future career was crystallised because of the way that his extraction from local values and practices during his overseas trip allowed him to question his assumptions. But the crucial point here is that despite Stuart's wealth of overseas contact, his economic and cultural resources, he remains a 'Northern lad'. He is able to place Manchester, its organisations and institutions in a broader, non-English context, but it does not lead him to question his own sense of belonging.

This sense that reflexivity allows local identities to be sustained comes over in most of the narratives of those who were globally reflexive. After an unhappy first marriage Ronald (R88) had for over a decade chosen to be single, but meeting a woman in a Chinese* restaurant changed this:

> This is my second marriage, I got married when I was quite young and it lasted for 2 years and I got divorced when I was 26 and I swore I'd never get married again and I stuck to it for a long, long time, I stuck to it for 12 years and it all changed for me the first time I ever went to China* and I went to Bangkok and it was pouring down with rain and me and a friend of mine went running in an English restaurant and the owner who was from Liverpool brought us a change of clothing and the person that brought the change of clothing is now my wife and that's how I first met her and that was the beginning of the holiday and I kept in touch after I came back and then I went back again on holiday 3 or 4 months later and to cut a long story short about 3 years later she came over here and we got married.

However, although married to a Chinese* woman, Ronald's lifestyles and values remained embedded in Ramsbottom routines. When asked if shared leisure interests with his wife he replied:

> No, I don't think we've got the same interests at all really. My idea of a night out is ... going out for a drink every night. The lifestyle in China* is completely different, they don't have pubs and clubs as such, so it's very much family orientated over there, whereas I was never like that, so she's more into having a night out at somebody's house, whereas I prefer to go out and socialise, so we've got two completely different ideas really.

A further example of this kind of relationship can be found among some Manchester United supporters who reported attending the team's games in Europe (see King 2000). One supporter reported how he regularly went to Old Trafford with people he had originally met at Barcelona:

> funnily enough in 1994 I went to Barcelona when United played Barcelona in Barcelona, I went with my lad I normally go with and we met three lads from London there who were sat with us in the stadium, and they go to every home game and we now meet them every home game, in this pub near the ground, only for about half an hour at about two o'clock on a Saturday, and they come up from London every game. But that comes from meeting them in Barcelona. (C46)

Here again we see the domestication of the non-English encounter back into the familiar local and national contexts. This even applied to those who had spent long periods of time abroad, such as Tom.

Tom: the 'homing instinct' of an international traveller

Tom (C136) was born and brought up in Cheadle, but had spent over a decade working in the Middle East, Sweden* and Indonesia* as a teacher, had married a Swedish* woman and had fathered a child who was now living in Sweden*. In some respects he insisted on his ability to move between places.

> I belong here, yes, I've grown up here, I've lived in Indonesia*, I've lived in the Middle East, I've lived in Sweden*, so no, to leave here would be quite easy.

However, he admitted that he could not settle or get a secure job in Sweden*, and had therefore returned to live with his father where he had resumed many of his youthful pastimes. His social life was now anchored around Cheadle where he belonged to the local social club and was a regular snooker player, and apart from the regular twice yearly visits he paid to his son and partner, showed little sign of missing his overseas ventures, though he did regret that he could no longer afford to keep up golf and membership of country clubs which he had been able to sustain in the Far East as part of the 'ex-pat' community. He retained the ability to place his life in wider context, but this did not shake his local identifications.

> I mean I was assaulted in Didsbury for no reason at eleven o'clock at night. ... Now if you go to Sweden* it's much safer and clearner, and you notice when you come back from there to here there has been a marked deterioriation here. ... I would chose Manchester over Stockport. ... I consider myself a Manchester person. When I came back from Saudi Arabia* it was Manchester City Council that took me on.

Other respondents, such as R66 explicitly defined their sense of belonging to the area in terms of rejection of overseas living. When asked if she belonged in Ramsbottom now, she stated:

> Definitely. And I've lived abroad, seven years in South Africa, and I know what it's like to belong to an area, I didn't really settle over there, but I have settled over here. And I'm originally from Doncaster, the other side of the Pennines.

Generally, people's accounts of their global reflexivity only shows the power of their localised identities, by providing them with an elaborated frame of reference in which to place themselves. There is however, a second group of 7 respondents (4% of the total) who show a more genuinely expansive sense of global awareness, to the extent that they could be seen as authentic cosmopolitans. These are people who place their own identities in some kind of explicit global frame, do not conceptualise England as their 'normal' home, and are able to reflect on global affairs from outside a national perspective. Although only a small proportion of our sample, it is worth examining their narratives in some detail to learn why they evinced a more developed cosmopolitanism.

Most of these cosmopolitans are unusual since they were not brought up in England, and migrated internationally during their lives. Probably the most striking case is that of a Frenchman, Serge.

Serge: internationalist reflexivity

Serge (D33) had come to Manchester because his Spanish* girlfriend, who he had met while working in the Caribbean, wished to develop her medical training in Britain. He had joined her and been recruited to work as a sales manager of a medium-sized local firm once he had arrived in Manchester. Serge had been to university in France and to graduate school in the United States. He exemplified a strongly internationalist outlook. He and his girlfriend planned to leave Manchester in two years and work together in the third world. At the age of 30 Serge had already lived in several nations, and planned to live in more in the future.

Serge strongly endorsed cosmopolitan ideals, and was attracted to Chorlton as an appropriate place for someone like him. Indeed, Serge's views about Chorlton were much less agonistic than were those of the northern cosmopolitans. In part, this was because his orientation was more tourist, in which Chorlton was a convenient site to visit parts of England he did not know.

What sort of things about it do you like?

I used to live in Paris and by comparison I like Manchester a lot because it's a big city from which you can get out quite easy, I like to go hiking, you can be in the Peak District in half an hour, once again there are no traffic jams to get out, no traffic jams to get back in and at the same time I like the night life and social life, I like cultural events and especially I like rock music and pop music, so it was definitely an ambition for me to come here and I really enjoy the scenery and on top of that price-wise its quite interesting because you've got good value for money, anything you buy or any cultural events you go to.

Do you like the countryside? How does it compare with France?

Its difficult to compare it with France, I come from Lyon and it's near the Alps so I'm quite familiar with the Alps, but here what I like it's very close from Manchester you can have decent hills like in the Peak District or little mountains, like in the Lake District. I like what I think are very typical in the British countryside all those little walls, stone walls separating sheep and all those sheep grazing, that's very pretty.

Serge had become actively involved in the Campaign for Real Ale, was a regular pub-goer, and waxed lyrical about the virtues of English beer. Yet at the same time he remained largely unconnected to the city. He had few friends, knew few of his neighbours and did not participate in any active local social life. Serge embraced Chorlton in part because he had so little investment in it: it was largely a site to live his life for three years (he planned to move away in exactly two years). For him, there was therefore not the kind of agonistic relationship between Manchester and London then there was for most of the northern cosmopolitans that we identified in Chapter 5.

A similar case is that of D16, an Anglo-Thai*. He had a partner living in Paris, who he visited regularly to see his son, and had family living in Spain. His response to being questioned about his identity was that:

Well I guess I'd just say I'm a product of quite a lot of influences, I'm ethnic, being from Thailand*, but then I've lived in quite a few places in Europe and Manchester, but yes I'd say if I came from anywhere in England it would be Manchester, it's the place I've lived in longest.

Several other similar, though less extreme, versions can be found. D11 was a middle-aged academic and consultant working in development, with particular experience of working in Africa. She was of English parentage but had lived in Egypt* and other nations when she was a child, though she was 'shipped back' to English boarding school between the ages of 4–13. Much of her testimony indicated a careful positioning of herself as oriented towards third world concerns, and there was consistent undercurrent of criticism of 'American' culture, such as that of American films or supermarkets. Hugh (W67) had been brought up in Belgium and had a Belgian mother, and was a strong Europhile. He was currently learning German and had long-been a member of the Anglo-German Medical society that encouraged interchange between British and German medics. He had German friends, was proud that his wife spoke French and said that he 'loathed and detested … the Colonel Blimp image'.

Leaving these aside, there were only three respondents who had been brought up in England yet who articulated a more expansive sense of global belonging. Two of these had jobs which involved large amounts of international travel. Dave reported that:

I'm happy here, but I'd like to wind it all up and go and find a villa in Spain, which inevitably I will do.

Is that a real possibility then?

Yes, for sure.

So you're definitely working towards that as a plan?

Yes, that's where all the investments and everything will be aligned to, I'm not talking something big, just somewhere with a small pool, walk down buy my fish at the market, come back and barbeque it of an evening, that kind of thing.

Is that because you've been on holidays there?

Well I see a lot because I travel a lot with the job and so I always have a look round and see what's what. I go to many different countries but I think Spain is probably the one. (R127)

Greg and James: English born cosmopolitans

Greg (R82) and James (D9) were the only two English born and raised respondents in our sample who had a developed global reflexivity. Yet, they could hardly be more different. Greg was brought up in Leeds, had worked in training in computing, and was unusual in clearly stating that he did not feel he belonged in Ramsbottom:

No I don't is the honest answer to that. But there are quite specific reasons for that. We did feel that we belonged here, and we're quite settled here to a degree, but we have a business in the Far East doing tours and travel and things, so part of our dedication or whatever the term is, is really over there rather than over here. So I guess we feel we've got dual loyalties because we spend a lot of time over there, we spend a lot of time here, and the aim is to spend 50:50 between the two really.

So do you actually have a place to live over there?

Yes, we have an apartment out there and a business …

And is that a normal sort of thing for you then, going to the Far East, or do you like to go to other places as well?

Well I do a lot of travelling, it depends, am I lucky or not, I can never quite work it out because it can be quite tiring and boring, but last year I went to Thailand and the Far East four times, for about two or three weeks each time. Coming back I might stop over in Turkey for a bit, last year I got to the Caribbean, the States and Europe, Spain, France, Belgium, Switzerland.

So that's a mixture of work and pleasure?

But the European stuff is mostly work, the Far East is a mixture of work and the States was ostensibly a business trip but it was a holiday really – but not for tax purposes!

In fact Greg's spatial identification was complex, in that he was very involved in local groups, such as a railway preservation society. Nonetheless, he was unusual in being distanced from his residence by his global connections. He was also gay and while he did not speak about how this might have been linked to his more expansive identity, it seems likely that this detached him from the strongly heterosexual Ramsbottom norm and helped generate more global attachments.

James, by contrast, was a retired manual worker who had lived in Chorlton most of his life, he began comparing his feelings about Chorlton with the US early in his interview:

In them early days it (Chorlton) did not have the traffic jams. Cars were few and far between, horse-drawn vehicles. More open space, parkland, not a lot of building. You can imagine going to Florida which was a swampland before they started building on it. You build on more land until eventually there are no open spaces and that is exactly how this has progressed over the years.

James is the only respondent who tried to explain what his or her residential area was like with reference to places outside Britain, in this case Florida. His interest in looking at things from outside England was clear at many points in his interview. When asked about whether Britain was becoming classless he responded that class is:

… just as important. The days of years and years ago you have already had that with Diana because you can talk to a person like that there is no snobbery but the old stages of the upper bracket, blue blood as we used to call it, realised they are a thing of the past, they are not respected any more or very little. They realise now, the public has more sway, people like that as a figurehead is OK but it is becoming, you are getting the same sort of thing in Australia. They are going the same way all those Commonwealth countries. Years ago Britain used to be there but slowly but surely they are all becoming independent, some to the good and again some not to the good. I think, I may be wrong, but I think that Bill Clinton after the last little hassle out in the Middle East, I think the biggest mistake, not necessarily that one, but when I was serving in the Canal Zone was the Balfour Declaration giving the Jews the right to live in Palestine, kick the Arabs out. There has been nothing but trouble since then. It will flare up again, it is a hot bed. He is hiding behind the UN. He is using the UN. I think he is ready for the chop. I don't think people here want to get involved in a war and the Arab nations certainly don't want to, apart from Kuwait.

This is most unusual testimony. Talking about class did not remain confined to a discussion about Britain, but triggered off a wide ranging discussion about world affairs, which evidently concerned him rather more than the parochial issue of whether Britain was still a class society. His concern about Americanisation was manifest at many points.

We have been to the Third World country which was the Dominican Republic but they are only trying. They are not geared up like Jamaica, there everything has been taken over by the Americans. Because slowly but surely they are taking over all the places. They are adding them to the flag. Bahamas, Hawaii, they are all Americanised. All these islands we have been you can see have been Americanised when you go in and see buffet meals, which is the way of having meals in America and Canada, you know where you can just help yourself.

It transpired that James had tried to emigrate to the United States in the past five years, but had not been able to sell his house at a price to allow him to buy a house in Florida. James was probably the most globally reflexive of all the English born people we talked to. He was also very untypical of Chorlton residents in having been a manual worker most of his life, having left school at 16, in having been brought up in Chorlton (indeed, in the same street where he was now living) and in being relatively poor. He is not the sort of person that one might expect to be globally reflexive if this is seen as the product of education and class. What was decisive in making James cosmopolitan was his war-time experience, where he had served in the army and travelled extensively in the Middle East.

James's case suggests that global reflexivity does not rub off from having routines that brings one into contact with global signs. You do not become globally reflexive by hanging around airport terminals or international conferences, for as we have seen such experiences can easily be domesticated into more localised identities. Rather, mobilisation into a global awareness appears to be linked to an intense personal experience, in his case serving in the Army in the aftermath of the Second World War.

Conclusion

In this chapter we have seen that many of our respondents had significant global connections. The vast majority of respondents travel abroad on holidays and substantial numbers have lived abroad, or have kin or friends abroad. They are implicated in wide-ranging global networks that tie them in to complex networks of global inter-dependency. However, once we consider the specific geography of such contacts, we can see them as indicative of a white, English speaking diaspora. They are not part of a globally dispersed population but have been formed through the geography of the British empire, with strong links to Canada, Australia, New Zealand and the United States. They are the inheritors of the British Empire. This is not to say that there are no contacts with other nations. However, where there is a comparative frame of reference with European or Asian nations, these are nearly always structured as 'exceptional' situations which confirm the normality of the white, northern English, world.

It is interesting that there is evidence for a limited kind of urban global consciousness, in which Manchester is related not to other British provincial cities but with other cities. There is some modest support here to Le Gales's (2002) arguments about the possibly enhanced significance of urban consciousness in a global world. We see this as related to the ability of cities to be key nodes that are networked to other cities in ways that by-pass national boundaries. People do not evince general global awareness but rather specific connections between places. However, global reflexivity does not, on the whole, disrupt people's sense of located identity. We have emphasised in other chapters that our sample connect their place to other salient places within England such as London or the northern countryside. Respondents often like and admire non-English places (hence, their enjoyment of holidays) but they would not see their residential area as connected with them. A significant number of respondents did draw comparisons outside England, but this enhanced local identities through allowing respondents to understand the specificity of their local with a wider range of spatial reference points. What stands out among our sample is the lack of any real evidence that their personal futures travel far from established, predictable, routes. To some extent people's desire for other places leads them to value the kinds of experiences in 'other' cultures. Interestingly, our respondents did not show any interest in moving to the United States, the most culturally significant nation for them, perhaps because it was deemed to be so close to home already. By contrast small numbers did talk about their desire to move to Spain or Australia.

There were a few more globally reflexive respondents who evince a more cosmopolitan outlook, who one might define as 'citizens of the world'. These are a diverse bunch of people, but all are unusual in having turbulent life histories. Those who exhibit global reflexivity have been 'recruited' into this awareness by particular extreme life experience, usually through having lived in different nations or having served in the armed forces overseas. Global reflexivity does not seep into people's lives because of the pervasive, power of global idioms and cues, but rather it depends on particular, indeed local and personal, circumstances. Furthermore these cosmopolitans were all, in important ways, highly unusual vis-à-vis other local residents, and mostly out of step with their current surrounds. For these reasons we think it is preferable to see global reflexivity as shaped primarily by a white, English speaking, diaspora rather than by any more far reaching cosmopolitanism.

Conclusion

In the late 1960s a group of eminent urban geographers, planners and sociologists associated with the Centre for Environmental Studies listened to a paper examining 'developing patterns of urbanisation' (Cowan and Diamond 1969). This provided an account of anticipated urban trends up to the century end, roughly the time when we conducted our interviews. Placing our findings against these expectations reveals how the expectations of 30 years before had largely been confounded. The paper outlined the dominant trend within Britain towards the creation of one large megalopolis. '(T)he dominance of London and the associated belt of almost contiguous urban development that stretches to Leeds and Liverpool will increase and the infant megalopolitan heart of Britain will have come to manhood. The currently projected motorway network will become its High Street'. They went on to add that 'we have to ask if there is still a discernible regional scale'.

This assumption of increased national homogeneity and urban centrality looks very different from the world conjured up by our respondents. The identities and practices we have examined are rooted in northern England. London is a long way away, and even those Chorlton residents who hankered after it did so under the assumption that it was a fundamentally different place than Manchester. However, Cowan and Diamond usefully suggested that four city regions would emerge within the large megalopolis. One of these was an urban corridor running from Merseyside, through Manchester, Bradford, Leeds to Humberside, and with a corridor running north to Preston.[1] In this book we have argued that the power of place is defined by a large group of those who 'electively belong' to a specific residential location which they can make congruent with their lives. This population is largely drawn from those brought up within this northern corridor (with the exception that few have come from Humberside, but they have in addition come from Newcastle-upon-Tyne, as well as parts of rural northern England and the Midlands), and is a group which challenges the traditional dichotomy between locals and cosmopolitans. The opportunities and scope offered by global communication and mobility has allowed the consolidation of a new kind of regional population, no longer defined with respect to a dominant local city, but with highly selective and partial global ties that create distinctive kinds of imaginary belongings.

This book has therefore been an empirical elaboration of the familiar argument that globalisation constructs local identities, attachments and belonging. However, we have sought to refine our understandings of the precise ways in which this occurs. We have distanced ourselves from any perspective which sees the local as an instance of the global, and have emphasised that it should be seen as an irritant. We do not seek to gloss local distinctiveness behind global generalisations. It is vital to comprehend the particularity of place. In this conclusion we pull together the threads of our analysis to offer our understanding of cultural globalisation in ways that may have broader relevance for other places and locations. We do this by critically reflecting on how our case studies relate to a series of common arguments evident within accounts of globalisation, before concluding with a statement of our own perspective.

In Chapter 1 we positioned our work as a critique of theories of globalisation that saw it as involving epochal social change. Let us indicate four ways in which our account poses serious problems for these kinds of globalisation theory before we elaborate our own alternative view:

1. *The local as defensive response.* In the work of Castells, Beck and Bauman, the local is a defensive response to the increasing general power of globalising forces. It thus reinstates the authenticity of the local as a means of challenging the claims of the global to by-pass place. We, however, see very little evidence that the local is historically constructed in this way as a kind of defensive identity. Indeed, historical claims imparting moral priority to long-term residents are rarely found and have limited significance in any of our areas. Most residents talk about their local belonging in terms of the connections which it allows with other places and its convenience for their everyday life. The local is thoroughly implicated in various kinds of global connection and the local can only be understood as a direct product of these. Theoretically, we see this as offering strong support for networked approaches to place identity, such as those championed by Appadurai (1996) and Massey (1994) which do not counterpose the local with the global, but explore how specific locals are interconnected to produce a complex range of particular geographies.

2. *The global as an awareness of the world.* From our and a half million words of transcript there is very little evidence that people imbue their narratives of everyday life with some sense of global concern. When talking about their everday lives people do not link their lives to issues of global warming, international relations, or a sense of the world as an arena with a shared destiny. In addition, our respondents had very little cultural contact with much of the world, especially Africa, Latin America, and parts of Asia. Insofar as globalisation is defined as a kind of generic global awareness, we must insist on its empirical limits. Global communications facilitate particular kinds of geographies which appear to reinforce longer term spatial relationships – in our case through elaborating the ties of the former British empire. Although this is theoretically consistent with the arguments of Robertson (1992, 1995) we see it as important to map out the actual kinds of diasporic identities that are fostered, rather than refer to generic 'global' identities.

3. *Global elite versus local mass.* Many theorists argue that globalisation has a clear class dimension which sets apart elites from other social groups. Castells distinguishes mobile elites from static populations. Against global flows, Castells emphasises that labour is organised in local settings, without being networked to other places, leading to conflict between global capital and local labour. Labour is thereby forced to use their stasis as a mobilising principle. This view is echoed by Bauman (1998: 19, 21), who writes that 'Elites travel in space and travel faster than ever before ... [but] the rest of the population finds itself cut off forced to pay the heavy cultural, psychological and political price of their new isolation. This kind of account can be seen in the work of Lash and Urry (1994) on the isolation of the underclass, as well as Friedman (1999). However, we see little evidence for this kind of distinction which rests on a crude class determinism. Many of our Wilmslow residents were members of a global corporate elite, yet it is not clear that they are more culturally mobile than respondents in our other three places. It is true that they are more likely to travel abroad with their work and report slightly higher levels of family and friends abroad. However, their cultural tastes are considerably more parochial and 'national' than those found in the other areas. They rarely have any developed sense of global reflexivity, and most of them explain their attachment to place in terms of their emotional investment in the north of England, where they were often brought up and have continuing kinship ties. The problem here is in part the remarkably crude distinction between elites and the rest, which is hardly convincing given the abundant evidence for more fine grained and complex differentiation between social groups.[2] More fundamentally than this, however, such writers appeal to a crude form of class determinism in order to account for the local, but they lack a theory of class as an integral aspect of contemporary globalisation. It is therefore odd that a writer such as Bauman who has staked his colours to the 'end of class' idea should in the end rely on some kind of class analysis – albeit one which has learned nothing from the sophisticated debate about meaning and nature of class relations which has raged in recent years.[3] It is not coincidental that those writers who have a class centred interpretation of global social change, such as Sklair (1997), are in fact sceptical of many of the claims of globalisation. Rather than assuming that labour is 'local' it is surely crucial to decompose different forms of 'labour', learning from the extensive debates about how to understand the nature of the middle classes (e.g. Abercrombie and Urry 1983; Savage et al. 1992; Butler and Savage 1995).

4. *Locals vs cosmopolitans.* If we have achieved one thing in this book, we hope it is to debunk the idea that the distinction between these two groups is of major contemporary significance. We have seen that there are few 'locals' who are still living in areas that they were 'born and bred', and where such locals do exist (notably in Cheadle) they often feel they do not belong but rather think of themselves as marginal. The weakness of these locals allows us also rethink cosmopolitan identities

in different ways to Hannerz (1996), Urry (2002) and Beck (2002), who see cosmopolitans in terms of 'their willingness to engage with the other' (Hannerz 1996: 103). Such accounts fail to register that given the limits of distinctively 'local' cultures, this willingness takes a particularly self-referential form, in which people seek security through identifying with other similar places. When distinctive local cultures can be detected, cosmopolitans can identify themselves in relation to them. This point is indeed made by Hannerz (1996) Beck (2002) and Urry (2002: 137), but they then fail to realise that when local cultures dissipate, the cosmopolitan project loses clear terms of reference, since it can no longer define itself against a bounded 'other'. Instead, it appears to become a search for reassurance which seeks sustenance through reference to 'other' similar cultures. Its dialogical qualities therefore have clear limits. Thus, Urry's (2002: 137) portrait of a cosmopolitan fluidity which involves 'the capacity to live simultaneously in both the global and the local, in the distant and proximate, in the universal and particular' fails to recognise that the 'global' becomes identified with other cosmopolitan 'proximates' (London), and that globalising processes actually lead to a circular frame of cosmopolitan reference in which encounters with the 'non-culturally privileged other' are foreclosed. We have traced the significance of this self-referential cosmopolitanism especially with respect to our Chorlton residents. This group claims a cosmopolitan identity, yet it is one that in some respects effaces the 'other'. Its members have little to do, practically, with local residents, and they have little awareness of the significance of other social groups living in the area. They are attracted to the idea of appreciating global cultures yet their actual cultural reference points show very little engagement with cultures outside the English speaking metropolises. They have intense local knowledge of the area and often moved to the place because of their range of face-to-face social contacts in the area. In short, they do not empirically sustain the kinds of claims that Beck (2002: 27), for instance makes of them in which cosmopolitanism is 'an imagination of a globally shared collective future'. Nor does this account support the arguments of Urry, Bauman and Turner that cosmopolitanism can be seen as related to 'irony' and distance from place. In fact, Chorlton cosmopolitans are highly at home in their surrounds and often have a dense range of social contacts near where they live. Empirically, 'actually existing cosmopolitans' do not seem to redeem the hope placed on them by contemporary social theorists.

An alternative approach

We are now in a position to lay out our alternative approach to understanding the dynamics of globalisation and belonging. This can most easily be done in the form of a series of points:

1. The precise form and nature of global connections depends strongly on the precise field of practice that is being studied. Rather than an epochal shift from a modern to global society, we need to recognise that fields vary in their spatial extension and scope. Some of these fields – for instance music and cinema – deploy IT to permit considerable spatial extension, yet other fields, notably that of residence, do not. Despite the claims of some post-modern theorists that we are witnessing the de-differentiation of fields (Lash 1990) we argued in Chapter 6 that fields are clearly differentiated from one another, with social networks of residence, work, and friendship, rarely overlapping. We are not in a position to assess whether these findings are new, since we have no historical data, but we would argue that our interpretation is consistent with a view that current globalisation is at best a deepening of long-term trends towards social differentiation.

2. Within these differentiated fields, residential space is a key arena in which respondents define their social position. If only because it remains rare to have multiple residences, residence plays an increasingly important role vis-à-vis other fields in defining one's own sense of social location. In addition, residential space is crucial also in allowing people access to other fields, such as that of education, employment, and vari-ous cultural fields. One's residence is a crucial, possibly *the* crucial, identifier of who you are. The sorting processes by which people chose to live in certain places and others leave is at the heart of contemporary battles over social distinction. Rather than seeing wider social identities as arising out of the field of employment it would be more promising to examine their relationship to residential location.

3. Places are defined not as historical residues of the local, or simply as sites where one happens to live, but as sites chosen by particular social groups wishing to announce their identities. While retaining the tradi-tional Chicago school emphasis on urban space as a habitat, we argue that places offer visions of living which do not depend on the character of face-to-face relationships, or the historical character of the place. In all four areas there are striking congruences between the capitals of the residents and their sense of feeling at home. Chorlton appeals to those with cultural capital and moderate amounts of economic capital. Wilmslow appeals to those with large amounts of economic capital and moderate amounts of cultural capital, while Ramsbottom is favoured by the upwardly mobile without large amounts of cultural capital.

4. Elective belonging involves people moving to a place and putting down roots. It evokes a distinctive form of temporality suspended between the 'glacial time' of long-term history, and the instantaneous time of the pre-sent through the way that people identify a moment when they commit to a place. People feel they belong when they are able to biographically make sense of their decision to move to a particular place, and their sense of belonging is hence linked to this contingent tie between themselves and their surrounds. We see the concept of elective belonging as preferable to that of 'outside belonging' (Probyn 1996) since the latter depends for

its analytical power on an alternative notion of 'inside belonging' which is largely absent. Elective belonging is a way of dealing, at the personal level with people's relative fixity in local routines of work, household relationships, and leisure on the one hand, and the mobility of their cultural imaginations on the other. Most respondents were embedded in their place of residence, and few could easily 'up sticks'. However, people routinely invoked a networked sense of place, comparing their locations with those that were meaningful and important to them through the infrastructure of global communications – tourism, the media, and so forth. We see these findings as exemplifying Appadurai's (1996) arguments concerning the significance of the organisation of the imagination, as well as Tomlinson's (1997) emphasis that globalisation is significant not so much in allowing new forms of mobility but in transforming places.

5. Identities are developed through the networked geography of places articulated together. In our research these can be seen to operate at a variety of spatial scales. Most globally, we have detected a white, Anglophone diaspora. Here respondents feel at home among the cultural values and objects of English, American and (to a much lesser extent) Australian and Canadian nations. Reference is occasionally made to cultures outside these zones, but they are nearly always seen as 'difficult' or 'exceptional'. Less powerful, and to some extent cutting across this, there are networks of global urban spaces, concentrating especially on the connections (or lack of) between Manchester and London, but sometimes extending into comparisons with other world cities, mostly in Europe. Thirdly, there is a powerful regional cultural geography enmeshed in our respondents' identities. The specific places to which they have moved offer a distinctive location within the north of England. The regional level is especially important since it is often within the broadly defined north (rather than the local level) that respondents have kinship ties and emotional connections. One of the striking and largely unexpected findings from our research is the limited significance of the national frame of reference in people's cultural imaginaries. Many of our respondents can be seen as being part of a 'northern English white middle class'.

These five points are all anchored in the empirical findings of our book but, we contend, offer an approach which might have application elsewhere. However, this is for others to judge.

Notes

1 The other three city regions were expected to be (a) the South East, with corridors running east to Ipswich, north to Northampton, west to Swindon, and south to Portsmouth and Southampton, (b) Severnside, running from Bristol west to Swansea, north to Gloucester and east to Bath and (c) the Midlands.

2 The use of the concept of elite, rather than class, is of course instructive here.

3 Examples of such work debates are to be found in Scott 1996, Crompton 1998, Crompton et al. 2000, Devine et al. 2003.

Appendix

List of Interviews

CHEADLE AREA

Interviewee	Gender	Age	Occupation	Household income	pages referenced
C2	Male	37	PVC window fitter	C	162
C6	Female	36	Cleaner/voluntary work	A	163
C4	Male	38	Accountant	D	81–2, 124
C10	Female	30	Housewife, prev. Staff Nurse	B	
C12	Female	55	Housewife, prev. Clerical worker	A	
C13 – Stuart	Male	49	Engineering manager	C	49–50, 135–37, 158, 163
C15	Male	33	Building worker	B	
C17	Male	33	Technical manager, Local authority	N/k	50, 73, 113, 148, 162, 163
C20	Female	74	Retired (retail assistant)	B	33, 98
C21	Male	39	Civil servant (Manager)	C	83, 109, 148
C24	Male	50	Gardener	B	
C26	Female	64	Retired clerical worker	N/k	47, 125
C27	Female	58	School mid-day assistant	N/k	
C29	Male	71	Retired leading tradesman	N/k	158
C32	Male	41	Computer software consultant	F	71
C34 – Edward	Male	49	F.E. Lecturer	C	26–7, 83, 143, 160
C38	Male	29	University lecturer	D	83, 87, 137, 166
C46	Male	43	Plumbing & heating merchant	D	32, 196
C48	Male	62	Unemployed (former sales manager)	C	158
C51	Female	43	Cleaning company proprietor	D	176
C52	Male	54	Unemployed, former miner	B	124–25, 158
C55 – Harry	Male	61	Security worker	B	91, 144, 158
C57	Male	60	Retired (chartered engineer)	B	
C60	Female	28	Solicitor	D	
C65	Male	29	Maintenance electrician	B	143
C70	Male	40	Building Contractor	D	70, 110, 142
C71	Male	54	Kitchen & bedroom fitter (s/e)	B	98, 148
C74	Male	51	Teacher	C	32
C78	Male	23	Tarmac layer	C	125, 158

(Continued)

CHEADLE AREA (Continued)

C79	Male	41	Driving instructor (s/e)	B	98, 147
C91	Female	31	Secretary	C	59, 158
C97	Female	39	Export administrator	B	71, 84, 158, 164
C98	Male	39	CCTV systems consultant (s/e)	D	48
C99	Male	57	Retired (drayman)	A	158
C100	Female	39	Retail assistant	C	
C101	Male	47	Maintenance administrator	D	33, 73, 147
C102	Male	55	builder (s/e)	B	110, 172
C110	Female	50	Education officer	F	132
C114	Female	32	Staff nurse	C	134
C118	Male	38	Fire fighter	C	
C120	Female	81	Retired (telephonist)	A	147
C136 – Tom	Male	42	Hospital porter	A	91, 148, 172, 196–7
C143	Female	65	Retired clerical worker	N/k	123

Total 43

Income codes: A: under £10,000
B: £11–20,000
C: £21–30,000
D: £31–40,000
E: £41–50,000
F: £51–60,000
G: £61–70,000
H: £71–80,000
I: £81–90,000
J: £91–100,000
K: over £100,000

Notes:

F.E = Further Education
(s/e) = self-employed

CHORLTON AREA

Interviewee	Gender	Age	Occupation	Household income	pages referenced
D4	Female	65	Admin. assistant	n/k	41
D9 – James	Male	65	Retired	A	143, 163, 199–201
D11	Female	43	Development consultant (s/e)	D	40, 86, 92, 139, 177, 186, 194, 199
D12 – Fiona	Female	37	Computer systems engineer	D	58, 92, 135, 162, 189–90
D13	Male	31	Hospital registrar	G	80, 95, 118, 126, 137
D14	Female	31	Optician (s/e)	C	85, 94, 126
D16	Male	40	Restaurant proprietor	E	43, 198
D20 – Steve	Male	36	Carpenter (s/e)	G	95, 97–8, 164
D23	Male	34	Operations manager	F	46, 140
D25	Male	39	Local auth. manager	D	67, 81, 158
D27 – Kerry	Female	35	Media professional	D	68–9, 150, 192–3

(Continued)

CHORLTON AREA (Continued)

D33 – Serge	Male	30	Export sales manager	n/k	114, 198
D34 – Joe	Male	27	PGCE student	C	86, 95, 117–8
D42	Male	52	Musician	B	139–40, 144, 192
D43	Female	41	Dentist	n/k	61, 145
D44	Male	49	Fork lift truck driver	B	59
D47	Female	44	Peripatetic teacher	n/k	59, 93, 96
D50	Male	40	Designer (s/e)	B	61, 94, 149
D51 – Sally	Female	45	Graphic designer (s/e)	D	42, 83, 149, 159–60
D52	Male	39	Orchestral musician	C	92, 112, 139, 164
D53	Female	43	Primary school teacher	C	43, 86, 186
D55	Female	49	Unemployed	A	47, 61, 113, 118
D56	Female	27	TV producer & director	D	140, 158
D59	Female	35	University lecturer	n/k	164
D63	Male	82	Retired (F.E. Lecturer)	B	108, 165
D64	Female	24	Administrator	n/k	41, 113, 163, 178
D66	Female	40	Manager, Local authority services	E	158
D68	Female	46	Childminder	D	50, 61–2, 113, 187, 164
D70	Female	51	Piano teacher (s/e)	A	92, 125, 158
D71	Male	N/k	Divisional leader F.E.	E	135, 158, 178
D74	Male	33	Software engineer	C	158, 162
D82	Female	51	F.E. coordinator	B (ind income)	
D84	Male	18	Retail assistant & student	n/k	158
D87	Female	29	Freelance editor	C	164
D89	Female	27	Actress	B	96
D92	Male	27	Medical biological scientist	C	147
D93	Female	34	Craft worker (s/e)	A	86
D94	Male	31	Science teacher secondary	D	
D98 – John	Male	47	Lecturer	C	67, 108–9, 126, 136
D100	Male	27	Project co-ordinator & manager	B	
D101	Female	69	Retired (BT clerical worker)	A	158, 163
D103	Male	37	NHS operations manager	E	162
D106	Female	43	Nurse	E	158, 161
D107	Male	30	Building site manager	F	42, 68, 191
D109 – Susan	Female	45	F.E. art teacher & NVQCo Ord.	E	23, 42, 43, 94, 96, 163
D110 – Jane	Female	30	Nursing student/ writer	A	47–48
D115	Female	32	Journalist	D	41, 42–3, 140

Total 47

RAMSBOTTOM AREA

Interviewee	Gender	Age	Occupation	Household income	pages referenced
R4	Female	30	Housewife	C	135
R12	Female	59	Housewife	B	158, 164
R13	Male	36	F.E. prog. dev. manager	D	60, 101, 132–33
R21 – Joanne	Female	49	Insurance adjuster	B	24–5, 34–5, 80, 119
R28 – Ronnie	Male	45	Landscape gardener (s/e)	D	36, 101, 128–29
R30	Male	37	Printer	D	136
R32	Female	72	Retired	A	158
R33	Female	38	Community nursing sister	B	166, 167
R37	Male	37	Dry cleaning co., proprietor	C	99, 161
R41	Female	61	Retired (teacher)	F	52
R42	Male	48	Insurance broker (s/e)	G	84
R43	Female	46	Secretary	G	
R47	Female	61	Retired (aux. nurse)	B	158
R48 – Joe	Male	53	Maintenance fitter	D	50–51
R51	Male	n/k	Retired (manager in manufacturing)	n/k	
R54	Male	50	Security manager	C	51, 165
R58	Female	n/k	Primary school teacher	D	
R59	Female	32	Freelance craft worker (s/e)	D	91, 140, 162, 163
R63	Female	70	Retired (secretary)	A	113, 122
R66	Male	39	Product manager	F	197
R67	Female	44	Care assistant	B	101
R76	Male	58	Self employed printer	D	35
R78	Male	n/k	F.E. lecturer	n/k	101, 145, 187
R79	Female	28	Secretary	C	
R80 – Bernie	Male	44	Computer services team leader	E	99–100
R81	Female	32	Health & safety consultant	G	101–2, 192, 193
R82 – Greg	Male	41	Senior trainer computing	G	60, 162, 167, 185, 199–201
R88	Male	43	Milkman (s/e)	C	196
R90	Female	n/k	Cleaner	C	37
R97	Female	26	Solicitor	E	90
R101	Male	40	Computer services	E	
R104	Male	34	Computer systems developer (s/e)	J	
R105	Male	34	Insurance sales manager	n/k	
R114	Female	38	Housewife (prev. Nurse)	D	59, 117, 158, 164
R127 – Dave	Male	48	Export sales manager	E	158, 167, 177, 199
R129	Male	49	District manager	n/k	
R135 – Stella	Female	33	Training consultant	E	57, 113, 128, 164
R138	Female	43	Accountant	G	82, 101, 163, 164
R139	Male	73	Retired (BT engineer)	B	163
R141	Male	48	Engineer	D	37, 70

(Continued)

RAMSBOTTOM AREA (Continued)

R145	Male	62	Chartered electrical engineer	D	162
R147	Male	39	BT customer advisor	E	82, 160, 161, 162
R148	Female	45	Teaching assistant	E	35
R149	Male	52	Specialist sales manger	D	70
R156	Male	58	Market trader (-)	C	158, 185
R158	Female	37	Housewife (prev. clerical and bank worker)	C	70
R164	Male	41	Bank official (call centre)	B	185

Total 47

WILMSLOW AREA

Interviewee	Gender	Age	Occupation	Household income	pages referenced
W1 – Ernest	Male	52	Managing director, Engineering Company	H	39, 60, 124, 138–39
W2	Female	36	Student	D	38–39, 81, 163
W3	Female	38	Retail assistant & buyer	B	38, 55, 93, 103, 103, 123, 163
W5 – Susan	Female	49	P-t administrator	K	55, 74
W7 – Deidre	Female	44	Training consultant	G	61, 87–8, 123, 126–7, 133–4, 158, 183
W10	Female	76	Retired (secretary)	n/k	103, 127, 158, 165
W12	Female	31	Facility assistant	F	74, 190
W13	Female	40	Communications manager: city Council	G	74
W14	Male	38	Solicitor	K	60, 115
W20	Male	75	Retired (electronics engineer)	D	47, 114–15
W21	Female	69	Retired (secretary)	n/k	38, 93, 166
W23	Male	49	Surveyor	D	127
W25	Female	42	Housewife (prev. software sales)	G	58, 163
W27	Female	n/k	Services manager, City Council	n/k	75–76, 91, 127, 192
W31	Female	45	Secretary	H	157, 163
W33	Female	51	Pharmaceutical dispenser	G	80, 163, 175
W34	Male	36	Purchasing manager	F	75
W35	Female	48	Head teacher	C	66, 81, 90, 120
W38	Male	56	Physician	J	184
W40	Female	54	Social worker	n/k	127
W42	Male	44	Air traffic controller	G	88, 143, 146
W50	Female	42	Dentist	G	117, 123
W51 – Peter	Male	48	Company Director	K	65, 89–90, 113
W58 – Betty	Female	70	Retired (partner. G.P.)	B	120–1, 163, 184
W59	Female	53	Housewife (partner. Textile Importer)	K	55, 127, 158, 164, 166

(Continued)

WILMSLOW AREA *(Continued)*

W60	Male	71	Retired engineering designer & agent	C	161–2
W62	Male	52	Secondary teacher	C	64–65, 112, 115
W67	Male	74	Retired (consultant physician)	F	164, 178, 198
W68	Female	80	Retired (housewife)	D	113, 175, 184
W69	Female	58	Co-owner textiles company	K	75, 117, 165
W70	Male	58	Retired (manager)	E	
W71	Male	68	Retired (hospital consultant)	H	
W73	Female	66	Retired (teacher)	D	119, 148, 164, 194
W74 – Stuart	Male	46	Senior executive in occupational medicine	n/k	22, 38, 82, 194–5
W82	Female	n/k	Retired (clerical worker)	n/k	158
W88 – Liz	Female	38	Pharmacist	K	56, 73, 148
W91	Female	52	Financial administrator	I	176
W93	Male	54	Managing director	K	99, 139, 147, 158, 185
W96	Female	58	Retired (shop proprietor)	G	162
W98 – Sarah	Female	50	Teacher (Prep. School)	K	63–4, 73, 164
W99	Female	50	Dental hygienist	H	146, 158
W100	Male	53	Cabin services director	F	
W106	Male	61	Retired senior manger	n/k	
W108	Female	43	Computer programmer	F	58–59, 64
W109	Female	49	Receptionist	I	162

Total 45

References

Abbott, A. (2000) *Time Matters*. Chicago: University of Chicago Press.

Abercrombie, N. and Longhurst, B. (1998) *Audiences: A Sociological Theory of Performance and Imagination*. London: Sage.

Abercrombie, N. and Urry, J. (1983) *Capital, Labour and the Middle Classes*. London: Allen and Unwin.

Abrams, P. (1968) *The Origins of British Sociology, 1834–1914: An Essay*: Chicago, Chicago University Press.

Adams, R. and Allan, G. (eds) (1998) *Placing Friendship in Context*. Cambridge: Cambridge University Press.

Adkins, L. (2002) *Revisions: Gender and Sexuality in Late Modernity*. Buckingham: Open University Press.

Albrow, M. (1996) *The Global Age*, Cambridge: Polity.

Albrow, M. (1997) 'Travelling beyond local cultures', in J. Eade (ed.) *Living the Global City*, London: Routledge. pp. 37–55.

Allan, G. (1979) *A Sociology of Friendship and Kinship*. London: Allen and Unwin.

Allen, J. (2003) *Lost Geographies of Power*. Oxford: Blackwells.

Amin, A. and Thrift, N. (2002) *Cities: Reimagining the Urban*. Cambridge: Polity.

Anderson, B. (1983) *Imagined Community*. London: Verso.

Ang, I. (1995) *Watching Dallas: Soap Opera and the Melodramatic Imagination*. London: Methuen.

Appadurai, A. (1993) 'Disjuncture and Difference in the Global Cultural Economy' in B. Robins (ed.) *The Phantom Public Sphere*. Minneapolis and London: University of Minnesota Press.

Appadurai, A. (1996) *Modernity at Large*. Minneapolis and London: University of Minnesota Press.

Audretsch, D. (1998) 'Agglomeration and the location of economic activity', *Oxford Review of Economic Policy*, 14 (2): 18–29.

Auge, M. (1995) *Non-places: Introduction to the anthropology of hyper-modernity*. Stanford: Stanford University Press.

Back, L. (1996) *New Ethnicities and Urban Culture: Racisms and Multiculture in Young Lives*. London: UCL Press.

Bacon-Smith, C. (1992) *Enterprising Women: Television Fandom and the Creation of Popular Myth*. Philadelphia: University of Pennsylvania Press.

Bagnall G. (1996) 'Consuming the past' in S. Edgell, K. Hetherington and A. Warde (eds) *Consumption Matters*. Oxford: Blackwell.

Bagnall, G. (1998) 'Mapping the museum: the cultural consumption and production of two north west heritage sites. Unpublished PhD thesis, University of Salford.

Bagnall, G., Longhurst, B. and Savage, M. (2003) Children, Belonging and Social Capital: The PTA and Middle Class Narratives of Social Involvement in the North-West of England, *Sociological Research on Line*.

Ball, S.J. (2002) *Class Strategies and the Education Market: The Middle Classes and Social Advantage*. London: Routledge Falmer.

Ball, S.J. and Vincent, C. (1998) 'I heard it on the grapevine: hot knowledge and school choice', *British Journal of the Sociology of Education*, 19 (3): 377–400.

Ball, S.J., Bowe, R. and Gerwitz, S. (1995) 'Circuits of schooling a sociological exploration of parental choice in social class contexts', *Sociological Review*, 43: 52–78.

Bartley, M. (2004) *Health Inequalities*. London: Sage.

Baudrillard, J. (1988) *Selected Writings*. Cambridge: Polity.

Bauman, Z. (1989) *Legislators and Interpreters: On Modernity, Post-Modernity and the Intellectuals*. Cambridge: Polity.

Bauman, Z. (1998) *Globalisation: The Human Consequences*. Oxford: Blackwell.

Baumgartner, M.P. (1991) *The Moral Order of a Suburb*. New York: Oxford University Press.

Beck, U. (2000) *What is Globalization?* Cambridge: Polity.

Beck, U. 2002. 'The cosmopolitan society and its enemies', *Theory, Culture and Society* 19: 17–44.

Beck, U. and Beck-Gersheim, E. (1995) *The Normal Chaos of Love*. Cambridge: Polity.

Bell, C. (1968) *Middle Class Families: Social and Geographical Mobility*. London: Routledge.

Bellah, R., Madsen, R., Sullivan, W., Swidler A. and Tipton, S.M. (1996) *Habits of the Heart*, 2nd edition. Berkeley: University of California Press.

Benjamin, W. (1973) *Illuminations*. London: Fontana.

Benjamin, W. (1999) *The Arcades Project*. Cambridge, MA: Harvard University Press.

Bennett, T., Emmison, M. and Frow, J. (2000) *Accounting for Taste: Australian Everyday Cultures*. Cambridge: Cambridge University Press.

Berman, M. (1983) *All That is Solid Melts into Air*. London: Verso.

Binnie, J. and Skeggs, B. (2004) 'Cosmopolitan knowledge and the production and consumption of sexualised space: Manchester's gay village', *Sociological Review*, 52 (1): 39–61.

Black, P. (2002) '"Ordinary people come through here": locating the beauty salon in women's lives', *Feminist Review*, 71: 2–17.

Black, P. and Sharma, U. (2001) 'Men are real, women are "made up": beauty therapy and the construction of femininity', *Sociological Review*, 49 (1): 100–116.

Blokland, T. (2003) *Urban Bonds*. Cambridge: Polity.

Bott, E. (1957) *Family and Social Network: Roles, Norms and External Relationships in Ordinary Urban Families*. London: Tavistock.

Bourdieu, P. (1977) 'Cultural reproduction and social reproduction', in J. Karabel and A.H. Halsey (eds) *Power and Ideology in Education*. New York: Oxford University Press.

Bourdieu, P. (1984) *Distinction: A Social Critique of Taste*. Cambridge, MA: Harvard University Press.

Bourdieu, P. (1987) 'What makes a social class: on the theoretical and practical existence of groups', *Berkeley Journal of Sociology*, 32: 1–18.

Bourdieu, P. (1996) *The State Nobility*. Cambridge: Polity.

Bourdieu, P. (1997) 'The forms of capital', in A.H. Halsey, H. Lauder, P. Brown, and A.S. Wells (eds) *Education: Culture, Economy, Society*. Oxford: Oxford University Press.

Bourdieu, P. (1998) *Practical Reason*. Cambridge: Polity Press.

Bourdieu, P. (1999a) *Pascalian Meditations*. Cambridge: Polity.

Bourdieu, P. (1999b) *The Weight of the World*. Cambridge: Polity.

Bourdieu, P. (1999c) 'The social conditions of the international circulation of ideas', in R. Shusterman (ed.) *Bourdieu: A Critical Reader*. Oxford: Blackwell.

Bourdieu, P. and Passeron, J.C. (1973) *Reproduction in Education, Society and Culture*. London: Sage.

Bourdieu, P. and Wacquant, L. (1992) *An Invitation to Reflexive Sociology*. Chicago: Chicago University Press.

Bourdieu, P. and Wacquant, L. (1999) 'On the cunning of imperialist wisdom', *Theory, Culture and Society*, 16: 41–58.

Bowlby, R. (1985) *Just Looking: Consumer Culture in Dreiser, Gissing and Zola*. New York: Methuen.

Brannen, J. and O'Brien, M. (1996) *Children in Families: Research and Policy*. London: Falmer Press.

Brenner, N. (2000) 'The urban question as a scale question: reflections on Henri Lefebvre, urban theory and the politics of scale', *International Journal of Urban and Regional Research*, 24: 361–378.

Brunsdon, C. (1991) 'Satellite dishes and the landscapes of taste', *New Formations*, 15: 23–42.

Bryson, B. (1996) '"Anything but heavy metal": symbolic exclusion and musical dislikes', *American Sociological Review*, 61: 884–899.

Buck, N., Gordon, I., Hall, P., Harloe, M. and Kleinman, M. (2002) *Working Capital: Life and Labour in Contemporary London*. London: Routledge.

Buck-Morss, S. (1989) *The Dialectics of Seeing*. Cambridge, MA: MIT Press.

Bulmer, M. (1986) *Neighbours: The Work of Philip Abrams*. Cambridge: Cambridge University Press.

Bull, M. (2000) *Sounding Out the City*. Oxford: Berg.

Burawoy, M. et al. (1991) *Ethnography Unbound: Power and Resistance in the Modern Metropolis*. Berkeley: University of California Press.

Burawoy, M., Blum, J.A., George, S., Gille, Z., Gowan, T., Haney, L., Klawiter, M., Lopez, S.H., O Riain, S. and Thayer, M. (2000) *Global Ethnography: Forces, Connections and Imaginations in a Postmodern World*. Berkeley: University of California Press.

Butler, T. and Robson, G. (2003a) *London Calling*. Avebury: Ashgate.

Butler, T. and Robson, G. (2003b) 'Plotting the middle classes: gentrification and circuits of education in London', *Housing Studies*, 18 (1): 5–28.

Butler, T. and Savage, M. (eds) (1995) *Social Change and the Middle Classes*. London: UCL Press.

Calhoun, C. (2003) 'The class consciousness of frequent travellers: towards a critique of actually existing cosmopolitanism', in Vertovec, S. and Cohen, R. (eds) *Conceiving Cosmopolitanism*, Oxford: Oxford University Press. pp. 86–109.

Carrabine, E. and Longhurst, B. (1999) 'Mosiacs of omnivorousness: suburban youth and popular music', *New Formations*, 38: 125–140.

Casey, C.S. (1997) *The Fate of Place: A Philosophical History*. Berkeley: University of California Press.

Castells, M. (1996a) *The Rise of the Network Society*. Oxford: Blackwells.

Castells, M. (1996b) *The Power of Identity*. Oxford: Blackwells.

Castells, M. (1997) *The End of the Millennium*, Oxford, Blackwells.

Castells, M. (2002) 'Conclusion: urban sociology in the twenty first century', in I. Susser (ed.) *The Castells Reader on Cities and Social Theory*. Oxford: Blackwells.

Caygill, H. (1998) *Walter Benjamin: The Colour of Experience*. London: Routledge.

Chaney, D. (1996), *Lifestyles*. London: Routledge.

Cheah, P. and Robbins, B. (eds) (1998) *Cosmopolitics: Thinking and Feeling Beyond the Nation*. Minneapolis: University of Minnesota Press.

Cloke, P. et al. *Writing the Rural: Five Cultural Geographies*. London: Paul Chapman.

Cohen, A.P. (ed.) (1982) *Belonging: Identity and Social Organization in British Rural Communities*. Manchester: Manchester University Press.

Cohen, A.P. (1985) *The Symbolic Construction of Community*. London: Tavistock.

Cohen, R. (1997) *Global Dispora*, London, UCL Press.

Corrigan, P. (1997) *The Sociology of Consumption*. London: Sage.

Cosgrove, D., Roscoe, B., Rycroft, S. (1996) 'Landscape and identity at Ladybower Reservoir and Rutland Water', *Transactions of the Institute of British Geographers*, 534–551.

Cowan, P. and Diamond, D.K. (1969) 'Emerging trends in urbanisation', copy found in box 14/1, Ray Pahl collection, Qualidata Archive: University of Essex.

Crompton, R. (1998) *Class and Stratification*, 2nd edition. Oxford: Blackwells.

Crompton, R., Devine, F., Savage, M., Scott, J. (2000) *Renewing Class Analysis*. Oxford: Blackwells.

Crossley, N. (2001) *The Social Body*. Cambridge: Polity.

Crow, G. and Allan, G. (1994) *Community Life*. Brighton: Harvester Wheatsheaf.

Crow, G. (2002) 'Community studies: fifty years of theorisation', *Sociological Research Online*, 7: 3 <http://www.socresonline.org.uk/7/3/crow.html>

Crow, G.A. and Summers M. (2002). 'Neither busybodies nor nobodies: managing proximity and distance in neighbouring relations', *Sociology*, 36: 127–147.

Davies, B. and Ward, P. (2002) *Managing Retail Consumption*. Chichester: John Wiley.

Davis, M. (1984) *City of Quartz*. London: Verso.

Dear, M. (2000) *The Postmodern Urban Condition*. Oxford: Blackwells.

De Certeau (1984) *The Practice of Everyday Life*. Berkeley: University of California Press.

De Nora, T. (2000) *Music in Everyday Life*. Cambridge: Cambridge University Press.

Deem, R. (1986) *All Work and No Play? The Sociology of Women and Leisure*. Milton Keynes: Open University Press.

Dennis, C. Henriques, F. and Slaughter, C. (1957) *Coal is our Life*. London: Tavistock.

Devine, F. (1992) *Affluent Workers Revisited*. Edinburgh: Edinburgh University Press.

Devine, F., Britton, J., Mellor, R. and Halfpenny, P. (2000) 'Professional work and professional careers in Manchester's business and financial sector', *Work, Employment and Society*, 14 (3): 521–540.

Devine, F., Savage, M., Crompton, R., Scott, J. (eds) (2004) *Class and Culture*. Basingstoke: Palgrave.

Dreyfus, H. and Rabinow, P. (1999) 'Can there be a science of existential structure and social meaning?', in R. Shusterman (ed.) *Bourdieu: A Critical Reader*. Oxford: Blackwells.

Drotner, K. (1994) 'Ethnographic enigmas: "the everyday" in recent media studies', *Cultural Studies*, 8 (2): 341–357.

Du Gay, P. (1996) *Consumption and Identity at Work*. London: Sage.

Duncan, S. and Smith, D (2002) 'Geographies of Family Formation: spatial differences and gender cultures in Britain', *Transactions of the Institute of British Geographers*, 27 (4): 471–493.

Eade, J. (ed.) (1996) *Living the Global City*. London: Routledge.

Edwards, J. (2000) *Born and Bred*. Oxford: Clarendon.

Elias, N. and Scotson, J. (1965) *The Established and the Outsiders*. London: Frank Cass.

Erickson, B. (1996) 'Culture, class and connections', *American Journal of Sociology*, 102 (1): 217–251.

Erikson, R. and Goldthorpe, J.H. (1992) *The constant flux: a study of class mobility in industrial societies*. Oxford: Clarendon.

Evans, G. (ed.) (1999) *The End of Class Politics? Class Voting in Comparative Perspective*. Oxford: Clarendon.

Falk, P. and Campbell, C. (1997) *The Shopping Experience*. London: Sage.

Featherstone, M. (1992) 'The heroic life and everyday life', *Theory, Culture and Society*, Feb, 159–182.

Featherstone, M. and Lash, S. (1995) 'Introduction' in Featherstone et al. (eds) *Global Modernities*, London: Sage. pp. 1–24.

Featherstone, M., Lash, S., Robertson, R. (1995) *Global Modernities*. London: Sage.

Fine, B. and Cohen, R. (2003) 'Four cosmopolitan moments', in Vertovec and Cohen (eds) *Conceiving Cosmopolitanism*, Oxford: Oxford University Press. pp. 137–62.

Finnegan, R. (1998), *Tales of the City*. London: Routledge.

Fischer, C.S. (1982) *To Dwell Amongst Friends: Personal Networks in Town and City*. Chicago: Chicago University Press.

Fiske, J. (1989) *Reading the Popular*. London: Unwin Hyman.

Fortier, A.-M. (2000) *Migrant Belongings*. Oxford: Berg.

Fowler, B. (1997) *Pierre Bourdieu and Cultural Theory*. London: Sage.

Frankenberg, R. (1957) *Village on the Border*. London: Cohen and West.

Frankenberg, R. (1966) *Communities in Britain*. London: Penguin.

Frankenberg, R. (1993) *White Women, Race Matters: The Social Construction of Whiteness*. London: Routledge.

Franklin, S., Lury, C. and Stacey, J. (2000) *Global Nature, Global Culture*. London: Sage.

Frazer, E. (1999) 'Unpicking political communitarianism: a critique of "the communitarian family"', in G. Jagger and C. Wright (eds) *Changing Family Values*. London: Routledge.

Friedmann, J. (1999) 'Reading Castells: zeitdiagnose and social theory', *Society and Space*, 17: 111–120.

Friedmann, J. and Wolff, G. (1982) 'World city formation: an agenda for research and action', *International Journal of Urban and Regional Research*, 6: 309–344.

Frisby, D. (1985), *Fragments of Modernity*. Oxford: Blackwells.

Fukuyama, F. (1992) *The End of History and the Last Man*. New York: Free Press.

Gans, H. (1962) *The Urban Villagers: Group and Class in the Life of Italian Americans.* New York: Free Press.

Gardiner, M.E. (2000) *Critiques of Everyday Life.* London: Routledge.

Gardner, C. and Sheppard, J. (1989), *Consuming Passion: The Rise of Retail Culture.* London: Unwin Hyman.

Gauntlett, D. and Hill, A. (1999) *TV Living: Televison, Culture and Everyday Life.* London: Routledge.

Giddens, A. (1973) *The Class Structure of the Advanced Societies.* London: Heinemann.

Giddens, A. (1990) *The Condition of Modernity.* Cambridge: Polity.

Giddens, A. (1991) *Intimacy and Self-identity.* Cambridge: Polity.

Gillespie, M. (1995) *Television, Ethnicity and Cultural Change.* London: Routledge.

Gilloch, G. (1996) *Myth and Metropolis: Walter Benjamin and the City.* Cambridge: Polity.

Gilroy, P. (1993) *The Black Atlantic.* London: Verso.

Giordino, B. and Twomey, I. (2002) 'Economic transitions: restructuring local labour markets', in J. Peck and K. Ward (eds) *City of Revolution.* Manchester: Manchester University Press, 50–75.

Glaser, B.G. and Strauss, A.L. (1967) *The Discovery of Grounded Theory: Strategies for Qualitative Research.* London: Weidenfeld and Nicholson.

Green, E., Hebron, S. and Woodward, D. (1990) *Women's Leisure, What Leisure?.* Basingstoke: Macmillan.

Grey, C. (1994) 'Career as a project of the self and labour process discipline', *Sociology*, 28 (2): 479–498.

Granovetter, M. (1973) 'The strength of weak ties', *American Journal of Sociology*, 78: 1360–1380.

Gregson, N. and Lowe, M. (1995) 'Too much work?, class, gender and the reconstitution of middle class domestic labour', in T. Butler and M. Savage (eds) *Social Change and the Middle Classes.* London: UCL Press.

Griffiths, S. (1998) *A Profile of Poverty and Health in Manchester.* Manchester: Manchester Health Authority and Manchester City Council.

Halford, S., Savage, M., Witz, A. (1997) *Gender, Careers and Organization: Recent Developments in Banking, Local Authorities and Nursing.* Basingstoke: Macmillan.

Hall, P. (1998) *Cities in Civilisation.* London: Weidenfeld and Nicholson.

Hall, S. and Jefferson, T. (eds) (1976) *Resistance Through Rituals: Youth Sub-Cultures in Post-War Britain.* London: Hutchinson.

Halsey, A.H., Heath, A.F., Ridge, J. (1980) *Origins and Destinations.* Oxford: Clarendon.

Hannerz, U. (1996) *Transnational Connections: Cultures, People, Places.* London: Routledge.

Harding, A. (1997) *Hulme City Challenge: did it work.* Liverpool European Institute for Urban Affairs.

Harrington, J. (1990) *The Outer City.* London: Edward Arnold.

Harvey, D. (1982) *The Limits to Capital.* Chicago: University of Chicago Press.

Harvey, D. (1985) 'The spatial fix', in D. Gregory and J. Urry (eds) *Social Relations and Spatial Structures.* Basingstoke: MacMillan.

Harvey, D. (1987) *The Condition of Postmodernity.* Oxford: Blackwells.

Harvey, D. (1993) 'From space to place and back again', in J. Bird et al. (eds) *Mapping the Futures: Local Cultures, Global Change.* London: Routledge.

Harvey, D. and Layter, T. (1993) *The Factory and the City: The Story of the Cowley Automobile Workers in Oxford.* London: Mansell.

Haylett, C. (2001) 'Ilegitimate subjects? abject whites, neoliberal modernisation and middle class multi-culturalism', *Society and Space*, 19: 351–370.

Heath, A.F., Jowell, R. and Curtice, J. (1985) *How Britain Votes.* Oxford: Clarendon.

Heath, A.F., Jowell, R., Curtice, J., Field, J. and Witherspoon, S. (1991) *Understanding Political Change: The British Voter, 1964–1987.* Oxford: Pergamon.

Held, D. (1995) *Democracy and the Global Order: From the Modern State to Cosmopolitan Governance.* Cambridge: Polity.

Held, D., McGrew, A., Goldblatt, D. and Perraton, J. (1999) *Global Transformations.* Cambridge: Polity.

Hermes, J. (1995) *Reading Women's Magazines.* Oxford: Polity.

Hetherington, K. (1997) *Badlands of Modernity*. London: Routledge.

Hetherington, K. and Law, J. (2000) 'After networks', *Society and Space*, 18 (2): 127–132.

Hills, H. and Tyrer, P. (2000) 'Half-forgotten streets: architecture and amnesia in Manchester' in N. Rudd (ed.) *Fabrications: new art and urban memory in Manchester*. Manchester: UMiM, pp. 32–39.

Hills H. and Tyrer, P. (2002) 'The fetishised past; post-industrial Manchester and intersticial spaces', *Visual Culture in Britain*, 3 (2): 103–18.

Hoschild, A. (1997) *The Time Bind: When Work Becomes Home and Home Becomes Work*. New York: Metropolitan Books.

Hoggart, R. (1957) *The Uses of Literacy: Aspects of Working Class Life with Special Reference to Publications and Entertainment*. Harmondsworth: Penguin.

Jameson, F. (1991) *Postmodernism, or the Cultural Logic of Late Capitalism*. London: Verso.

Jamieson, L. (1998) *Intimacy: Personal Relationships in Modern Societies*. Cambridge: Polity.

Jenkins, H. (1992) *Textual Poachers: Television Fans and Participatory Culture*. London: Routledge.

Jenkins, R. (1992) *Pierre Bourdieu*. London: Routledge.

Joyce, P. (2003) *The Rule of Freedom*. London: Verso.

Kearon, A.T. (2001), Older People and Fear of Crime: Towards an Understanding of the Roles of Social Networks and the Impact of the Media, Unpublished PhD Thesis, University of Salford.

Kidd, A.J. (1993), *Manchester*, Keele: Ryburn.

King, A.C. (2000) 'New directors, customers and fans: the transformation of English football in the 1990s', *Sociology of Sport Journal*, 14 (3): 576–593.

Kracauer, S. (1995) *The Mass Ornament*. Harvard: Harvard University Press.

Krugman, P. (1991) *Geography and Trade*. Cambridge, MA: MIT Press.

Krugman, P. (1995) *Development, Geography and Economic Theory*. Cambridge, MA: MIT Press.

Kumar, K. (1978) *Prophecy and Progress*. London. Penguin.

Kumar, K. (2003) *The Making of English National Identity*. Cambridge: Cambridge University Press.

Lamont, M. (1992) *Money, Morals and Manners: The Culture of the French and American Upper-middle class*. Chicago: University of Chicago Press.

Lamont, M. and Askartova, S. (2002) 'Ordinary cosmopolitanism: strategies for bridging racial boundaries among working class men', *Theory, Culture and Society*, 19: 1–27.

Lasch, C. (1995) *Revolt of the Elites and Betrayal of Democracy*. New York: Norton.

Lash, S. (1990) *The Sociology of Postmodernism*. London: Routledge.

Lash, S. (2002) *Critique of Information*. London: Sage.

Lash, S. and Urry, J. (1987) *The End of Organised Capitalism*. Cambridge: Polity.

Lash, S. and Urry, J. (1994) *Economies of Signs and Spaces*. London: Sage.

Latour, B.S. (1993) *We Have Never Been Modern*. New York: Harvester Wheatsheaf.

Layder, D. (1993) *New Strategies in Social Research*. Cambridge: Polity.

Le Gales, P. (2002) *European Cities: Social Conflicts and Governance*. Oxford: Blackwells.

Lefebvre, H. (1991) *The Production of Space*. Oxford: Blackwells.

Longhurst, B.J. and Savage, M. (1996) 'Social class, consumption, and the influence of Bourdieu: some critical issues', in S. Edgell, K. Hetherington and A. Warde (eds) *Consumption Matters*. Oxford: Blackwells.

Longhurst, B.J., Bagnall, G. and Savage, M. (2001) 'Ordinary consumption and personal identity: radio and the middle classes in the north west of England', in A. Warde and J. Gronow (eds) *Ordinary Consumption*. London: Routledge.

Longhurst, B.J., Bagnall, G. and Savage, M. (2004) 'Audiences, museums and the English middle class', *Museum and Society*, in press.

Lopez, J. and Scott, J. (2000) *Social Structure*. Milton Keynes: Open University Press.

Lull, J. (ed.) (1988) *World Families Watch Television*. London: Sage.

Lull, J. (1990) *Inside Family Viewing*. London: Routledge.

Lury, C. (1997) *Consumer Culture*. Cambridge: Polity.

Lury, C. (2003) 'The game of loyal(o)y, diversions and divisions in network society', *Sociological Review*, 51 (3): 301–320.

Lynch, K. (1960) *The Image of the City*. Cambridge, MA: MIT Press.

McNay, L. (1999). 'Gender, habitus and the field: Pierre Bourdieu and the limits of reflexivity', *Theory, Culture and Society*, 16: 95–117.

McRobbie, A. (1998) *British Fashion Design: Rag Trade or Image Industry?* London: Routledge.

Marshall, G., Swift, A. and Roberts, S. (1997) *Against the Odds: Social Class and Social Justice in Industrial Societies*. Oxford: Clarendon.

Mason, J. (1996) *Qualitative Researching*. London: Sage.

Massey, D. (1984) *Spatial Divisions of Labour*. Basingstoke: Macmillan.

Massey, D. (1993) 'Power geometry and a progressive sense of place', in J. Bird et al. (eds) *Mapping the Futures, Local Cultures, Global Change*. London: Routledge.

Massey, D. (1994), *Space, Class and Gender*. Cambridge: Polity.

Matless, D. (1998) *Landscape and Englishness*. London: Reaktion.

May, T. (2001) *Social Research: Issues, Methods and Process*. Milton Keynes: Open University Press.

Medhurst, A. (1997) 'Negotiating the gnome zone: versions of suburbia in British popular culture', in R. Silverstone (ed.) *Visions of Suburbia*. London: Routldge.

Mellor, R. (2002) 'Hypocritical city: cycles of urban exclusion', in J. Peck and K. Ward (eds) *City of Revolution*. Manchester: Manchester University Press.

Meyrowitz, J.A. (1985) *No Sense of Place: The Impact of Electronic Media on Social Behaviour*. New York: Oxford University Press.

Miller, D. (1995) *Acknowledging Consumption: A Review of New Studies*. London: Routledge.

Miller, D. (1998) *A Theory of Shopping*. Cambridge: Polity.

Miller, D., Jackson, P., Thrift, N., Holbrook, B. and Rowlands, M. (1998) *Shopping Place and Identity*. London: Routledge.

Miller, S. (1995) 'Land, landscape, and the question of culture: English urban hegemony and research needs', *Journal of Historical Sociology*, 8, 1, 94–107.

Mills, C.W. (1951) *White Collar*. New York: Oxford University Press.

Monbiot, G. (2000) *Captive State: The Corporate Take Over of Britain*. London: Pan.

Money, A. (2003) Consumption in the Home: Cultural Capital, Family Gift Cultures and Place, Unpublished PhD Thesis, University of Salford.

Moores, S. (1996) *Satellite Television and Everyday Life: Articulating Technology,*

Moores, S. (2000) *Media and Everyday Life in Modern Society*. Edinburgh: Edinburgh University Press.

Morley, D. (1986) *Family Television: Cultural Power and Domestic Leisure*. London: Comedia.

Morley, D. (2000) *Home Territories: Media, Mobility and Migrancy*. London: Routledge.

Morris, R.J. (1990) *Class, Sect and Party: The Making of the British Middle Class*. Manchester: Manchester University Press.

Morris, R.J. (1990) 'Clubs, societies and associations', in F.M.L. Thompson (ed.) *The Cambridge Social History of Britain*, Vol. 3. Cambridge: Cambridge University Press.

Munro, R. (1998) 'Belonging on the move: market rhetoric and the future as obligatory passage', *Sociological Review*, 46 (2): 208–243.

Newby, H. (1980) *Green and Pleasant Land? Social Change in Rural England*. Harmondworth: Penguin.

Nisbet, R. (1953) *The Quest for Community*. London: Oxford University Press.

O'Connor, J. and Wynne, D. (1996) 'Left loafing: city cultures and postmodern lifestyles', in O'Connor J. and Wynne, D. *From the Margins to the Centre: Cultural production and consumption in the post-industrial city*. Aldershot: Arena.

Pahl, J. and Pahl, R. (1971) *Managers and Their Wives*. London: Penguin.

Pahl, R. (1965) *Urbs in Rure*. London: LSE, Geographical Papers.

Pahl, R. (1970) *Patterns of Urban Life*. London: Longman.

Pahl, R. (2000) *On Friendship*. Cambridge: Polity.

Papastergiadis, N. (2000) *The Turbulence of Migration*. Cambridge: Polity.

Parker, S.R. (1976) *The Sociology of Leisure*. London: Allen and Unwin.

Parker, S.R. (1983) *Leisure and Work*. London: Allen and Unwin.

Paxman, J. (1999) *The English: A Portrait of a People*. London: Penguin.

Peck, J. and Tickell, A. (1994) 'Searching for a new institutional fix: The after fordist crisis and global-local disorder', in A. Amin (ed.) *Post-Fordism: A Reader*. Oxford: Blackwells.

Peck, J. and Tickell, A. (1995) 'Business goes local: dissecting the business agenda in Manchester', *International Journal of Urban and Regional Research*, 19: 55–78.

Peck, J. and Ward, K. (eds) (2002) *City of Revolution*. Manchester: Manchester University Press.

Penley, C. (1992) 'Feminism, psychoanalysis and the study of popular culture' in L. Grossberg, C. Nelson and P. Treichler (eds) *Cultural Studies*. London: Routledge.

Peterson, R.A and Kern, R.M. (1996) 'Changing highbrow taste: from snob to omnivore', *American Sociological Review*, 61: 900–907.

Phillips, M. et al. (1995) 'The new middle classes and social constructs of rural living', in T. Butler and M. Savage (eds) *Social Change and the Middle Classes*. London: UCL press.

Poggi, G. (1978) *The Development of the Modern State: A Sociological Introduction*. London: Hutchinson.

Poovey, M. (1995) *Making a Social Body: British Cultural Formation 1830–1864*. Chicago: University of Chicago Press.

Power, S. Edwards, T. Whitty, G. and Wigfall, V. (2003) *Education and the Middle Class*. Buckingham: Open University Press.

Probyn, E. (1996) *Outside Belongings*. New York: Routledge.

Putnam, R. (2000) *Bowling Alone*. New York: Touchstone.

Quilley, S. (1998) 'Manchester first: from municipal socialism to the entrepreneurial city', *International Journal of Urban and Regional Research*, 24: 601–621.

Quilley, S. (2002) 'Entrepreneurial turns: muncipal socialism and after', in J. Peck and K. Ward (eds) *City of Revolution*,. Manchester: Manchester University Press.

Rapoport, R. and Rapoport, R.N. (1995) 'Leisure and the family life cycle', in C. Critcher, P. Bramham and A. Tomlinson (eds) *Sociology of Leisure: A Reader*. London: E & F N Spon.

Reay, D. (2000) 'A useful extension of Bourdieu's conceptual framework? emotional capital as a way of understanding mothers' involvement in their children's education', *Sociological Review*, 48 (4): 568–585.

Reay, D. and Lucey, H. (2003) 'The limits of "Choice": children and inner city schooling', *Sociology*, 37 (1): 121–142.

Regional Trends 36 (2001) London: HMSO.

Ribbens, J., McCorthy, J. Edwards, R. and Gillies, V. (2000) 'Moral tales of the child and the adult: Narratives of contemporary family lives under changing circumstances' *Sociology*, 34 (4): 785–803.

Robbins, B. (2001) 'The village of the liberal–managerial class', in V. Dharwadker (ed.) *Cosmopolitan Geographies: New Locations in Literature and Culture*. New York: Routledge.

Roberts, R. (1971) *The Classic Slum*. Harmondsworth: Penguin.

Roberts, K. (1995) 'Work and its corollaries', in C. Critcher, P. Bramham and A. Tomlinson (eds) *Sociology of Leisure: A Reader*. London: E & F N Spon.

Roberts, K. (1999) *Leisure in Contemporary Society*. Wallingford: CABI.

Robertson, R. (1992) *Globalisation*. London: Sage.

Robertson, R. (1995) 'Glocalisation: time-space and homogeneity-heterogeneity', in M. Featherstone, S. Lash and R. Robertson (eds) Global Modernities. London: Sage.

Robson, B. (2002) 'Mancunian ways: the politics of regeneration', in J. Peck and K. Ward (eds).

Robson, G. and Butler, T. (2001) 'Coming to terms with London: Middle class communities in a global city', *International Journal of Urban and Regional Research*, 25 (1): 70–86.

Roediger, R. (1991) *The Wages of Whiteness*. London: Verso.

Rojek, C. (1995) *Decentering Leisure Theory*. London: Sage.

Rose, J. (2001) *The Intellectual Life of the British Working Classes*. Yale: Yale University Press.

Samuel, R. (1998) 'Country visiting: a memoir', in R. Samuel, *Island Stories: Unravelling Memory*. London: Verso.

Sassen, S. (1991) *The Global City*. London: Routledge.

Savage, M. (1995) 'Walter Benjamin's urban thought: A critical analysis', *Society and Space*, 13: 201–216.

Savage, M. (1999) 'Sociology, class and male manual work cultures', in J. McIlroy, N. Fishman, and A. Campbell (eds) *British Trade Unions and Industrial Politics: The High Tide of Trade Unionism, 1964–1979*. Aldershot: Ashgate.

Savage, M. (2000) *Class Analysis and Social Transformation*. Milton Keynes: Open University Press.

Savage, M. (2005) 'Bureaucracy and social capital', in P. du Gay (ed.) *The valuer of Bureaucracy*. Oxford: Oxford University Press.

Savage, M., Bagnall, G., Longhurst, B.J. (2001) 'Ordinary, ambivalent and defensive: Class identities in the north west of England', *Sociology*, 35 (4): 875–892.

Savage, M., Bagnall, G., Longhurst, B.J. (2004a) 'The comforts of place: Belonging and identity in the north-west of England', in T. Bennett and E. Silva (eds) *Everyday Cultures*. London: Sociology Press.

Savage, M., Bagnall, G., Longhurst, B.J. (2004b) 'Local habitus and working class culture', in F. Devine, M. Savage, R. Crompton and J. Scott (eds) *Rethinking Class*. Basingstoke: Palgrave.

Savage, M., Bagnall, G., Longhurst, B.J. (2005) 'Social capital in suburbia', in T Blokland and M. Savage (eds) *Social Capital on the Ground*. Forthcoming.

Savage, M., Barlow, J., Dickens, P. and Fielding, A.J. (1992) *Property, Bureaucracy and Culture: Middle Class Formation in Contemporary Britain*. London: Routledge.

Savage, M., Warde, A. and Ward, K. (2003) *Urban Sociology, Capitalism and Modernity*, 2nd edition. Basingstoke: Palgrave.

Sayer, A. (1992) *Method in Social Science: A realist approach*. London: Routledge.

Scannell, P. (1996) *Radio, Television and Modern Life*. Oxford: Blackwells.

Schlereth, T.J. (1977) *The Cosmopolitan Ideal in Enlightenment Thought*. Notre Dame, IN: University of Notre Dame Press.

Scott, J. (1996) *Stratification and Power*. Cambridge: Polity.

Scraton, S. and Watson, B. (1998) 'Gendered cities: women and public leisure space in the "postmodern city"', *Leisure Studies*, 17 (2): 123–137.

Seabrook, J. (1971) *City Close Up*. London: Penguin.

Seale, C. (1999) *The Quality of Qualitative Research*. London: Sage.

Sennett, R. (1998) *Flesh and Stone: The City in Western Civilization*. Allen Lane: London.

Shields, R. (1991) *Places on the Margin*. London: Routledge.

Shields, R. (1992) *Lifestyle Shopping*. London: Routledge.

Silva, E. (2000) *The Politics of Consumption @ Home: Practices and Dispositions in the Uses of Technologies*. Open University: Pavis Papers in Social and Cultural Research, No. 1.

Silver, A. (1989) 'Friendship and trust as moral ideals: an historical approach', *European Journal of Sociology*, 30: 274–297.

Silver, A. (1990) 'Friendship in commercial society: Eighteenth-century social theory and modern sociology', *American Journal of Sociology*, 25: 1474–1504.

Silverman, D. (2001) *Interpreting Qualitative Data: Methods for Analysing Talk, Text and Interaction*, 2nd edition. London: Sage.

Silverstone, R. (1994) *Television and Everyday Life*. London: Routledge.

Silverstone, R. (ed.) (1997) *Visions of Suburbia*. London: Routledge.

Simmel, G. (1964) 'The metropolis and mental life', in K. Wolff (ed.) *The Sociology of Georg Simmel*. New York: Free Press.

Simmel, G. (1990) *The Philosophy of Money*. London: Routledge.

Sklair, L. (2001) *The Transnational Capitalist Class*. Oxford: Blackwells.

Smith, M.P. (2001) *Transnational Urbanism*. Oxford: Blackwells.

Smith, M.P. and Feagin, J. (eds) (1987) *The Capitalist City: Global restructuring and community politics*. Oxford: Blackwells.

Social Trends 31, (2001) London: HMSO.

Soja, E. (1989) *Postmodern Geographies*. London: Verso.

Solomos, J. (1989) *Race and Racism in Contemporary Britain*. Basingstoke: MacMillan.

Southerton, D. (2002) 'Boundaries of "us" and "them": class, mobility and identification in a New town', *Sociology*, 36 (1): 161–193.

Souza Briggs, de X. (1998) 'Doing democracy up close: culture, power, and communication in community building', *Journal of Planning Education and Research*, 18: 1–13.

Spigel, L. (2001) *Welcome to the Dreamhouse: Popular Media and Postwar Suburbs*. Durham and London: Duke University Press.

Stacey, M. (1960) *Tradition and Change: A Study of Banbury*. London: Oxford University Press.

Stacey, M., Batstone, E., Bell, C. and Murcott, A. (1975) *Power, Persistence and Change: A Second Study of Banbury*. London: Routledge.

Stoker, G. (1998) 'Governance as theory: five propositions', *International Social Science Journal*, 155: 17–28.

Strathern, M. (1981) *Kinship at the Core: An Anthropology of Elmdon, A Village in the North-West of Essex in the 1960s*. Cambridge: Cambridge University Press.

Strathern, M. (1990) *After Nature*. Cambridge: Cambridge University Press.

Strathern, M. (1991), *Partial Connections*. Savage, Maryland, Rowman and Littlefield.

Sullivan, A. (2001) 'Cultural capital and educational attainment', *Sociology*, 35 (4): 893–912.

Swartz, D. (1997) *Culture and Power*. Chicago: University of Chicago Press.

Taylor, I. (1995) 'Private homes and public others: an analysis of talk about crime in suburban south Manchester in the mid 1990s', *British Journal of Sociology*, 35 (2): 263–285.

Taylor, I., Evans, K., Fraser, P. (1996) *A Tale of Two Cities*. London: Routledge.

Tester, K. (ed.) (1994) *The Flaneur*. London: Routledge.

Therborn, G. (1976) *Science, Class and Society*. London: Verso.

Thrift, N.J. (1993) 'Giddens's theory of structuration: A critical appreciation', *Progress in Human Geography*, 17 (1): 111–121.

Tomlinson, J. (1997) *Globalisation and Culture*. Cambridge: Polity.

Tomlinson, J. (2003) 'Interests and identities in cosmopolitan politics', in S. Vertotec and R. Cohen (eds) *Conceiving Cosmopolitanism*. Oxford: Oxford University Press.

Tornqvist, G. (1983) 'Creativity and the renewal of regional life', in A. Buttimer (ed.) *Creativity and Context: A Seminar Report*, Lund.

Tulloch, J. and Jenkins, H. (1995) *Science Fiction Audiences: Watching 'Doctor Who' and 'Star Trek'*. London: Routledge.

Turner, B.S. (2002). 'Cosmopolitan virtue, globalisation and patriotism', *Theory, Culture and Society*, 19: 45–65.

Turner, B.S. and Rojek, C. (2001) *Society and Culture: Principles of Scarcity and Solidarity*. London: Sage.

Urry, J. (1990) *The Tourist Gaze*. London: Sage.

Urry, J. (1995) 'A middle class countryside?', in Butler and Savage (eds) *Social Change and the Middle Classes*. London: UCC Press.

Urry, J. (2000) *Sociology Beyond Societies*. London: Routledge.

Urry, J. (2002) *Global Complexity*. Cambridge: Polity.

Vertovec, S. and Cohen, R. (eds) (2003) *Conceiving Cosmopolitanism*. Oxford: Oxford University Press.

Vester, M. (2000) 'The transformation of social classes: from "deproletarianisation" to "individualisation"', in G. Van Gyes, H. De Witte and P. Pasture (eds) *Can Class Still Unite?* Aldershot: Ashgate.

Vincent, C. (2001) 'Social class and parental agency', *Journal of Education Policy*, 16 (4): 347–364.

Vincent, C. and Ball, S.J. (2001) 'A market in love? Choosing pre-school childcare', *British Educational Research Journal*, 27 (5): 633–651.

Vincent, C. and Martin, J. (2002) 'Class, culture, and agency: researching parental voice', *Discourse: Studies in the Cultural Politics of Education*, 23 (1): 109–128.

Warde, A. (1997) *Consumption, Taste and Food: Cultural Antinomies and Consumer Culture*. London: Sage.

Warde, A., Martens, L. and Olsen, W. (1999) 'Consumption and the problem of variety: cultural omnivorousness, social distinction and eating out', *Sociology*, 33: 105–127.

Warde, A. and Martens, L. (2000) *Eating Out*. Cambridge: Cambridge University Press.

Wasserman, S. and Faust, K. (1994) *Social Network Analysis: Methods and Applications*. Cambridge: Cambridge University Press.

Watson, W. (1964) 'Social mobility and social class in industrial societies', in M. Glucksmann and F. Devons (eds) *Closed Systems and Open Minds*. Edinburgh: Oliver and Boyd.

Wellman, B. (1979) 'The community question: the intimate networks of east Yorkers', *American Journal of Sociology*, 84: 1201–1231.

Wellman, B. (2001) 'Physical space and cyberspace: the rise of personal networking', *International Journal of Urban and Regional Research*, 25: 227–252.

Werbner, P. (1990) *The Migration Process*. Oxford: Berg.

Werbner, P. (2002) *Imagined Diasporas among Manchester Muslims: The Public Performance of Pakistani Transnational Identity Politics*. Oxford: James Currey.

Whyte, W.S. (1957) *The Organisation Man*. New York: Touchstone.

Williams, G. (2002) 'City building: developing Manchester's core', in Peck and Ward (eds) *City of Revolution*. Manchester: Manchester University Press.

Willmott, P. (1987) *Friendship Networks and Social Support*. London: Policy Studies Institute.

Wilson, J. and Kelling, G.L. (1982) 'Broken windows', *The Atlantic Monthly*, September, pp. 72–88.

Wittel, A. (2001). 'Toward a network sociality', *Theory, Culture and Society*, 18: 51–76.

Wolfe, A. (1998) *One Nation, After All: What Middle Class Americans Really Think About God, Country, Family, Racism, Welfare, Immigration, Homosexuality, Work, the Right, the Left and Each Other*. New York: Viking.

Woolf, J. (1987) 'The invisible flaneuse: Women and the literature of modernity', in A. Benjamin (ed.) *The Problems of Modernity*. London: Routledge.

Woolgar, S. (2002) *A Virtual Society*. Oxford: Blackwell.

Wynne, D. (1996) *Leisure, Lifestyles and the New Middle Class: A case study*. London: Routledge.

Yeo, E. (1996) *The Contest for Social Science: Relations and Representations of Gender and Class*. London: Rivers Oram.

Young, M. and Wilmott, P. (1957) *Family and Kinship in East London*. London: Routledge.

Name Index

Subject Index

Page numbers in *italics* refer to figures and tables.